A HISTORY

OF YUGOSLAV

LITERATURE

ANTUN BARAC

LEARNED SOCIETIES ·

THE AMERICAN COUNCIL OF

the Joint
Committee
on Eastern
Europe
Publication
Series
Number 1.
THE SOCIAL

SCIENCE RESEARCH COUNCIL

Translated by
PETAR MIJUŠKOVIĆ

This volume is sponsored by the Joint Com-
mittee on Eastern Europe of the American
Council of Learned Societies and the Social
Science Research Council and is published
through the cooperation of Michigan Slavic
Publications, Department of Slavic Languages
and Literatures, University of Michigan, Ann
Arbor. Cover by Leonard Zamiska.

CHAPTER ONE

THE PAST OF THE YUGOSLAVS
AND THEIR LANGUAGE

1. A SURVEY OF THE POLITICAL AND SOCIAL HISTORY OF THE YUGOSLAV PEOPLES

Yugoslav literature comprises the literatures of the Serbs, Croats, Slovenes and Macedonians united in the Federal People's Republic of Yugoslavia. The literatures of the Yugoslavs are as closely related as the Yugoslav peoples are by tongue and origin. Political, social, economic and cultural factors, however, kept the Yugoslavs parted for centuries. In consequence of this some Yugoslav groups, living a separate life, evolved into separate nations. Their literatures were affected in the same fashion: the conditions being different, they followed paths different in many respects. Notwithstanding this, they preserved many common features.

The Yugoslavs are not autochthonous on the territory which they inhabit. Coming from beyond the Carpathians, they settled in parts of the Balkan Peninsula and Central Europe during the migration of nations, chiefly during the sixth century. They came in groups, large and small, and in successive waves. Some of them were forced to flee before superior warrior nations, like the Avars; others came as a part of those hosts; still others were warriors and conquerors in their own right. Their mightiest onslaught carried them as far south as the Peloponnesus.

The Yugoslavs entered the territories of Byzantium, and lived later under the direct influence of the Franks of that period; but several centuries passed before they became consolidated and settled in their new country. Gradually, they also founded independent and semi-independent states: the Slovenes founded a principality in the eighth century; the Croatian State developed in the tenth century from a principality into a kingdom, its nucleus being in Dalmatia; the Serbian State of the Middle Ages under the Nemanjić dynasty was a very strong state between the twelfth and the fourteenth century. These and other Yugoslav states, however, disintegrated before stronger and better-organized invaders. The Slovenes came under the Germans as early as the ninth century, and remained under them till 1917; the Croatian kingdom, vanquished in 1102, acknowledged the Hungarian kings, but still preserved some semblance of a state. It entered into a union with Hungary in an Austrian State under the Habsburgs early in the sixteenth century. Serbia, Zeta (Montenegro), Herzegovina, and Bosnia were overrun by the Turks.

After having lost their independence, the Yugoslavs lived for centuries under the Hungarians, Germans, Italians and Turks. The penetration of the Turks into Europe was especially fateful for them. The Turks occupied Bosnia, Herzegovina, Serbia, Macedonia, most of Croatia and all of Dalmatia but a narrow strip of the coast and the islands. Early in the fifteenth century Venice bought these regions from the King of Hungary and held them till 1797, when it had to surrender them to Austria as the price of its defeat at Napoleon's hands. Only Dubrovnik enjoyed relative independence through the centuries as a city-republic under the formal protection either of the kings of Hungary or of the Turkish sultans. Montenegro also enjoyed a degree of freedom thanks to the inaccessibility of this mountainous country.

Their lands exposed to the clashes of warring nations, the Yugoslavs were ever open both to invasion by foreign conquerors and to plundering by their own lords. Most of the Croatian regions were ravaged in the thirteenth century by the Mongols. During several subsequent centuries, the Croatian and Serbian regions, as a border area between the Turks and the West, were continually an arena of war. In consequence, for centuries the Yugoslavs had to live a special kind of life, the primitive life of the warrior. In the border areas, the men were forced to be soldiers from childhood up to old age. Although the Serbs and Croats were as numerous in the twelfth century as any of the bigger nations of Western Europe, the population decreased during later developments, for many of the people were slain.

At the same time, strong pressure was brought to bear on the Yugoslavs by various European nations: by the Germans in their advance eastwards, by the Italians in their striving to gain a firm foothold on the eastern shores of the Adriatic, by the Hungarians in their endeavours to break out westwards to the sea. Pressure was exerted in various forms: by means of military aggression, commerce, cultural and religious propaganda, immigration. In Austria, the authorities themselves Germanized and Magyarized the Yugoslavs, especially the Slovenes and Croats, during some periods. Although living in their own countries, these people were regarded at best as second-class citizens. No fundamental change occurred in

4

this respect during the centuries: from the Mongolian invasion in the thirteenth century up to the fascist invasion during the second world war, conditions underwent hardly any change.

The social structure of the Yugoslavs passed through radical changes during the centuries. When they arrived in the Balkan Peninsula and Central Europe, they were organized in loosely-knit tribes. As time passed, they accepted feudal forms after the West-European model. The majority of the people were the subjugated peasantry. In the Slovene regions, the nobility were of German nationality; in the Croatian regions, the feudal masters were mostly Croats. Since the official language in the country, as in the whole of Hungary, was Latin till 1848, there was a very wide gap between the nobility and the peasant masses. The pressure of the Croatian feudalists on the peasantry was as intolerable as the pressure of the foreigners. Dalmatia was ruled by Venetian envoys and by the local nobility against the interests of the majority of the people. The regions under Turkey (Serbia up to the beginning of the nineteenth century, and Bosnia and Herzegovina up to almost the end of it) were ruled by Turks or by local Moslems as the ruling class, while the people generally were a rightless *raia*.

For centuries, the history of the Yugoslavs was on the whole one of political and social thraldom. The situation was aggravated by their division into two religions and three creeds: the Orthodox and the Catholic, and the Moslem. Members of the same nation belonging to one of these creeds often persecuted members of the same nation belonging to another with a bitterness which exceeded that fomented by war against an outside nation. Relations between the Christians and the Moslems were especially bitter. Regarding religion as an essential part of the human being, the Moslems often subjugated their Christian countrymen more bitterly than did the Turks themselves.

Economic conditions among the Yugoslavs varied both from century to century and during the same century. For example, medieval Serbia had developed handicrafts and mining, activities which were almost entirely ruined with the coming of the Turks, for most of the Serbs were forced to resort to agriculture and live-stock breeding as a livelihood. Livestock breeding was the only practicable type of economy during the years of war and the periods of plunder by the invaders, for the refugees were able to save only their livestock. Up to the middle of the nineteenth century, the feudalists in Austria favoured primitive agriculture among the majority of the Yugoslavs, exploiting the unpaid labour of the peasantry; handicrafts and commerce were carried on only in the towns, which had begun to flourish in the nineteenth century. The majority of the town population, however, were of foreign nationality. Only in Dalmatia and on the islands of Hvar, Rab, Korčula and Brač did the towns reach higher levels of development, thanks to their favourable geographical position. Dubrovnik was the most prosperous, having in the course of several centuries become one of the strongest commercial centures on the Adriatic.

One of the characteristics of the economic and social relations of most of the Yugoslavs were the peasant cooperatives. They were exclusive economic units consisting of relatives by blood, in which, according to a strict hierarchical division and a division of labour, the members produced whatever the community required.

Owing to the political and social relations prevalent in those times, the history of the Yugoslavs is marked by frequent rebellions against their oppressors. From the sixteenth century, when the feudal yoke had grown intolerable to the peasants, uprisings alternated in Dalmatia, Croatia and in the Slovene areas. But up to the nineteenth century they were always cruelly suppressed.

The Yugoslavs began to demand their complete liberation, both political and social, in the eighteenth century (Montenegro). In the nineteenth century their struggle had reached its peak. After two insurrections early in the nineteenth century, Serbia gradually gained complete independence. Montenegro had become independent at the beginning of the same century. In the areas under the Habsburgs, movements for political and national freedom followed each other during the nineteenth century. The Yugoslavs under the Habsburgs repeatedly fought throughout the nineteenth century and the first decade of the twentieth for their political rights, and for the unification of the areas which they inhabited, scattered as they were under several governments. Originally these movements were tolerated, for it was considered that their purpose was not secession from the state in which these people lived. But as the efforts to quell these movements increased, the Yugoslavs, also turning radical, saw a solution of their national problems outside Austria. A revolutionary movement had developed among them during the years preceding the first world war, advocating the political unification of all the Yugoslavs. One of the results of the first world war, which broke out with the attack of Austria on Serbia, was the creation in 1918 of Yugoslavia, which for the first time in their history incorporated all the Yugoslavs, except the Croats and Slovenes in Istria, who came under Italy in accordance with the peace treaties.

2. CULTURAL INFLUENCES

The Yugoslavs moved to this part of Europe during the migration of nations, bringing their beliefs and their culture with them. In this new land, they entered the realm of Christianity and the sphere of Greco-Roman culture. The towns of Dalmatia, however, clung to their Romanesque character for several centuries after the arrival of the Yugoslavs. Byzantine and Italian influences began to affect the Yugoslavs from the very beginning in such a way that they were compelled to fight for their individuality. However, the division of the Christian world between Rome and Byzantium had unfortunate consequences for them. When they became part of the Frankish Empire, the Slovenes and Croats adopted Catholicism, while the Serbs, who were under Byzantine influence, except for a period of hesitation during the early centuries, accepted the Orthodox creed. Similar influences spreading from the neighbouring nations affected them later as well. Strong elements of German culture prevailed in the northern regions, while Italian culture affected the south. The Turks introduced strong Oriental elements among the Yugoslavs, which have survived in some parts till quite recently.

Accordingly, the principal task of the Yugoslavs, both in their cultural and in their political life, was to accept the beneficial elements of foreign cultures while preserving their own individuality. Their cultural life, consequently, evolved in accordance with the economic and political conditions in which they lived: during times of complete national independence it flourished; during centuries of political thraldom, on the other hand, they had to make every effort to preserve their bare existence. The Serbs won renown with their medieval art, the Croats with their art of the thirteenth century and later in Dalmatia and Dubrovnik. Even during the later unfavourable social and political developments, the Yugoslavs continued in different parts of present-day Yugoslavia to cultivate their artistic aptitude (the Slovene architecture of the sixteenth century, the architecture and painting of the Croatian baroque in Zagorje).

During the period of Turkish rule, the cultural level of the Yugoslavs varied. Illiteracy and primitive ways of life were the general curse of the Yugoslavs under the Turks, for while the nobility of Croatia and of the Slovene regions enjoyed a standard of living which equalled that of the nobility of Western Europe, the broad peasant masses, suffered from cultural neglect. The people in the Dalmatian towns endeavoured to live according to West-European models; but the villages, especially in the more remote districts of the country, suffered from extreme backwardness.

The adverse cultural conditions forced many of the boldest and gifted individuals, particularly in Dalmatia, Croatia and in the Slovene regions, to leave for foreign parts. The majority of them went to Italy, where they distinguished themselves as architects, painters, poets or scientists. This state of affairs went on till the

7

nineteenth century, when the political and social changes in what is today Yugoslavia brought more favourable conditions for cultural activity.

3. THE LANGUAGE AND DIALECTS

Owing to their tongue, the Yugoslavs have always been regarded by other nations on the whole as a single entity, which they usually designated by one name. The Yugoslavs, however, as far back as the time when they migrated, have always possessed some distinct features by which they have differed from each other. As a consequence of these and some other factors, they gradually evolved into several nations. But there have never been any rigid territorial or lingual boundaries separating them: the medieval Yugoslav states occupied different territories, which never coincided with the division into Serbs, Croats and Slovenes. The Croatian State was founded in Dalmatia, but later its centre shifted to Pannonia, to Zagreb. The heart of medieval Serbia was in Macedonia, but it slowly moved northwards with the northerly advance of the Turks, while Albanians and Turks settled in the southern regions. Driven by the Turkish onslaughts, the Croats also moved northwards from the regions they had inhabited, while the Serbs from Serbia settled in Croatia, Hungary, Dalmatia. Accordingly, the numerical relation of the several Yugoslav nations frequently changed in the same area.

Today northwestern Yugoslavia, west of the river Sutla, is inhabited by Slovenes. In Croatia, Slavonia and Dalmatia the Croats are a majority, with numerous Serbs. In Bosnia and Herzegovina the population is mixed, while in Serbia the Serbs are in the majority. The areas along the rivers Danube and Tisa, which were Hungarian up to 1918, are inhabited by the Serbs with numerous Croats. Macedonians form the majority in Macedonia.

The whole of Yugoslavia speaks a language which varies only in negligible differences of dialect. The Croats and the Serbs speak the same tongue, known to the former as Croatian and to the latter as Serbian. Its scientific name is Serbian or Croatian, Serbo-Croatian or Croato-Serbian. It differentiates three dialects and three speech developments. The fundamental difference between the dialects lies in the word used for the interrogative pronoun "what", which is *što* in some parts, *ča* in others, and *kaj* in still other parts. Accordingly, the three dialects of Serbo-Croatian are known as *štokavski*, *čakavski*, and *kajkavski*. These three dialects are also differentiated into three speech developments, which depend on whether the root vowel in the same word in the three dialects takes the form of *i, e,* or *ije,* and are known as *ikavski, ekavski* and *ijekavski.*

8

The most widespread dialect is the *štokavski*. It is spoken by all the Serbs and by most of the Croats. The *čakavski* is the oldest dialect, and it is spoken by the Croats along the coast and on the islands, while *kajkavski* is spoken by the Croats in the northwest, in the vicinity of Zagreb. The Slovene speech resembles that of the *kajkavski* Croats, but they have evolved a literary language of their own.

In the past a dialect became a literary language if literary life was able to unfold in the region where it was spoken. For a long time, the attempts of the Yugoslavs generally, or of the Serbs and Croats at least, or of the Croats alone, to overcome territorial fragmentation with the assistance of a common literary language were in vain. Only the nineteenth century united the Serbs and Croats in a single literary language and orthography, and the Slovenes and Croats in orthography, which marked the foundation of their modern literatures.

CHAPTER TWO

THE LITERATURE OF THE MIDDLE AGES

1. THE BEGINNINGS OF SLAVIC LITERATURES; CYRIL AND METHODIUS

The conversion of the Yugoslavs to Christianity marks the beginning of literacy among them. They began to accept the new faith on settling in these regions, especially in the eighth century, having been initiated in it by the Greeks, Italians, and Germans, whose cultural, political and religious spheres they had entered. The new faith was imparted to the Yugoslavs in the tongues of the Christians or in Latin. Since Christian propaganda was simultaneously an element of national propaganda, the preachers of the new faith encountered many obstacles in their work. Only towards the end of the ninth century and in the tenth did the new faith take firm root among the Yugoslavs, the disciples of the missionaries Cyril and Methodius having popularized it among them in a Slavic tongue. It was in this period that the first monuments of their literacy originated. The Yugoslavs were compelled, however, to continue to combat the endeavours of the Greek and the Roman Catholic Church to dominate them.

What was significant for the cultural and religious life of the Yugoslavs, were just those movements which had originated during the early centuries after their conversion. They assumed different forms and were known by different names; but they had the common feature of resisting the endeavours of the Greek and the Roman Catholic Church to denationalize them, and of striving for church autonomy and religious independence. The most radical among these movements was *Bogomilism*, which resembled the West-European *Patarines and Cathari*. *Bogomilism* spread to a considerable number of Yugoslav regions after the ninth century. In Bosnia it was a species of established church; its doctrines: to resist the opportunistic doctrines of Christianity, the official church, splendour, wealth, immorality; to promote the moral values of the people, and the idea of equality among them. *Bogomilism* was so strong in Bosnia that crusades were instigated against it by the Pope. But all endeavours to stamp it out were futile. Finally, it vanished with the downfall of the independent Bosnian State, in the fifteenth century, when the *Bogomils* accepted Islam.

It is to similar causes that the successes of Cyril and Methodius among the Slavs, the origin of the Croatian *Glagolitsa*, and the inception of the autonomous Serbian Church should be attributed.

German clerics began to preach Christianity in Moravia, a Slavic State, in the ninth century, and to spread German influence by this means. Prince Rostislav, consequently, requested the Emperor Michael of Byzantium to send missionaries to teach the new faith to his people in a tongue which they would be able to understand. Michael chose the brothers Constantine and Methodius for this work. Methodius, the elder, had been a scribe for some time. Later he became a monk. Constantine, on the other hand, inclined to meditation, philosophy. As missionaries, both of them had a good name. Being Greeks from Salonika, they spoke the tongue of the local Macedonian Slavs, which differed little at that time from the other Slavic tongues.

Since the Slavs had had no alphabet with which to represent all their vocal sounds, Constantine invented the required characters. Besides this, the two brothers translated the most essential sacred books into the Slavic tongue of their region. In Moravia, they preached their faith with success, and taught a number of disciples. They soon came into conflict, however, with the local German clerics. Accused by them of spreading a heresy, the two brothers went to Rome to clear themselves before the Pope. The Pope praised their work and approved the use of the Slavic tongue in the Church. In 869 Constantine died in a monastery in Rome which he had entered and taken the name of Cyril. Methodius, on the other hand, continued the work which the two brothers had begun.

In the meantime a change had taken place on the throne of Moravia: Rostislav was overthrown, and Svatopluk, the new ruler, persuaded by the German clerics, evicted Cyril and Methodius' disciples. In consequence Methodius worked for a time in the small state of Prince Kocel in Pannonia near Lake Balaton, as Pannonian archbishop. After Prince Kocel's death, he returned to Moravia, where he was the victim of continual persecution. His enemies intrigued against him, and in the end he was imprisoned. After he died in 885, Svatopluk again expelled his disciples, who scattered on all sides, the majority of them going to the territories of the southern Slavs. In those times there were two major independent states in these parts: Croatia under King Tomislav, and Bulgaria under Emperor Simeon. Religious and literary work now began to develop in the two countries, and in time all the Slavic literatures sprang from this seed.

12

The manuscripts of *Cyril* and *Methodius,* written in Macedonian, were liturgical manuscripts: missals and translations of the most important sacred books (the Gospels, the Psalter, the euchology, etc.). In addition to the sacred books, a number of original legends were written later also in Macedonia, two of which were about Cyril and Methodius and their work. The writer was probably Bishop *Kliment* of Ohrid, a disciple of the two missionaries. Besides this, there is an important manuscript defending the Slavic script from its opponents. It was written by a monk named *Hrabar.*

At the very beginning, the Slavic alphabet and the Slavic ritual had bitter opponents both in the Catholic Church and among the German and Greek clerics. They alleged that the liturgy was admissible only in one of the consecrated languages: in Latin, Greek, or Hebrew. In point of fact, they feared that the work of the Slavic preachers would encroach on their interests, for up to then the Slavic regions had been under their ecclesiastical jurisdiction. But, since one Pope had already sanctioned the use of the Slavic alphabet and tongue in the Church, nothing could ever again abolish this custom, which had become settled by now. Besides, the Greek Church was more tolerant towards the use of other languages in the liturgy. In Bulgaria under Emperor Simeon (the tenth century) various aspects of fruitful literary work developed freely. Concurrently, a significant formal change also took place: Cyril's original Slavic alpabet, the difficult *Glagolitsa,* was abandoned for a new alphabet based chiefly on the Greek uncial letters. It derives its name *Cirilica* from Cyril, the founder of the Slavic alphabet. In time it became the script of all the Slavs of the Orthodox denomination. It was later adopted in the Catholic regions as well.

The writers of the first books in Macedonian referred to their language as Slavic. Hence, in science it is known as Old Slavic. Its other names are Church Slavic (used in the Church), Old Bulgarian (used among the Bulgars).

The Old Slavic manuscripts probably reached the Croatian areas in more than one way: they were written either by Cyril and Methodius themselves during their journey to Rome, or by others who were influenced by Methodius while he was in the small neighbouring State of Prince Kocel, or by his disciples who had been evicted from Moravia. On the other hand, the Old Slavic manuscripts reached the Serbian areas from Bulgaria, of which the Serbs formed a part for a time. Because of the specific conditions in which the Yugoslav peoples lived, the beginnings of literacy among them and the further development of their literatures followed devious courses.

2. THE EARLIEST RECORDS OF SLAVIC SPEECH

The Slovenes, who lived from the ninth century in the Frankish Empire, were dominated by one or another foreign bishopric — that of Salzburg or of Acquileia. The church hierarchy being German in most of the Slovene lands — in Krain, Styria, Carinthia — the Slovenes were unable even to initiate any literary work of consequence. Indeed, it is from the tenth century that the first written documents in Slovene derive, the *Brižinski Spomenici* [Freisingen Texts], so called after the Bavarian town in which they were found. These are fragments of a general confession, written down on the Latin text by the hand of an unknown cleric. It is obvious in the face of this evidence that the Catholic clerics were compelled to use the Slovene tongue in their works among the Slovenes. The Slovenes were a considerable nation numerically: in the tenth century, they formed the majority also in the Carantania (Caranthia) of the Franks. At his investiture, the local *Voivode* had to take the oath of office before the people in the Zollfeld Plain near the village of Maria Saal, known in Slovene by the name of *Gosposvetsko Polje*, in Slovene and in the Slovene peasant costume. This custom survived up to 1414. But the Slovenes being thinly populated, the Germans settled among them in increasing numbers. But for a few manuscripts, till the sixteenth century, there was no Slovene literature deserving of the name. Most of the church hierarchy and the greater part of the nobility were German and Italian. The ignorant and illiterate Slovene peasants were neglected culturally.

3. CROATIAN MEDIEVAL LITERATURE

The Croats, on the other hand, having a State of their own during the time of Cyril and Methodius in the ninth century, were free to adopt *Glagolitsa* and the Old Slavic language. In less than a century *Glagolitsa* spread throughout the Croatian kingdom. Literature with Old Slavic texts for copying was cultivated especially in many Benedictine monasteries, particularly in the northern parts — in Istria, the Croatian Littoral, and on the island of Krk. Elements of the living popular speech soon began to penetrate into the language adopted from Cyril and Methodius' disciples. It is from the close of the eleventh century that the first written monuments of the Croatian language derive: for example, the stone tablet found in the town of Baška on the island of Krk, which says that King Zvonimir gave a field to the small church of Saint Lucia at Baška.

The Glagolitic alphabet with the popular language was not, however, freely admitted to the Church. The Dalmatian towns were still Romanesque, their religious services in Latin. As the popes, save a few at the beginning, were opposed to the use of Slavic in the liturgy, they were of accord with the clergy of the Latin denomination in the Dalmatian towns in this respect. Besides, the bishops of these towns insisted on the territorial jurisdiction they had had before the coming of the Croats. The inevitable consequence would have been that *Glagolitsa* and the Slavic liturgy would be prohibited in the whole of Croatia. In order to win the favour of the Dalmatian towns, the Croatian rulers pursued an opportunistic policy, and allowed the church councils in Croatia to prohibit the use of Slavic in favour of Latin. Neither they nor the council decisions, however, were able to overcome the resistance of the Croatian Glagolitic clergy, who stubbornly cultivated *Glagolitsa* with the popular speech on the whole territory of Croatia, notwithstanding the pressure exercised by the secular and ecclesiastical authorities. Nor did they yield when Croatia became a part of the Hungarian crown, or when Dalmatia and the Istrian islands fell under Venice. Moreover, in some regions, as in the Bishopric of Senj and on the island of Krk, there were hardly any other clerics besides the *Glagolashi*. And so the popes were compelled to acknowledge the fact, and allow the Slavic liturgy in the bishoprics in which it was in use and in which the clergy were ignorant of Latin (1244). Then followed a period of relative calm for *Glagolitsa* and the popular tongue, which have survived in the Church till the present day in spite of persecution by Italian priests in Istria and by the Austro-Hungarian authorities.

Owing to the unfavourable conditions of development, the confines of *Glagolitsa* and its use in the Church neevrtheless gradually narrowed. In the twelfth century the Hungarian kings introduced Latin on the territory of the Bishopric of Zagreb; the Cyrillic alphabet pressed northwards from Serbian Zeta; and the Roman alphabet spread from the Romanesque towns of Dalmatia. Thus, *Glagolitsa* remained as a rare manifestation confined to a narrow strip of Croatian soil.

The first books written in Croatian Glagolitic literature were those required in church: missals, breviaries, books of prayer, hymnals, homilies, etc. The copying of books had reached a high standard of perfection in Croatia, and there were many manuscript books. A number of manuscripts were produced during the centuries preceding the art of printing. They were transcribed by veritable artists, as is testified by the *Missal of Prince Novak* (1368), the *Missal of Voivode Hrvoje* (the early fifteenth century). The art of printing books was adopted also by the *Glagolashi*. Glagolitic printing-presses were founded at Senj and Rijeka. The first Croatian missal in *Glagolitsa* was printed in 1483.

Besides being used in church, *Glagolitsa* became the universal script among the Croats, in everyday use and in secular literature. Whereas the Old Slavic script survived in sacred books, the living *čakavski* dialect of the western Croatian regions prevailed in the secular books.

Numerous sacred and didactic books were compiled in Croatian *Glagolitsa*, such as books about the lives of the saints, hymnals, etc. Various legends about the saints, and especially about the Virgin Mary, were a species of literature of a limited nature; the apocrypha, which are typical of Yugoslav literature, were related to them. The medieval romances known in every literature in Europe (about the *Trojan War, Alexander the Great)* belong to literature proper. The first Croatian experiments in sacred drama after German and Italian models which preceded the fifteenth century were also written in *Glagolitsa.*

Like the other literatures of that time, most of the Croatian medieval literature written in *Glagolitsa* was not original. The majority of the books were adaptations or translations of works generally familiar in all the medieval literatures of Europe. They invaded Croatian literature either from the west, as translations from Latin or Italian, or from the east, from Byzantine sources. Most of these manuscripts are significant for literature in that the Croatian literary language gradually evolving in them became increasingly capable of artistic expression.

The Roman alphabet began to win popularity in the early Croatian literature of the fourteenth century. It does not signify, however, that the Croatian writers who had adopted the Roman alphabet were now hostile to *Glagolitsa.* Rather, they borrowed from it, or found inspiration in it. With the influence of the secular and ecclesiastical authorities, the Roman alphabet gradually suppressed *Glagolitsa* almost everywhere, and became the universal Croatian script.

The beginnings of Croatian poetry also lie in Croatian medieval literature. Its original purpose was sacred; later, however, the poets were distinguished by individualistic features. The first known verses were recorded in the *Missal of Prince Novak,* already referred to, while the first known more complete and personal poems had their origin in the fourteenth or fifteenth century. They expressed, not only sacred, but secular sentiments also.

A similar process may be observed also throughout Croatian Glagolitic literature: instead of the usual strict adaptations, the writers gradually came to express individual features in individual ways.

Among the earliest works distinguished by their originality, which offer a picture of Croatian social and cultural conditions, the most important are various codices, for example the *Codex of Vinodol* of 1288, the oldest of all Slavic codices. A manuscript which may be said to be the purest national manuscript in old Croatian literature is *Ljetopis Popa Dukljanina* [The annals of Father Dukljanin], written probably in the twelfth century in Duklja (Montenegro), the existence of which came to be known from fifteenth-century manuscripts. It describes events from the coming of the Yugoslavs down to the writer's time. Many scientists doubt its historical authenticity; its literary significance, however, is indisputable: the language is already polished, the style is flowing, fancy often takes prominence over objective truth. Moreover, it is suggestive of the folk poems.

The Glagolitic literature of the Croats began to decline with the sixteenth century. Neglected by the superior secular authorities, suffering the persecution and disdain of the Roman Curia and the high church hierarchy, the *Glagolashi* were left to fend for themselves. Their books being rarely printed, they were often compelled to content themselves with performing the service from antiquated manuscripts. But they were adamant, and they performed their work steadfastly at least in a part of Croatia.

The protagonists of Croatian Glagolitic literature were mostly the lower clergy, who were often without sufficient theological training and general education. Attempts were occasionally made to assist them by printing new sacred books and by opening schools for them. It was not until the nineteenth century, however, that these endeavours produced palpable results. By then *Glagolitsa* had already been confined to the Church.

In the history of the Croatian people *Glagolitsa* was of literary, national and social significance.

The literary significance of *Glagolitsa* lies in the fact that the structure of the Croatian literary language was conceived and built on the foundations of its Old Slavic manuscripts.

National credit must be given to the *Glagolashi* for having raised an almost impenetrable bastion, during centuries of continual political and cultural pressure, against the influences radiating from the Appenine Peninsula towards Istria, Dalmatia and the Croatian Littoral with the purpose of denationalizing these regions with the assistance of the Church and Latin.

The social significance of Glagolitic literature lies in that it was a literature cultivated by the lower clergy and by the broad sections of the people. Whereas the feudalists and higher clergy sought to gratify their cultural needs in Latin or Italian, the works which were written in *Glagolitsa* were in the tongue of the common people.

17

4. SERBIAN MEDIEVAL LITERATURE

The most flourishing literature in the Middle Ages was that of the Serbs. They succeeded in substituting the Cyrillic alphabet for *Glagolitsa* during the beginnings of their literature thanks to favourable political conditions. They had given proof of their remarkable literary faculty *(Miroslavljevo Jevandjelje* — the Gospel of Prince Miroslav) as far back as the twelfth century. Serbian literature began to develop especially with the strengthening of the Serbian State under the Nemanjić dynasty, which, during the reign of Emperor Dušan, attained almost European significance. Serbia had expanded its boundaries well-nigh to the bastions of Constantinople and incorporated most of the Balkan Peninsula. Unlike the conditions among the Slovenes, in Serbia the Church was administered, not by aliens, but by the Serbs themselves. Sava, the youngest son of Stevan Nemanja, the Serbian Zupan, retired when he was a youth to a monastery on Mount Athos. Later he was canonized. Having returned to his country, he organized the life of the Church and won autonomy for the Serbian Church. Sava was also the initiator of intensive literary work among the Serbs.

As distinct, again, from conditions in Croatia, in Serbia the protagonists of Serbian medieval literature were the members of the dynasty and the most learned monks.

Spreading on a territory rich in the remains of Greco-Roman culture, and directly in contact with the highly advanced Byzantium, medieval Serbia became the focal-point of extensive cultural and artistic work during the period of its independence. It was prosperous; the members of the Serbian dynasty and the nobility promoted the closest relations with the courts of Europe, they cultivated elegant tastes in the style of their times, and founded libraries. The Serbian rulers built beautiful votive monasteries and provided the monks with the material means they required to carry on literary scientific work in peace. A considerable number of these dazzling thirteenth- and fourteent-century monuments still survive. In addition to architecture, painting also flourished in medieval Serbia.

Indeed, in their main trend, both the architecture and the art of ancient Serbia are distinguished by Byzantine features, which are, after all, common to the whole Orthodox world. Their distinction is an emphasis on line and a wealth of colour and form. But step by step the builders and the painters, Serbs all, succeeded in endowing their works with both personal and national features.

The Serbian monasteries were the cradle of literary activity. Their monks, often educated abroad, especially at Mount Athos, copied and translated books primarily for the requirements of their monasteries and of the Serbian Orthodox Church. There were many highly educated men among them, with the highest theological culture which the Middle Ages could offer. The Serbian monasteries gained in importance in the fifteenth century, when many educated Bulgars fled to Serbia following the defeat of Bulgaria by the Turks in 1393.

Founded by churchmen for the Church, the Serbian literature of the Middle Ages originally consisted of translated sacred literature. It included every possible manuscript known in Byzantine literature, starting with ritual books and ending with philosophical, ethical, and oratorical works. In addition to these books, it included also history (annals, chronicles, chronographies), as well as hagiographies, legends, apocrypha. Sacred verses, such as the *Kondakion* and the *Troparion*, were also composed. Almost everything of importance in Byzantine literature was rendered into Serbian. Among the more remarkable secular works are medieval romances and tales, such as *Alexander the Great, The Trojan War, Varlaam i Joasaf* (Barlaam and Josaphat), *Stefanit i Ihnilat, Salamun, Carica Teofana* [The Empress Theophana]. There are also some humorous stories, such as *Muke Blaženog Grozdija* [The agonies of the blessed Grozdije].

Most of these literary works are of Byzantine and not of Serbian origin. Serbian literature, however, did develop a characteristic literary form in the biographies of the Serbian rulers and church dignitaries. Its initiator was Sava, the founder of the autonomous Serbian Church. It was continued by King Stevan, his brother. They were succeeded by the learned monks and high church dignitaries Domentijan, Teodosije, Danilo, Grigorije Camblak, Constantine the Philosopher.

At the beginning of the thirteenth century *Sava* wrote a biography of his father Nemanja, who terminated his long reign by retiring to a monastery, where he took the name Stevan. Sava only described the few years of his father's life in the monastery, and his death. In 1216 his brother *Stevan* wrote the life-story of their father from his birth to his death. In the middle of the thirteenth century *Domentijan*, a monk from Mount Athos, described the lives of Stevan Nemanja and Sava at great length and with many elaborations. Both biographies were revised at the close of the century by *Teodosije*, another monk, who rid them of their excess of pathos and rhetoric.

Serbian biographical literature was set upon a new course by the Archbishop of the Serbian Church, *Danilo*. In the fourteenth century he wrote the lives of the Serbian rulers and of a number of Serbian archbishops. His biographical works are definitely historical in character. His work was continued by others.

At the beginning of the fifteenth century *Grigorije Camblak*, a Bulgar, wrote the life of King Stefan Dečanski of Serbia. In 1432 probably, *Constantine the Philosopher,* likewise a Bulgarian refugee, described the life of Despot Stevan, the most important Serbian ruler after the Battle of Kosovo Plain.

In view of their origin, the Serbian biographies are in fact hagiographies. The majority of the Serbian rulers gained renown by building churches and monasteries and by providing for the monks. Towards the end of their lives some of them even took orders. They were, consequently, canonized by the Church, and their lives were written by the learned monks. But it has been ascertained that the writers cut the bonds which held them to the church patterns, and gradually accustomed themselves to independent literary ways. Some of their manuscripts constitute a precious source for the study of Serbian history. They wrote other manuscripts, again, with an eye exclusively to literature, with a personal world outlook, and with a specific style, which is especially evident from a comparison of the different biographies of the same persons (for example, Sava's and Stevan's biographies of their father Nemanja, or Domentijan's and Teodosije's biographies of Sava and Nemanja).

Besides their religious and historical value, the Serbian biographies are also of special national significance. They steadily raised the consciousness of Serbdom, the consciousness of its mission, of the aggrandizement of the Serbian State and of the difficulties its rulers encountered. They are often suggestive of the life of the Serbian people in those times: the relations prevailing among the nobility, the position of the Church, the way of life of the average Serbian folk. They become more comprehensible if they are studied side by side with Serbian architecture and painting, and with the legal order in Serbia, which is best exemplified by the *Zakonik Cara Dušana* [The codex of Emperor Dušan] of 1349.

The Serbian biographers had no literary objective as they wrote their works: they were simply doing their religious duty. Sava, the founder of Serbian medieval literature and the organizer of the Serbian Church, was no professional writer; he was a religious worker, an organizer of Church and State. Principally he wanted to strengthen the Serbian State and to organize the autonomous Serbian Church. To this end he composed a number of manuscripts on the organization of some monasteries (Hilandar, Studenica). He wrote his father's biography as a part of the *Typicon* for Studenica Monastery, which was founded by Nemanja. It is distinguished by an unusually warm, tender narrative of the last days of Sava's father. Parts of Danilo's biographies of the lives of the Serbian kings and archbishops are distinguished by extremely realistic descriptions. They give a clear picture of the conditions in the Balkan Peninsula in those times: the dangers threatening the traveller on the roads, the attacks of highwaymen. Moreover, Constantine the Philosopher dwelt on matters of literary language and orthography.

Medieval Serbian literature reached its highest level during the peak of prosperity of the medieval Serbian State. With the death of Emperor Dušan, however, his State began to fall to pieces: the feudalists, who had always clung to their independence as far as possible, went to war with each other. The Turks turned their differences to account: in two disastrous battles — on the river Maritsa in 1371, and on Kosovo Plain in 1389 — the Serbian rulers lost their lives, King Vukašin on the Maritsa, Prince Lazar at Kosovo. The Serbian State dwindled to a mere despotism under the rule of Lazar's erudite son Stevan.

The Serbs considered the Battle of Kosovo as a national disaster. It was important inasmuch as both the Turkish Sultan and Prince Lazar were killed in it, the sultan being slain by Miloš Obilić, a Serbian hero, as he is called in folk poetry.

Serbian literature did not cease to live, although the Serbian State had been reduced to its smallest bounds. *Despot Stevan* himself was a writer. He went beyond the bounds of the Serbian literature of his day, which was influenced by the Church, by composing a species of lyric poem, *Slovo Ljubve* [A song of love]; while *Jefimija*, the unhappy widow of one of the Serbian nobles killed in the Battle of the Maritsa, who had retired to a monastery, embroidered a shroud for Prince Lazar, on which she represented the woes of vanquished Serbdom (1399).

Owing to the influence of the Church, Serbian literature, albeit unhampered in its development, also had its disadvantages. The language of the sacred books in Old Slavic remained unchanged for the sake of tradition. Unlike Croatian literature, it did not accept the living popular speech, so that the tongue of the ordinary people and the literary language parted ways. Besides this, it was the narrow class literature of the feudalists and the Church.

With the invention of printing, the Serbs founded printing-presses at Obod in Zeta (Montenegro) in 1493, at Gračanica, and in Belgrade.

Creative literary work among the Serbs ceased when, in 1459, the remnant of the Serbian State became a Turkish pashalik. The Turks systematically destroyed every document concerning Serbian national life in order to force the Serbian people to be an obedient *raia*. And they succeeded in their design: the leading Serbian class, the feudalists, was either destroyed or its members fled to other countries. The few monks who survived in the remaining monasteries were mostly illiterate. It was only infrequently that books were copied. The Serbian people as a biological unit survived only through the peasantry, devoted as they were to their land, and living a patriarchal way of life in the remote villages. They had to bear heavy burdens in taxes and levies, and lived a simple, primitive life with few needs. In the battle for their bare survival, literature was out of the question. Artistic expression did not go beyond the spoken word, the unwritten folk poem and folk tale. Before Serbian literature could revive, it had to await new times with their new conditions. And it was the eighteenth century when these arrived.

CHAPTER THREE

THE SIXTEENTH CENTURY

1. THE POLITICAL AND SOCIAL CONDITIONS; THE TURKS; HUMANISM AND THE RENAISSANCE AMONG THE YUGOSLAVS

The Yugoslavs were going through the most difficult period in their history while European art and literature were flourishing during the period of humanism and the Renaissance. In their advance westwards the Turks had seized most of the Yugoslav territory. Only the Slovene regions and the greater part of Croatia had still escaped their grasp. Venetian Dalmatia had been reduced to the narrow belt along the coast and to the islands. The Yugoslav territory, which was a border dividing the Turks from the countries of Western Europe, was the scene of perpetual war. The Turkish detachments made incursions as far north as Krain and Styria, and as far west as the Dalmatian islands. Fire, plunder, massacre or Turkish captivity were an everyday part of life in the Yugoslav areas. Croatia, reduced to an insignificant territory — *reliquiae reliquiarum* — came to be known in the course of the unceasing wars with the Turks as the farthest outpost of Christianity — *Antemurale Christianitatis* — an honour for which it paid with untold sacrifices in human life and material wealth.

The hardships of the war were rendered worse by the social conditions. The peasantry especially had to bear the burden of endless warfare. To make things worse, the feudalists continued to imitate the way of life of the European nobility, notwithstanding the hard times. It often happened that the very persons who had distinguished themselves in battle against the Turks exploited their peasant subjects, impoverished though they were, even worse than the Turks did.

Cultural work came to a complete standstill in the Yugoslav regions seized by the Turks. Nor could there be question of any systematic literary work in the regions outside Turkish control. Croatia, Dalmatia and the Slovene areas were in a perpetual state of turmoil: the population was restless, fleeing before the Turk from the eastern and southern parts to regions in the west and north. Of the whole Croatian territory, only the northernmost part, in the vicinity of Zagreb, preserved its original population. Owing to the war, aliens kept penetrating even to this part of Croatia, where they gained power and suppressed the Croatian population.

The conditions were quite different in the Dalmatian towns under Venice, especially in Dubrovnik. These towns gradually turned Croatian with the influx of people from the hinterland (Zadar as early as the twelfth century). But they did not renounce their old ways of life with the autonomy they enjoyed as corporate towns and with their special statutes. What is more, Dubrovnik succeeded in ridding itself completely of Venetian authority. Acknowledging the sovereignty of the Hungarian kings or Turkish sultans, as the case may be, and paying them tribute, it preserved its full internal freedom, and maintained diplomatic and commercial relations with most of Europe.

The Turks launched repeated attacks against Venetian Dalmatia. The people were forced to leave their homes, fleeing to the islands or to Italy. In the sixteenth century, the whole mainland of Venetian Dalmatia, including the towns of Zadar, Šibenik and Split counted only about sixty thousand people. On the other hand, the island towns (Hvar, Rab, Korčula) flourished.

During the centuries of Turkish oppression endured by most of the Yugoslav peoples, the Dalmatian towns, especially Dubrovnik, lived in the sphere of West-European culture, with all its advantages and characteristics. Their social and political conditions resembled those of Venice. Power was in the hands of the numerically small but closely knit nobility. The rest of the population, the people in the towns and the peasantry in the environs, had no political rights. Unlike the nobility in the Croatian interior, the nobility of the Dalmatian towns lived, not from agriculture, but chiefly from commerce, often having widely ramified business relations with the commercial towns of Italy and Europe as a whole. In view of the language of intercourse and the political privileges they enjoyed, the nobility endeavoured to imitate the Venetians in every way. Most of the population, however, remained Croatian. The government of Venice, primarily seeking economic gain from Dalmatia, was not concerned over national matters. Yet it persecuted any movement smacking of disobedience or rebellion. And the most significant disorders in the life of Venetian Dalmatia did occur because of social relationships.

Like Dubrovnik, the Dalmatian towns had cultural traditions of long standing. They had achieved a richly developed architecture and painting of a very high order long before the fifteenth century. Although artists from Italy had contributed to these achievements, native artists had also advanced step by step. Two sculptors of repute who demonstrated their creative skill were Radovan (at Trogir) and Buvina (at Split).

The geographical position of Dalmatia and Dubrovnik, as well as their political and social conditions, endowed their cultural development with special qualities. The *Glagolashi* had continued their work in the Dalmatian towns, especially in Zadar and in the towns of Istria. Some towns of Dalmatia were familiar with the Cyrillic script as well. The influence of the Catholic Church, however, helped the Roman script and Latin to gain sway. The government of Venice and contact with Italy abetted the penetration of Italian literature and Italian folk poetry into Croatia. From the immediate hinterland, on the other hand, came the peasant folk poetry of the Croats and Serbs among the townsfolk by dint of its own strength.

Humanism and the Renaissance, with their source in the immediate vicinity of the Yugoslav territories (in Italy), soon echoed among the Yugoslavs, particularly among the Croats and Slovenes. Humanism was able to take root among them the more easily as the language of officialdom in Hungary and Croatia was already Latin. In the fifteenth and the sixteenth century, the Yugoslav areas produced quite a number of humanists, most of whom had been educated in Italy. They were distinguished for their works written in Latin. Among the most prominent were *Ivan Česmički* (Janus Pannonius, 1434–1472), of Slavonia, a writer of odes and epigrams in Latin; *Jakov Bunić* (Jacobus de Bona, 1469–1534), of Dubrovnik, a writer of epic poems; *Ilija Crijević* (Aelius Lampridius Cerva, 1463–1520), of Dubrovnik, a lyric poet; *Juraj Šišgorić* (Georgius Sisgoreus, fifteenth century), of Šibenik, a writer of elegies, odes and prose pieces. They assumed Latinized names and surnames, and considered themselves part of the great family of humanists. They had, however, a highly developed feeling for their own people and their way of life. Thus, Šišgorić (Sisgoreus) extolled the peasant folk poems of his region, although he was a humanist. On the other hand, he also described the actual circumstances of his times, which were aggravated by the penetration of the Turks into his native town.

During the Renaissance, the Yugoslav regions produced a number of sculptors, painters and scientists whose works brought them fame in other lands, their Latinized surnames always denoting their origin, such as *Andrija Medulić* (Andrea de Mendola Schiavone), a painter, and *Matija Grbić* (Mathias Garbitius Illyricus), a professor of Greek in Germany.

25

2. THE BEGINNINGS OF CROATIAN LITERATURE
IN DALMATIA AND DUBROVNIK

Poetical works in Croatian, with accomplished modes of expression, appeared during the period of humanism and the Renaissance. They appeared in different regions more or less at the same time: at Senj in Croatia, at Venetian Split, and in free Dubrovnik. The poem *Transit Sv. Jeronima* [The translation of Saint Jerome] was written at Senj in 1508; Marko Marulić wrote his epic poem *Judita* at Split in 1501; Dubrovnik had at least two lyric poets, Šiško Menčetić and Džore Držić, towards the close of the fifteenth and at the beginning of the sixteenth century. In spirit these works differ; their verse, however, is more or less identical: the twelve-syllabled verse, which rhymes in the middle and at the end. They also have differences of language. It is obvious that they did not appear suddenly, but were the fruit of a considerable period of evolution. Although in different ways, they reflect the conditions of the Yugoslav peoples in those times.

A poetic form of expression had already taken shape in the Croatian Glagolitic and Latin literatures some time before the sixteenth century. The poetic language was specially nurtured in the church brotherhoods, one of whose tasks was also to concern themselves with church singing. The religious drama also had developed a taste for more meritorious poetical works before the sixteenth century. A literary language based on the *čakavski* dialect had been created simultaneously in several northern Croatian regions (Istria, the Croatian Littoral), which spread slowly southwards to Zadar and Dubrovnik.

The lively economic and political connexions with Italy and the rest of Europe encouraged fruitful cultural exchanges between the population of the Dalmatian towns and Dubrovnik. Many young men from Croatian regions studied in Italy and visited that country again on more than one occasion during their later years. Furthermore, teachers and artists came from Italy to Dalmatia, where they worked in the towns for long periods. Thus, towards the end of the fifteenth and at the beginning of the sixteenth century, the way of life of the Yugoslav peoples was marked by two extremes: by general illiteracy along the border and in the areas occupied by the Turks, and by Central European luxury in the towns on the coast and in the feudal castles of Croatia and Slovenia, a condition which influenced the first-known Croatian poetical works.

Transit Sv. Jeronima does not go beyond the characteristics of a medieval work. It was printed after an earlier manuscript. Its subject-matter is not original. Its fundamental quality is that of all medieval Croatian literature: piousness. But its verse resembles works more modern in spirit.

Unlike *Transit Sv. Jeronima*, the earliest-known poetical works of Dubrovnik breathe a definite secular, Renaissance spirit. The first acknowledged poets of Dubrovnik, *Šiško Menčetić* (1457—1527) and *Džore Držić* (1461—1501) are simultaneously the earliest-known representatives of Petrarchan lyrics with their expressions of secular love, with their courting, emotion, disappointments. Besides this, the layman Menčetić is more realistic, sensuous, the cleric Držić more retiring, circumspect; Menčetić is stereotyped, Držić uninhibited. Although their manuscript collections of lyrics hardly demonstrate sincerity or real poetry, they are important, for they developed, or at least adopted and passed on, a poetic idiom which proved significant for the entire later literature of Dubrovnik and Dalmatia. Time was required before it could be mastered. It is interesting to observe, however, that Menčetić, the patrician, is more conventional in ideas and expressions; Držić, the priest of the people, is more sensitive, spontaneous. Although their lyrics are, to a certain extent, related to the characteristics of the subject-matter and idiom of the Italian poetry of their time, nonetheless they express national characteristics. Držić goes so far as to attempt to group his verses in an original fashion, which is reminiscent of the species of national epic known by the name of the *Bugarštica*. Still, regardless of its foreign models, their poetry reflects real life: the happy, extravagant, carefree life that could have been lived in those days only in Dubrovnik of all the Yugoslav regions.

The most eminent poetic figure in Croatian literature at the beginning of the sixteenth century was *Marko Marulić* (1450—1524). Probably the descendant of a patrician Romance family from Split, which had been Croatized, he was highly learned, and a prolific writer in Latin and Croatian. A number of his moralistic writings, chiefly compilations, spread throughout Europe in numerous editions, some of which are *De institutione bene beateque vivendi, Evangelistarium, De humilitate et gloria Christi*. He also wrote lyric and epic poems in Latin. His most extensive work of this type, an epic, *King David*, was not printed.

Educated in a humanistic spirit, and exceedingly pious besides, Marulić preached Christian morality, sacrifice and virtue in his works. He deprecated the manifestations engendered by the Renaissance. Yet he was a man who had keen discernment for the conditions prevalent in his town and in Europe generally. He was especially concerned for the social conditions and vices among the classes which should have been leading the people. A sincere Croatian patriot in his public work, he realized in time the danger from the Turks that threatened Western Europe, particularly his own people.

Split had been under Venetian rule for thirty years when Marulić was born. During his maturity, the Turks had advanced so far westwards that they even stormed the walls of the town. In order to warn the western Christian world of all the horrors which his fellow Christians and countrymen were enduring at Turkish hands, he sent a public message in Latin to Pope Hadrian IV, hoping to inspire him to organize a crusade for defence against the Turk. His appeal failed. He also demonstrated his patriotism by translating *Ljetopis Popa Dukljanina* into Latin.

Marulić's poetical works in Croatian are the fruit of his humanistic education, of his Christian morality, and of his outlook on conditions in Europe and in his own country.

In his shorter poems, which did not go beyond the manuscript stage, Marulić, in a fashion, preaches piousness and Christian morality, as he does in his works in Latin. In most of them he severely criticized the social conditions of his times, execrating the depravity reigning in the ranks of the Catholic Church, among the friars and nuns. The most touching of his shorter poems, *Molitva suprotiva Turkom* [A prayer against the Turk] is a realistic picture of the horrors caused by the Turks in the Croatian regions.

Marulić wrote his most extensive work, the epic *Judita* [Judith], in 1501, and printed it in Venice in 1521. It soon reached a third edition.

In subject-matter *Judita* is an epic poem about the biblical character, the widow Judith who saved her town Bethulia from disaster. Aware of the enemy's superiority, she seeks admission to the enemy general, Holofernes, wins his confidence, enchants him, and, one night while he is under the influence of alcohol, kills him and takes his head to her people. Discovering their general dead, the enemy take flight.

Marulić neither expanded nor deepened the plot. Keeping to the biblical story, he adorned it with many descriptions, in accordance with the style of his day and in the spirit of Petrarchan lyrics. His principal work in Croatian is obviously the result of the conditions in Dalmatia. With the horrors perpetrated by Holofernes' army, Marulić indirectly illustrated those perpetrated by the Turk. Simultaneously, by the example of Judith he endeavoured to sustain the faith of his people in deliverance from the enemy.

Marulić wrote *Judita* in mature twelve-syllabled verse, the middle of each verse rhyming with the end. He was not the first poet to adopt this type of verse, which was probably devised after the medieval Latin sacred poetry and the folk poetry: he evidently inherited it from his predecessors, writers with whom we are still unfamiliar. He mentions them in the introduction of his poem, alluding to them as *Začinjavci* — poets.

Marulić was not an exceptional artistic creator. He mostly adapted familiar motifs, which he expressed in his own idiom. He was endowed with a sense for motion, action. His comparisons are vivid, taken from real life. His main work reflects the duality of Croatian conditions: in Dubrovnik, and rather less so in the rest of Dalmatia, the splendour and the gaiety of the Renaissance; in the immediate hinterland, the bloody reality of the Turkish onslaughts. *Judita* is the fruit of anxiety: what will become of the Croatian people under the blows of Turkish might? Unlike the imitations of Petrarchan lyrics from Dubrovnik, it is pervaded by ideas of struggle for freedom, by faith in Croatian strength, which soon brought Marulić a fame outside Split that continued undiminished in Croatian literature for centuries.

The works of the first Croatian poets soon gained renown outside their part of Dalmatia. Dalmatian poets began to sing love poems after the style of Menčetić and Držić, some repetitions of their modes being interspersed with an occasional personal note. Some of them, however, following Marulić in a fashion of their own, continued his patriotic and moralistic line. The second generation of Croatian poets is headed by Hanibal Lucić and Petar Hektorović, of the island of Hvar; Mavro Vetranović, Andrija Čubranović and Marin Držić, of Dubrovnik; and by Petar Zoranić, of Zadar. Although from different regions, they cultivated personal and literary ties, exchanged their experiences, and criticized each other's works.

Hanibal Lucić (1485—1553), a nobleman from Hvar, was the author of love poems and of the drama *Robinja* [The slave girl]. His verses are less formal, and are distinguished by more conciseness than the poetry of the first poets of Dubrovnik. His most outstanding work is *Robinja*. Lucić introduced a secular note into Croatian drama, which had been bound till then to the Church in subject-matter, while being medieval in spirit. Another important point is that its writer, like Marulić, portrayed the bloody reality of his time. As a play it is a failure, for instead of unfolding on the stage, the plot is simply recited. Pirates abduct the daughter of a nobleman and take her to some unknown destination. Her former admirer seeks her, at length finding her a slave on the market-place in Dubrovnik. They reveal their love for each other, he frees her, and they wed.

Elements of Petrarchan lyrics are obvious in *Robinja*. But it also contains the unmistakable marks of folk poetry, for it mentions personages sung of in the national epics. Simultaneously it reflects conditions prevailing in the Balkans and Central Europe, when bands of robbers often abducted the unwary and sold them in slavery. Lucić, who esteemed Dubrovnik both for its cultural and literary importance, and for its political organization, purposely took it as the setting for his plot.

Petar Hektorović (1487–1572), a wealthy nobleman from Hvar, also wrote love poems. His most important poem is *Ribanje i ribarsko prigovaranje* [Fishing and fishermen's talk]. He was well-advanced in age when he wrote this poem in 1568. He describes a three-day excursion on the sea with two fishermen. The poem is a sincere and realistic picture of the impressions he gathered on the fishing-trip, inspired by the warm sense of democracy with which he portrays ordinary people as his equals. Feudalism had reached its height, and the peasants often rose against the nobility even on the island of Hvar. Yet Hektorović expressed himself in terms of admiration for the mind of the simple fishermen. He is also the first poet in Croatian literature to have included three lyric and two epic folk poems, the *Bugarštice*, in his work, as he heard them from his companions on their excursion. He also wrote down their melody, which he said was Serbian.

As a model Hektorović's *Ribanje* is related to Italian fishermen's eclogues. But it primarily contains traits belonging to its own country and to its own period. Hektorović also possessed a definitely artistic quality: the faculty of perceiving and expressing the everyday, small things of life, and an ability of intimate expression. He drew his comparisons from reality, from the real life of the seamen.

Petar Zoranić (1508–c.1550), of Zadar, continued on the course set by Marulić's *Judita* and *Molitve suprotiva Turkom*. Little is known about his life. He wrote a number of works, only one of which, *Planine* [The mountains], was printed after his death, in 1569. In the view of Croatian historians of literature, *Planine* is the first Croatian novel, a remote imitation of Jacopo Sannazaro's *Arcadia*. It contains the fundamental elements of Croatian Petrarchan lyrics. The theme of the work is a description of the poet's journey through the Croatian mountains in order to forget his unhappy love. He describes the regions he passed through, as well as the towns in which he stopped. Love stories with metamorphoses in Ovidian fashion are a part of his descriptions. Actually, the work is an allegory on Croatian life. Security reigns on a narrow strip of territory, on the coast, and life is imbued with love and song. On the other hand, poverty, fear, gnawing cares dominate the hinterland, for the rapacious wolves continually break in. Zoranić's work expresses profound Croatian patriotism as the severe afflictions of the Turkish onslaughts endured in the hinterland by the people loomed on the horizon.

Zoranić also skilfully interwove Marulić's *Molitva suprotiva Turkom* into his work.

Its literary form makes *Planine* the first complete document of Croatian prose to appear during a period when verse predominated in literature. It is distinguished by charming narration, clear-cut representation, and by a warmth with which the writer depicts the Croatian regions. He preserves a multitude of typically Croatian geographical names which were later Italianized during the long Venetian rule.

The poetical and social conditions in Dalmatia under Venetian rule disfavoured Croatian literature. The local nobility curried favour with the ruling sections; the peasant masses were left to provide for themselves in the wilderness of their neglect and ignorance; Turkish pressure from the hinterland was intensified — all this rendered cultural work difficult in Croatia. The first notable writers were followed by a long intermission without any continuators meriting mention. Dubrovnik became the centre of literary activity as it steadily won freedom.

One of the most interesting works in the literature of Dubrovnik is *Jedjupka* [The gypsy], by Andrija Čubranović. It is the story of a gypsy telling some ladies of Dubrovnik their fortunes. The entire subject revolves around love and fidelity. The most important and eloquent is what she foretells the sixth lady — it is in fact a proposal by the poet himself, who is disguised in gypsy costume. *Jedjupka* is a love poem, it resembles Petrarchan verse; but it is devoid of the stereotyped requisites of expression employed by the first poets of Dubrovnik, for it is written in the lively octosyllable. In fact, this type of poetry has now reached its acme. Although short-lived, it was highly popular in Dubrovnik and frequently imitated.

Mavro Vetranović (1482–1576) was a Benedictine friar, and occupied many offices in his order. He withdrew for a time to the lonely island of Sveti Andrija, where he lived as a recluse. He cultivated two traits all his life: a bent for meditation, and critical philosophy.

Vetranović was the first writer in Dubrovnik to occupy himself systematically with writing all his life. He wrote drama, lyric and reflective poems, and tried his hand at epic poems.

As a playwright, Vetranović continued the traditions of Croatian sacred drama. He dramatized biblical events, such as *Posvetilište Avramovo* [Abraham's sacrifice], and *Od poroda Jezušova* [The tribe of Jesus]. His works are more concise and contain more drama than similar medieval religious plays by anonymous writers.

In some of his poems Vetranović waxes eloquent in offering religious guidance, and paraphrases prayers. These poems, however, have no artistic value. But in many of his poems he also expressed his own feelings, his bitter disappointment with people, his loneliness on his desert island. These poems are pure lyricism, full of personal elements. His most important poems are his reflective poems, with the sentiments of the meditator who is confronted with the social and political manifestations of his period. He stigmatized the immorality of the higher social classes in Western Europe, the disunity and egoism of the Christian rulers as the crimes of the Turks loomed on the horizon. He flailed the evils which rent the Catholic Church. He perceived the growing might of the Turkish empire and the desperate position of the Christian nations. During the stubborn defence of Klis, the last Christian bulwark before Split, Vetranović openly warned its defenders that they must not expect help from the Christian West; and he blamed, not the Turks, but the egoism and incompetence of the Christian rulers for those conditions. A patriot and a realist, Vetranović, consequently, paid the highest tribute to the policy of Dubrovnik, his native town, which had adapted itself to the situation, living in peace with the Turk. He demonstrated his patriotism also by being the first writer in Dubrovnik to rise against the insatiate endeavours of Venice to dominate the eastern, Croatian, shore of the Adriatic.

Vetranović is the greatest thinker in the Croatian literature of the sixteenth century. He added depth to the poetry of Dubrovnik of his day in an endeavour to elevate it to universal human coigns of vantage. Unfortunately, most of his poems give the impression of being verbalism rather than real poetry.

Vetranović endeavoured to embody the experiences of a lifetime and his ideas of morality in an epic called *Piligrin* [The pilgrim]. It tells the reader allegorically that with each sin the sinner transforms into a beast which is the symbol of his sin. Vetranović failed to complete the poem.

Marin Držić's (c. 1520) physiognomy, life and literary road differed from Vetranović's. A commoner by birth, a cleric who disliked his occupation, Držić regarded people, not from the standpoint of his own moral and religious upbringing, but as they really were. Although he accepted different ecclesiastical offices, he lived on the whole untrammelled. He studied at Siena, travelled, wrote comedies in Dubrovnik for the entertainment of his fellow countrymen. Restless and rebellious, towards the end of his life he organized a plot against the government of his native town and enlisted the aid of Florence against its patricians. He died in Venice in 1567.

At the beginning of his literary work, Držić followed in the footsteps of the older writers of Dubrovnik. He composed love poems, he attempted to introduce himself as a dramatist with a play intended to be an improved religious representation. His dramatic beginnings were so unfortunate, however, that his contemporaries even accused him of being a plagiarist. Nevertheless he soon found his best field of self-expression in the pastoral play and comedy.

Držić had watched pastoral plays at Siena; he must have become familiar with comedy by reading the writers of Rome and by attending the Italian *commedia dell'arte*. At the height of his literary powers he wrote a number of pastoral plays *(Tirena, Venera i Adon, Ljubmir, Plakir)* and the comedies *Novela od Stanca* [The story of Stanac], *Dundo Maroje* [Uncle Maroje], *Skup* [Skup], *Tripče de Ustolče*. Some of them were published during his lifetime *(Venera i Adon, Novela od Stanca)*, some have been preserved in manuscript, others have perished.

Držić wrote his pastoral plays and comedies, not to be read, but to be acted. He created them hastily, on various occasions. They were performed by amateur companies in Dubrovnik. Indeed, Držić was the founder of the theatre in his native town. He took popular subjects as the basis of his works *(Aulularia, Menaechmi)*, and introduced his own experiences and views into them. There is hardly any difference in this respect between his pastoral plays and his comedies; they differ only in the costumes of the characters and in the place of action: the settings of the comedies were towns (Dubrovnik, Rome, Kotor); the settings of the pastoral plays were the groves. The characters of both are pervaded by the same feelings, by the feelings of the writer himself and of the people of his day.

Držić was a man of the Renaissance. He was sensible of the richness of life in every aspect, and he presented it in his works as he experienced it. His characters hanker for pleasure, entertainment. There is no difference between the old and the young, the rich and the poor, the peasant and the nobleman, between the cleric and the layman. Most of them lived for women, for good food, for pleasure. Adultery and love intrigues were considered, not a sin, but a human trait. To deceive a stupid husband, to substitute a poor lover for a rich one were not offences, but a sign of profound wisdom. Držić's dramas extol youth, gaiety, adroitness, beauty, fun; and scorn old age, weakness, parsimony.

Marin Držić's literary expression reflects the milieu presented in his plays. He is luxuriant, brilliant, with many words and comparisons. Držić's monologues and dialogues are full of wit. His characters move in their atmosphere with animation and ease. Though we meet satyrs and fairies in his pastoral plays, they are actually *Dubrovčani,* old and young, handsome and ugly, the townsfolk and the peasants from the surroundings. In his comedies, on the other hand, Držić intentionally portrayed his contemporaries:

33

the young men of Dubrovnik in quest of pleasure; the elder townsmen with their parsimony and avarice; the relations between the nobility and the peasantry, fathers and children, masters and servants. His works give the most complete picture of Dubrovnik in the period of its prosperity. His contemporary, Nikola Nalješković, tried to present this picture also in dramatic form; but he only contrived to produce the raw material. It required a Držić to shape with the sovereign ease of a creator characters so complete that they have survived the many centuries since their creation.

It seems that in writing his comedies Držić was not content to be merely a painter: he wanted to be a critic as well. As he presents his senile, selfish, stingy old men, he seems to ask how they contrived to obtain the right to rule Dubrovnik. His last action — a political one — owing to which he died far from his native town, seems to be the result of this question.

During the period of Mavro Vetranović and Marin Držić there were several other writers in Dubrovnik and elsewhere who in some way broadened the bounds of literature or altered its course in accordance with the spirit of the times. The most outstanding in Dubrovnik were *Dinko Ranjina* (1536—1607), and *Dinko Zlatarić* (1558—1609). In his lyric poems *(Pjesni razlike* — Different poems — 1563) Ranjina shows a definite desire to break away from the tradition of the older lyrics as had developed from Šiško Menčetić and Džore Držić. He rightly contended that each period creates its own form of expression. His poems contain more life than the poems of his predecessors from Dubrovnik. Dinko Zlatarić, on the other hand, distinguished himself by his renderings of Sophocles' *Electra*, Tasso's *Aminta*, Ovid's *Pyramus and Thisbe*. The struggle with the Turk is treated in Dubrovnik in the work of *Antun Sasin (Razboji od Turaka* — The crimes of the Turks).

There were writers in sixteenth-century Dubrovnik who wrote both in Croatian and in Italian. A literary academy had also already been founded there at that time. One of its members, Miho Monaldi, wrote both philosophical dissertations and poems in Italian.

There was only one eminent writer outside Dubrovnik during Marin Držić's lifetime. He was *Brno Krnarutić* (c.1515—c.1572), of Zadar. He wrote the epic *Vazetje Sigeta grada* [The capture of Szigetvár], which was printed in 1584, and *Smrt Pirama i Tizbe* [The death of Pyramus and Thisbe], printed in 1586. *Vazetje Sigeta grada* for the first time in Croatian literature describes the fall of Szigetvár in Hungary, which was valiantly defended from the Turk by the Croat Nikola Šubić Zrinski, who preferred death to surrender. *Smrt Pirama i Tizbe* is the first independent poetic story in Croatian literature, a belated reflection of Petrarchan lyricism. Both works have documentary rather than poetic significance.

34

Krnarutić dedicated his works to Croats outside Dalmatia: *Vazetje* to Juraj Zrinski, the son of the defender of Szigetvár; *Smrt Pirama i Tizbe* to Antun Vrančić, the Archbishop of Észtergom. In *Vazetje* the writer indicated, not only the danger threatening from the Turk, but also, in his opinion, the evils of Protestantism. He thus touched upon a question which opened new horizons and roused the Slovenes and Croats to new efforts.

3. PROTESTANT LITERATURE AMONG THE SLOVENES AND CROATS

The Reformation moved, in the sixteenth century, from Germany as far south as the Croats and Slovenes, among whom it acquired specific Slovene and Croatian traits. It made the greatest headway in the regions till then devoid of written literature, or whose written literature, if they had any, was frowned on or banned by the authorities.

In the sixteenth century, when Turkish pressure on the Yugoslav people was the severest, social conditions in the Croatian and Slovene regions became steadily worse. Burdened by the war and by feudal levies, the peasantry were deprived of all rights and also neglected culturally. While skirmishes were fought almost continually on the border with the Turk, dissatisfaction grew among the peasantry in feudal Croatia, Krain, and Styria. It was demonstrated most markedly in the Slovene peasant rebellion in 1525, and in the Croatian and Slovene rebellion in 1573. The peasantry took up arms for economic and social liberation and for human dignity. Following initial successes, the rebellions were quelled, their leaders being executed in the cruelest fashion.

The German Reformation was primarily the expression of class relations; it sprang up out of the struggle waged by the German nobility for an independent economic area. Consequently, in relation to the peasantry it remained a strictly class affair. The Slovene areas being under German rule, the movement spread to the local German population. It was adopted also by the Slovenes among whom it gained another significance. Of all the principles of the Reformation the Slovenes most readily favoured the printing of sacred books in the language of the people. Accordingly, it received a more national and social significance among the Slovenes.

The Slovenes entered the sixteenth century as social and political slaves, no less than they had been in the fifteenth century. The nobility and the high church dignitaries, as well as the townspeople, thought and felt like Germans. The few Slovenes who had succeeded in reaching a higher social rung with the help of schools took for granted the use of German and Latin in cultural intercourse. They too considered that Slovene was unfit for literary expression. After the tenth century, to be sure, some scribes, as in the Stična Monastery (1428, 1440), wrote down a negligible number of compositions in Slovene, but these compositions were far from literature. Among the more educated sections, only the lower clergy maintained contact with the despised, illiterate peasantry.

The German Reformation won followers among the nobility and clergy of Krain and Styria, and later among the clergy of Istria and Croatia. Having for a time enjoyed the favour of court circles in Vienna, the Reformation met with no obstacles in Krain and Styria. It was joined by a number of Slovene and Croatian intellectuals at the German universities, who later occupied prominent positions in Germany. Some of them also became outstanding theorists and practicians in the struggle against Catholicism in Germany itself. The most notable was *Matija Vlačić* (Flacius Illyricus, 1520–1575), from Labin in Istria, a writer of works in Latin supporting the Reformation. He spent his mature years in Germany, where he married and carried on significant literary and religious work.

A different path of life was followed by *Primož Trubar* (1508–1586), the son of a peasant from Raščica in Krain. Having accepted the Reformation as a cleric under the protection of his bishop at an early period, Trubar worked for it as a preacher in Ljubljana, his native town, and later in Germany, where he had gone into exile. To him the Reformation was not so much a matter of dogma and relations towards the Pope as it was an opportunity to help his culturally backward peasant people. He concentrated his efforts, in keeping with Protestant principles, on enabling the Slovenes to acquire religious conceptions in their own tongue. Before books were written and printed in Slovene it was necessary to develop a Slovene literary language and orthography. This was accomplished by Trubar with the assistance of his closest friends. His first books, which were also the first books in Slovene, his *Catechism* and his *Abecedarium* (with catechism) were printed at Tübingen in 1550 (or 1551). He signed his books, not with his own name, but with his nom de plume *Philopatridus Illyricus*, the Friend of all the Slovenes. He wrote both works in the dialect of his native land, using the Gothic script.

Trubar found encouragement in his work both in Germany and in his own country. His patron in Germany was Herzog Kristoff von Würtemberg. His position became even stronger with the arrival in Germany of Baron Ivan Ungnad as a refugee from Styria. Ungnad financed a printing-press at Urach for the publication of books in Slovene and Croatian. In his native country he enjoyed the support of almost everyone who was related to the Slovene people.

Trubar's chief task was to supply the Slovene Protestants with the most essential sacred books: the gospels, homilies, hymns. His most important manuscript consisted of rules for the Slovene Protestant Church. All his works, except his first two, were written in the Roman alphabet, which thus also became the Slovene script.

Trubar carried on his religious and literary work in extremely unsettled conditions. He returned to Ljubljana in triumph, after fourteen years in exile, as the head of the Slovene Protestant Church. In Ljubljana he continued his literary work with the assistance of other writers, particularly with the assistance of *Juraj Dalmatin*, the translator of the Bible into Slovene, and *Adam Bohorič*, the founder of the Slovene orthography and the writer of the first Slovene grammar in Latin *(Arcticae horulae;* 1584). Moreover, there was, for a short time, a Protestant printing-press in Ljubljana, in which books in Slovene were printed.

At this time a number of Croatian *Glagolashi* clerics from Istria had fled to Germany. At first they worked with Trubar. The German protectors of the Slovene and Croatian Protestants requested that Protestant books should be written in a language which could be understood by the majority of their readers. They wanted to bring the Slovene texts as near to the Croatian as possible. Realizing, besides, that Serbo-Croatian was spoken in the greater part of the Balkans, they held that this might be used as a mighty propaganda weapon in their work against the Turks. Accordingly they helped the Croatian Protestants. Trubar, however, refused to have anything to do with the project, for he realized that it would prevent him from attracting the Slovene peasants to his literature.

When the Austrian authorities began to persecute the Protestants again, Trubar fled from the country. He died at Deredingen, Germany. The Protestant preachers were exiled from Austria in 1598, the Protestant nobility in 1628, and the movement was thus finally suppressed among the Slovenes.

The conditions for the Reformation were more difficult among the Croats than among the Slovenes. The authorities in the country were opposed from the very outset to every new religious movement, and allowed no other besides the Catholic faith. The followers of the new movement came from the ranks of the lower clergy, from Istria and the Croatian Littoral, primarily from among the *Glagolashi*. In the Catholic Church they had had a feeling of oppression, of being despised. Unable to work at home openly for their movement, the Croatian Protestants fled to Germany, where they organized their work under the patronage of Baron Ungnad and with Trubar's group, translating and printing Croatian Protestant books. Several years later they printed a translation of the New

Testament and a number of other sacred writings. The most prominent among these *Glagolashi* were *Antun Dalmatin* and *Stjepan Konzul Istranin*.

Being *Glagolashi*, the Croatian Protestant writers at first printed their books in the *Glagolitsa*. But knowing that the Croats used the Roman as well as the Cyrillic alphabet, they prepared some of their editions in these scripts. They realized how widespread the use of their tongue was and how related the Yugoslav peoples were; and they endeavoured to write in a language which could be understood on the whole Yugoslav territory.

4. THE BEGINNINGS OF CROATIAN LITERATURE IN THE *KAJKAVSKI* DIALECT

The Croatian Protestant writers were remarkably successful in their work, particularly among the lower clergy. But strong resistance came from the Catholic Church and from the State authorities. The Protestant books, which had been smuggled into the country, were burnt publicly, the Protestants being persecuted and arrested. After the death of Baron Ungnad, the patron of the Slovene and Croatian Protestants, they dispersed in Germany, where they died one after the other in different parts of the country. The movement was soon suppressed.

The success of the Slovene and Croatian Protestants and their propaganda weapon, the written popular tongue, spurred the Catholic reaction to employ the same weapon as a means of spreading the influence of the Catholic Church among the broad masses. It was at first unsuccessful. But later, having defeated its rival, it was no longer concerned with the position of the faithful. Spiritual desolation followed, especially among the Slovenes. With his companions Trubar had sown the seed of Slovene literature with a literary language and orthography. After his death only an occasional book in Slovene, intended chiefly for religious requirements, was printed in the course of two centuries. But even the Catholic writers were compelled to have recourse to the traditions which had been initiated by the Protestants.

Conditions among the Croats improved after the disappearance of the Reformation movement. Although the Catholic reaction did not replace the Protestant books at first, signs of literacy began to appear during the period of the Reformation and later in those regions where till then there had been none. Considerable literary activity showed itself in the seventeenth century, especially when Rome realized what a significant role the Yugoslav peoples played in the Balkan Peninsula.

During the Reformation, literature began to develop in the political centre of the country (near Zagreb and Varaždin), a part of Croatia which had never been conquered by the Turks. It was then that the *kajkavski* dialect of the region came to be used in written literature. Its founders were *Antun Vramec* (1538—1587), a cleric who wrote a chronicle and a collection of stories, and *Ivan Pergošić* (d. 1592), a jurist and the translator of the basic codex of Hungary, Verböczy's *Decretum tripartitum*, into Croatian.

CHAPTER FOUR

THE SEVENTEENTH CENTURY

1. THE LITERATURE OF THE CATHOLIC REACTION

The outstanding problem for the Yugoslav people in the seventeenth century was the continued Turkish rule over most of their territory and the unceasing Turkish attacks upon the regions still unconquered. Besides this, new problems were added by Roman Catholic propaganda in the Yugoslav areas and by the endeavours of the Austrian authorities to weaken the power of the feudal lords with the assistance of the bourgeoisie.

The Turks began to suffer defeats in Europe towards the end of the sixteenth century. For all that, they were still strong. Moreover, in 1683 they advanced as far as Vienna. Only towards the end of the century was Slavonia freed. Instead of being united to Croatia, however, it was governed from Vienna as a special territory under military administration. In Serbia conditions had improved so far that, thanks to Mehmed Sokolović, the Grand Vizier, who was of Bosnian descent, the Turks allowed the Patriarchate of Peć (1557—1766) to be revived, and tolerated at least some semblance of religious life.

In view of the fact that the Turks were obviously weakening, and as signs became evident that the day of national liberation from Turkish oppression was approaching, bonds of Slavic kinship and unity steadily grew between the Croats and the Serbs, who began to feel the need to combat the oppressors. Rebellions even broke out against the Turks in some regions of Serbia; and it was due to the fear of ensuing persecution that in 1690 the Serbs migrated, under the leadership of Patriarch Arsenije Čarnojević, to the uninhabited regions of Hungary near the Turkish border and deeper inland.

In 1525 *Vicko Pribojević*, a Dominican friar, delivered a lecture at Hvar on the subject, *De origine successbusque Slavorum*, which was printed in Venice in 1532. In it he extolled Slavdom in the past and during his day. In 1601 *Mavro Orbini* printed *Il regno degli Slavi*, a historical work imbued with the same spirit. Ideas of Slavdom and Yugoslavdom penetrated into literature more and more in the seventeenth century; but its development was uneven owing to the fragmentation of the Yugoslav territory.

The Croatian literature in the *kajkavski* dialect, which originated in the sixteenth century, produced a number of distinctive writers in the seventeenth century, such as *Juraj Habdelić* (Staro Čiče at Turopolje, 1609 — Zagreb, 1678). A Jesuit and teacher at the Jesuit secondary school in Zagreb, he had no literary pretensions. But his books of sermons *(Zrcalo Marijansko* — Marienglas; *Prvi oca našega Adama Grijeh* — The first sin of our father Adam) contain eloquent observations on the social life of the period, written with taste and elegance.

On account of the small number of readers, the literature of the Croatian *kajkavci* encountered difficulties in gaining popularity. Even the few purchasers of books were unwilling to accept the literature of the *kajkavci* because each purchaser wanted a book written in the dialect of his own region. Consequently, Habdelić was compelled to occupy himself with the problem of finding an orthography and language acceptable to all. But in spite of all difficulties, the *kajkavski* dialect succeeded in surviving in literature. Works of literary significance, in verse and prose, were written in the *kajkavski* dialect; in time dictionaries in this dialect were also compiled. Since it was the dialect of a part of the country which was considered to be the Croatian State, it gradually came to be identified as Croatian.

The main representatives of the Counter Reformation and of Roman Catholic propaganda for the consolidation of Catholicism in the Balkan Peninsula came from Venetian Dalmatia because of its nearness to Italy and Rome and of its contact with the interior of the Peninsula. Having stamped out the Reformation among the Yugoslavs, the Catholic Church resorted to the same propaganda weapon as that employed by the Protestants: the written word. The most prominent of its representatives in Dalmatia was *Bartol Kašić* (1575–1650), from the island of Pag. Aware of the significance of Croatian in the church propaganda disseminated among the people in the Balkan part of the Turkish empire, he could not but discover that its most widespread dialect was the *štokavski*. As a man of foresight he recommended it as the general Yugoslav literary language. He also wrote its first grammar *(Institutiones linguae Illyricae;* 1604), and a number of sacred books of changing significance and subject-matter. As a teacher and missionary, he lived at Dubrovnik and in Belgrade. He died in Rome.

The beginnings of literature in Bosnia under the Turks were also associated with the work of the Roman Catholic propaganda. In their onslaught, the Turks had destroyed most of the monuments of older culture in the country and continually persecuted the infidel. In order to save their positions, the Bosnian feudal lords had embraced Islam. In their religious fanaticism they regarded themselves as Turks, and gave the Turkish State exceptionally zealous officials, while the peasant Christian masses were disfranchized subjects. Only the Franciscans had remained with their people during the centuries of Turkish power in Bosnia. From among them, in the seventeenth century, came the beginnings of literature in Bosnia as they pressed onwards to spread the influence of the Catholic Church eastwards. The representatives of the Catholic Church primarily wanted to give its followers material for religious education. *Matija Divković* (Jelaška, Bosnia, 1563 — Olovo, 1631) had the most success in this work. He was adept at connecting religious instruction with appropriate stories *(Besjede — Sermons — 1616)*.

Divković and his followers were not completely original writers. They took the material for their works from those of the Croatian *Glagolashi* and from various West-European writings. But theirs was a new literary language: the Bosnian *štokavski* dialect. Their books were printed in the Cyrillic script, which they had adapted to the vocal qualities of the living tongue.

The cultural work of the Slovene and Croatian Protestant and Counter Reformation writers contains what appear to be contradictory features. On the one hand, it spread literacy in regions till then ignorant of the written word, and raised local dialects to the level of literary languages. On the other hand, it roused feelings of kinship among the Yugoslav peoples, the result being that the first attempts were made to unite them in literary language. Therein lies the unquestionable cultural, historical and national significance of their work.

2. THE SEVENTEENTH - CENTURY WRITERS OF DUBROVNIK

During those times of memorable conflicts and trials, only Dubrovnik preserved its peace and intensified its feelings of freedom. The golden period of its history was the transition between the sixteenth and seventeenth century: a period of economic prosperity, comfort and almost untroubled happiness. Naturally, its wealth had unpropitious effects: luxury, gaudy adornment in dress, loose morality. This state of affairs endured till the great earthquake of 1667, which destroyed most of the town and caused the death of a large part of the population. During its period of prosperity, Dubrovnik produced its greatest writers, the first of whom was Gundulić.

Ivan Gundulić (1588—1638) came of a patrician family of Dubrovnik. He successively occupied all the offices in Dubrovnik to which he was eligible by reason of his social standing. He was primarily a writer. He wrote lyric poems and a number of plays; but only fragments of some of these have been handed down to us. We know of the existence of others only through their titles. In his plays he dramatized episodes from Ariosto's and Tasso's epics, or motifs from the classics. The poet himself has said that they were performed in Dubrovnik with success. Rarely, however, do they suggest anything personal: with them the poet merely pays tribute to his period and then, in a fashion, casts them aside. Gundulić is famous for three works: the poem *Suze sina razmetnoga* [The tears of the prodigal son], the drama *Dubravka*, and the epic *Osman* which, unfortunately, he did not complete.

Two elements which are evident in Gundulić's art are Christian morality and nationalism.

As a man of his period, Gundulić was convinced that all the things of this world are transient, that all pleasures are evanescent, that it is necessary to concentrate all one's thoughts on religion. This conviction especially pervades *Suze sina razmetnoga*. His lengthiest work, *Osman*, a poem about the transience of everything worldly, is also inspired by it. In *Suze sina razmetnoga*, based on the biblical story, he reflects upon the vanity of pleasure, and on the necessity of seeking and finding God. Their underlying idea is similar to that in some Italian works (Tasso and Tansillo). They are original for their refined expression, sonorous syllables, resounding rhythms.

But Gundulić was also very well aware of the position of his town and of the Slavs as a whole in the Europe of his day. In *Dubravka* and in *Osman* he is a poet of freedom, a champion of Slavdom, of struggle. *Dubravka* (1628) is obviously a pastoral play, recounting love between shepherds and shepherdesses, the intrigues of satyrs, the mishaps of the neighbouring peasants, etc. It has no real dramatic action, but only concentrates on extravagant word-play, colour, light, gaiety. The most beautiful girl, who should be adjudged according to tradition to the handsomest youth, is given by the bribed judges to a rich, ugly man. At the moment, when the unfortunate youth is resolved to commit suicide, the unjust decision is righted by the will of the gods, and everything ends happily and in good humour, and with a hymn to freedom. Instead of the plot unfolding on the stage, the story is recited.

Gundulić is skilful in not allowing human vices to be exposed on the stage in the raw. The spectator is invited to watch and listen only to joy, song and dance. But Gundulić hints that behind the bright façade there is darkness: the pressure of the rich on the poor, the evils of money, the hatefulness of corruption. Beneath the veil of his pastoral play he alludes to social life in Dubrovnik, to its vices, to conditions in Venetian Dalmatia, to the relations between the nobility and the peasantry. Apparently the drama takes place in an imaginary place; but it divulges the reality of Gundulić's period. Gundulić was the first writer in Dubrovnik to sound a warning that Venetian power was pressing heavily upon the population.

> "Primorja naša sva u ništa sila zbi."
> ("Power our coastland into nought has crushed.")

But *Dubravka* is full of optimism: the intrigues of the depraved rich are wrecked, and in the end freedom triumphs as the supreme good which is inherent of every other good.

Gundulić's lengthiest work, *Osman,* is much more forceful in expressing the idea which underlies *Dubravka:* the significance of freedom. But instead of an imaginary world, as in *Dubravka, Osman* contains fresh events of European significance, and dwells at the same time upon the most important problems of Europe: the position of Slavdom, the relation of Christianity towards Islam.

Gundulić was inspired to write *Osman* by the violent death of the sultan of that time. Defeated in 1621 in the Battle of Hotin by the Poles, Osman desired to rejuvenate his army and revive the strength of his empire. But malcontents, learning of his intentions, killed him.

Gundulić brought out the event in his epic, not because of Osman, but in order to illustrate the decay of Turkish power under the blows of the Slavic state during his reign, and to inspire hope for the liberation of all Slavs.

There are some elements in Gundulić's *Osman* which resemble Tasso's and Ariosto's epics. In it vagrant girls also act the part of knights; it recounts a duel for love, jealousy, abductions, etc. There are many Marinoan features in Gundulić's idiom: he indulges in heterogeneity, richness of expression, numerous similes. But the subject-matter of his epic is realistic. In it Gundulić portrays the life of the Turks and Poles with almost photographic precision. Besides this, Gundulić endeavoured to cast his characters psychologically, explaining their successes and their setbacks as being the result of the social environments in which they lived. Osman, the representative of Turkish power, comes to grief, not because he has been conquered, but because his whole environments are depraved. Moreover, Gundulić also brought the inferno into his story as an obstacle to Christian successes. But he seems to have been incapable of bringing this element into accord with the distinctly realistic parts of his epic.

In considering the whole of the earlier literature of Dubrovnik, Gundulić's works, and especially *Osman*, are distinguished by his magnificent ideas. Gundulić dealt with the religious, political and national problems of his day. He portrayed his characters in the whirlpool of the struggle among the supreme ideas of his time: the nation, freedom, Slavdom, humanity.

Gundulić felt especially deeply for Slavdom. Whatever had been revealed about Slavdom since *Pribojević*, Gundulić accepted in the noblest spirit. He extolled the Polish prince, Vladislav, the victor of Hotin, as the champion of the liberation of all Christianity. With particular warmth he described medieval Serbia and the enslaved Serbian people who had to live the life of shepherds, although they were descended from kings. To his mind the folk poetry of the Yugoslav peoples was the supreme treasure, strains from Orpheus' lyre. He spoke of his people as Slavs, and regarded all the Slavs as being one whole.

Gundulić expressed his views and feelings in a rich, brilliant idiom, unequalled by any writer before him. His rhythms are full of frolic, his rhymes are like water drops from a fountain. And in each of his works he succeeded in achieving the proper mood: in *Suze sina razmetnoga*, he is dreary and depressive; in *Dubravka*, the freshness of the breezes of spring; in *Osman*, the verse is like the current of a river, with the echoes of sorrow and fatalism.

Junije Palmotić (1606–1657) was considered a great playwright in Gundulić's time. He wrote a number of comedies and tragicomedies on themes taken from classic mythology, the Italian epics, and national traditions. His best work is *Pavlimir*, with which he extolled his town and its founders. Otherwise, all his works are overburdened with rhetoric, fantasy and loquacity.

The best-known lyric poet in Dubrovnik in Gundulić's day was *Dživo Bunić Vučić* (1594–1658). Like the earlier poets of Dubrovnik, he was chiefly a singer of love. He also has something in common with the troubadours, singing about love disappointments, piety and similar subjects. But although his predecessors often wrote conventional verses, Bunić Vučić revealed his anacreontic sentiments with conciseness and pithiness: the gaiety of youth, the strength of love even in old age, the omnipotence of the feelings, the value of pleasure, side by side with the transience of worldly things. He endeavoured to rid himself of stylistic stereotypes, seeking to give vent to that very feeling in his verse of which it was the source. His poetry, consequently, is impressive in its freshness. The name which he gave his verses is also characteristic: *Plandovanje* [Idling]. During his lifetime he published only one poem, *Mandaljena pokornica* [The repentant Magdalene], in 1630.

During Gundulić's and Bunić's lifetime there appeared two more interesting, but not very prolific, poets in Dubrovnik. They were *Stijepo Djordjić* (1579—1632) and *Vladislav Menčetić* (c. 1600—1666). Djordjić wrote a short poem called *Derviš* [The dervish], in which he parodied Petrarchan lyricism in a novel fashion. By presenting a love-sick old dervish and his wooing realistically, but in the style of the troubadours and followers of Petrarch, he succeeds in showing the reader how silly they are. In addition to other works, Menčetić wrote the poem *Trublja slovinska* [The Slavic trumpet], in which he extolled the Croatian Ban Petar Zrinski for his heroism in the battle against the Turks. Gundulić expected that the Poles would deliver Slavdom; Menčetić destined his hero for this mission. He revealed the stand of the Croats in defence of the West as both tragic and magnificent. He said that Italy would long have been conquered,

> "Were it not that Othman Sea
> "On Croatian headland dashed itself."

3. THE SEVENTEENTH - CENTURY CROATIAN WRITERS

Petar Zrinski (Vrbovac, 1621 — Wiener Neustadt, 1671), Menčetić's hero, was also a writer. A member of one of the wealthiest and most famous Croatian feudal families, the count was the owner of many estates in Croatia. He was also the Ban of Croatia, the political and military head of the country. For his courage and many successes in border clashes with the Turks he earned widespread renown both in his own country and abroad. He had connexions with the most distinguished families of Europe. On the battlefield most of his life, he defended his own estates and protected the whole country from the Turks. In its struggle against the feudal lords, the Austrian court was reluctant to see Turkish might over-weakened for fear the feudal lords would become stronger. Aware that Austria was deceiving both him and the other noblemen, after the death of his elder brother, Petar Zrinski took the lead in the plot against the Habsburgs in association with Louis XIV. He was even prepared to reach a compromise with the Turks. The plot being discovered, he was summoned to Vienna, arrested, condemned to death, and executed at Wiener Neustadt. His brother-in-law *Knez Fran Krsto Frankopan*, a member of another distinguished Croatian feudal family, was executed with him. He was just twenty-eight years of age at his death, but a famous soldier for all that. He too was a poet.

Petar Zrinski and Krsto Frankopan wrote in Croatia proper, in which no distinctive literary works, apart from didactic and

religious writings, had yet been written. Both Zrinski and Frankopan were familiar with European literature. Petar Zrinski was also
in contact with the writers of Dubrovnik. Zrinski and Frankopan
were aware of the living power of folk poetry, and they were not
content with the negligible literature of the Croatian *kajkavci*.
Consequently, as writers, no less than as soldiers, they kept the
whole nation in view as they wrote.

Apparently Petar Zrinski was not an original poet. The only
book he published, *Adrianskoga mora sirena* [The siren of the
Adriatic], is a paraphrase on the work written in Hungarian by
his elder brother Nikola. It consists chiefly of a description of the
battle of Szigetvár. The whole work is pervaded by a tendency
which, being the result of experience, guided Zrinski in his political work as well. He presented Nikola Zrinski, the hero of Szigetvár, as the victim of Austrian treachery: he died because the
emperor refused to send him relief. The theme of the poem is that
one should place as little faith in the Germans as in the sun of a
winter's day. The book is also imbued with democratic feelings.
According to his own statement, Zrinski wrote the book for his
comrades-in-arms. The poem is in the twelve-syllable verse familiar
in the literature of Dubrovnik and Dalmatia.

The young, inexperienced, temperamental *Fran Krsto Frankopan* (1643—1671) was involved in the plot, he himself knew not
how. None of his books were published during his lifetime. Perhaps
no one even knew that he occupied himself with writing. His
manuscripts were preserved in Vienna, together with the files of
the inquiry conducted against him, and published two hundred
years after his death. They indicate Frankopan's broad literary
tastes. For example, he was engaged in translating Molière's *Georges
Dandin* even before it was published in France. But the most
important of all are his lyric poems called *Gartlic za čas kratiti* [The
garden of repose]. The collection contains some conventional
verses of love written after the fashion of the day. But many of
his verses contain distinctively personal outpourings. As a member
of his family and as a soldier who fought against the Turks, Frankopan wrote sincere poems of war, which are a truthful picture of
the times. The most touching and the profoundest are the verses
he wrote in prison. They contain the complaints of a young man
who had scarcely begun to live, who had lost his father and mother
early, and who had now been snatched also from his wife, friends,
from everything dear to him, leaving him neither alive nor dead.
One of Frankopan's media was also the verse of folk poetry; thus
he attained a simplicity and directness of expression rare in any
Croatian writer in that period.

Two writers significant of the ideological trends in Croatian cultural and national life are Juraj Križanić and Pavao Ritter Vitezović.

Juraj Križanić (1618–1683) was born at Ribnik near Zagreb. He was a Jesuit. He pursued some of his studies in Rome. Entrusted with the task of popularizing a union between the Orthodox and the Catholic Church, he went twice to Russia. After his first stay, he evidently forgot the purpose of his journey, for he was carried away by the idea of Slavdom and the unification of all the Slavs. The Russian authorities, suspecting sedition, exiled him to Siberia. It seems they released him just before his death, for his body was found among the Polish dead during the Turkish siege of Vienna.

Križanić was a prolific writer. His works in manuscript were left behind in Russia. In his most important work, *Politika*, he advised the Slavs, particularly the Russians, to improve their economic and cultural level. He denounced their social deficiencies, their state of neglect, their backwardness. But more than anything, he condemned their tendency to admire whatever came from abroad, and to despise whatever was their own. He told them what they ought to learn from the West-European nations, and encouraged them to aspire towards greater heights.

A similar fate befell *Pavao Ritter Vitezović* (1652–1712). Born at Senj, he developed differently from most of the Croatian writers who were clerics by profession or feudal lords by social standing. Highly educated, he worked in his country, especially in Zagreb, as a poet, historian, printer, publisher, lexicographer, editor of a calendar, etc. He wrote in Latin and Croatian. His most extensive work is his poem in Croatian *Odiljenje sigetsko* [The resistance of Szigetvár], describing the battle for that town. He wrote the first scientific history of Serbia, *Serbia illustrata*. He was the first Croatian professional man of letters. Concerned for the Yugoslav peoples, who were partitioned by many rulers, he worked out a plan according to which Austria was to free all the Yugoslavs from the Turks and unite them in a single nation, justifying their unification by means of historical legal documents. Besides this, he occupied himself with the problems of the literary language and orthography, in connexion with simplifying writing with the Roman alphabet and uniting the Yugoslavs in a single literary language.

He failed to publish all his works. His fate in his own country resembled that of Juraj Križanić in Russia. A poor intellectual, living by his work, he hoped to become economically independent on being presented by the emperor, whose official historian he was, with the estate of an insane canon from Zagreb. But the

Croatian nobility were against him. Evicted from the estate, he fled to Vienna to seek the protection of the Court. In Vienna he died in poverty.

4. PAJSIJE

In the seventeenth-century Serbian culture under the Turks, the most prominent personality was the Patriarch of Peć, *Pajsije* (c. 1550—1647). He travelled from monastery to monastery, collecting old manuscripts and encouraging the surviving monks to copy books. He wrote the biography of Uroš, the last of the Serbian emperors, which is a legend rather than a life story.

CHAPTER FIVE

THE EIGHTEENTH CENTURY

1. THE POLITICAL AND ECONOMIC CONDITIONS

The most obvious discrepancy of the European eighteenth century — the extravagance of the ruling classes and the extreme poverty and backwardness of the broad sections of the population — also affected the Yugoslav peoples. The difference was that the Yugoslav peoples had no prosperous, progressive bourgeoisie like the bourgeoisie of Western Europe to do away with obsolete views and to fight for better social conditions. In the western Yugoslav regions, the bourgeoisie came from nationalities other than Yugoslav, or was still in its infancy. Besides this, the majority of the population in regions newly liberated from the Turks still lived in primitive conditions.

The eighteenth century in Austria was still feudal. While it degenerated, its pressure on the subjugated peasantry became heavier. Even during the most unpropitious economic periods, the feudal gentry affected all the comforts available in those times. The picture of social relationships is clear at first sight: in the centre of the country were baroque palaces and churches of inestimable artistic value; side by side with them were the tumble-down hovels of the ragged and under-nourished peasantry. The majority of the eighteenth-century aristocrats did not live in Croatia. They received their rents from their holdings in Croatia and spent them in Vienna. It was the same case in the Slovene areas. As a result a number of peasant rebellions broke out in the eighteenth century. The effect of these social conditions reverberated in Slavonia, which had just been liberated from the Turks. Coming under Austrian rule, the Slavonian peasantry expected to gain economic independence. Instead, their fertile land was divided among alien feudal lords, and they became serfs again. The new masters often exploited their subjects even more ruthlessly than their old masters had. Many a Slavonian peasant, preferring Turkish thraldom, fled to Bosnia.

A rich cultural life began to bloom in Zagreb during the latter half of the eighteenth century. During the eighties a permanent German theatre was founded in the town by a company of good actors. It also had a newspaper, which was published in German. The theatre presented plays which were in vogue in Central Europe. But the Croatian townspeople could not regard the theatre as other than a foreign theatre. Meanwhile, the pupils of the Catholic seminary organized a company, which performed plays in Croatian. Some *kajkavski* writers adapted plays by popular playwrights, such as Goldoni, or wrote plays of their own.

The eighteenth century brought a change particularly to that section of the Serbian people who had moved to Austria towards the close of the seventeenth century. The Austrian authorities had promised the Serbs national and religious freedom in exchange for military service. The Serbs had slowly allowed themselves to be assimilated into the new regions, many of them taking up vocations which they had never followed in Serbia. Most of the people continued to till the land. Others engaged in crafts, commerce and banking, and became a considerable economic factor in their adopted country. Many young Serbs went to Austrian schools and obtained a Central-European education.

Living as they did in a multi-national State, which Austria in fact was, the Serbs did not confine themselves to the border territory adjacent on the Turkish empire, but slowly spread inland. There were important colonies of Serbs even in Budapest, Vienna and Trieste. Near Budapest there were towns with Serbian majorities (Szentendre).

In the regions under Austrian rule the Serbs established a bourgeoisie of their own, which was prosperous and nationally aware. As the Orthodox faith was the only mark which distinguished the Serbs from the ruling Germans and Hungarians, the Church came to be almost a synonym for Serbdom, and the supreme authority among the Serbs. The views and decisions of the high ecclesiastical authorities were tantamount to final judgment. The Serbian Orthodox Church was, therefore, not only a religious, but also a secular and educational authority. It was an economic force as well. Some church dignitaries owned considerable property; even more considerable was the property owned by the many Serbian monasteries, upon which gifts were lavished by the prosperous Serbs, who considered them the symbols of Serbdom.

Life in those parts of the Yugoslav territories which were still held by the Turks (Serbia, Bosnia and Herzegovina, Macedonia) was vastly different. The life of the Christians worsened as the Turkish power in Europe declined. Plunder, murder, rape, the abduction of healthy children to Turkey, exorbitant taxes, total lawlessness were the order of the day. Conditions were especially bad in the border areas, where various officials held arbitrary sway, disregarding the real policy of the central authorities in Constantinople. These conditions were the cause of repeated rebellions, which invariably ended in the defeat of the rebels and in the bloody vengeance of the conqueror. Consequently, many people took to the woods, while the more intrepid among them joined the *Hajduks* to take their revenge on the oppressors.

In these conditions literary work was impossible. The peasantry were wholly illiterate; even the rare clerics were poorly educated. Folk poetry, which extolled the champions of freedom and cherished the memories of the past, was the only sign of literary creation.

The second half of the eighteenth century, with its general economic and social restlessness, was an important turning point for all the Yugoslav peoples. The Austrian rulers continued to consolidate their power by suppressing the nobility and strengthening the bourgeoisie. The reign of Maria Theresa (1740—1780) was distinguished by many progressive cultural and social decrees. Her policy was continued even more radically by her son Joseph II (1780—1790). Both Maria Theresa and Joseph II endeavoured to lessen class and religious differences, to abolish class discrimination, to promote prosperity and to raise the standard of education. Joseph II was especially renowned for his liberal and educational reforms. He closed the monasteries whose monks did not occupy themselves with school work or charity. His cultural and social reforms in Austria were named *Josephinism* after him.

The reign of Maria Theresa and Joseph II was also to a considerable extent advantageous for the Slovenes: decrees were issued in Slovene, attempts were made to teach Slovene in schools. Furthermore *Josephinism* had champions in Croatia. In spite of this, however, Joseph II, on the whole, caused resistance. Desirous of simplifying the administration, both he and his mother centralized the government by concentrating power in Vienna, and in this way violated the rights of the several nations constituting the empire. Besides this, they gave preference to German to the detriment of Latin, which was the official language, and to that of the national tongues. Joseph II's reign marks the beginning of systematic Germanization of the non-German parts of his realm, including Croatia. This was especially supported by the well-to-do in the Croatian towns. In Croatia the second half of the eighteenth century was characterized by the growing hatred of sincere patriots for everything introduced by foreigners, including even those things which were in essence beneficent.

Towards the end of the century, the Yugoslavs in Austria, as well as the Yugoslavs under Venice and in Dubrovnik, learned of the French Revolution, which inspired enthusiasm in the oppressed and horror in the privileged.

2. CROATIAN EIGHTEENTH - CENTURY LITERATURE

Owing to the political fragmentation of the Croatian territory, Croatian literature continued in the eighteenth century in four dialects, in four orthographies, and with various problems confronting it. There were apparently four literatures: one in inner Croatia, one in Dubrovnik, one in Venetian Dalmatia, and one in Slavonia. There were stirrings of literature also in Bosnia.

Dubrovnik was steadily losing its prominence owing to the declining importance of the Adriatic in world trade. The earthquake of 1667 had dealt a heavy blow to its economy, and dessimated its ruling class. The bourgeoisie of Dubrovnik, on the other hand, gained in strength in the eighteenth century. Some wealthier members of the bourgeoisie were even admitted into patrician society. Cultural life in the town continued to be intensive. It is significant, for instance, that many of Molière's comedies, adapted to conditions in Dubrovnik, were performed in Dubrovnik in that century. On the other hand, creative work in the popular tongue declined. In the new conditions, the educated *Dubrovčani* wrote either in Latin or Italian, and some of them left their country and went to France, Italy, etc. The most prominent among them was *Rudjer Bošković* (1711—1787), a physicist, mathematician and poet. On the other hand, others who wrote in foreign languages, dealt nevertheless with national topics. One of them was *Djuro Ferić* (1739—1820), who translated folk poetry into Latin.

The most European of the Croatian writers of the eighteenth century were those who, notwithstanding the proximity of the Turkish State, and the backwardness of most of the people, wrote in the baroque style of the European literature of that period. In Dubrovnik there was Ignjat Djurdjević, in Slavonia Antun Kanižlić. Obviously they wrote for the most educated section of the people: for the clergy and the nobility.

Ignjat Djurdjević (1675—1737) was the last noteworthy poet from Dubrovnik. He began to write while he was very young. He was twenty-two years of age when he joined the Jesuit order and burnt most of his poems. Later he joined the Benedictines and held various ecclesiastical offices in Dubrovnik and in Italy. During his lifetime he cherished literature more than anything else, composing poems, translating, studying science. He wrote in Latin and Italian.

Most of his works, however, are in Croatian. He was the first to attempt to give a complete picture of the literary past of Dubrovnik (*Vitae et carmina nonnullorum illustrium civium Ragusinorum*), and was the author of the first major scholarly work in Croatia, the *Life of Saint Benedict*, the founder of the Benedictine order. Out of all his works Djurdjević published only the poem *Mandaljena Pokornica* [The repentant Magdalene] and a translation of David's Psalms, *Saltijer Slovenski* [The Slavic psalter], both of which were printed in 1728.

Djurdjević's lyric verse, including *Mandaljena Pokornica*, in the main typifies the baroque. The writer strove, not to disclose his personal feelings, but to set out his own peculiar modes of expression. For example, he sang to the fire-fly, whose glow, for want of a better light, helped a lover to read a note from his beloved. He sang about a maiden who accidentally caused the death of her lover by giving him a flower to smell, which a serpent had filled with venom. In his *Različite zgode nesretne ljubavi* [The various trials of an unhappy love], Djurdjević went out of his way to invent the strangest and most unusual story. And in all his works, he employed a medium luxuriant and rich in attributives. Yet he always wrote with so much care, and demonstrated such a degree of ingenuity that his poems are impressive in their charm and loveliness.

Mandaljena Pokornica is a poem about a woman who repents of her sinful past and passes her days in a cave, far from her country. The work is distinctive for the richness of its expression rather than for the psychology of the penitent.

Although outwardly a follower of the West-European style, Djurdjević also showed a profound understanding of the events which were taking place among his own people. He was enthusiastic about the idea of Slavdom, referring to his tongue as Slavic, as Gundulić had before him. In some of his poems he uses the rhythms of the folk poems and alludes to its heroes.

Antun Kanižlić (1699–1777), from Požega in Slavonia, resembled Djurdjević in trend and in style. He wrote short poems and the epic *Sveta Rožalija* [Saint Rosalia], which was published in 1780. The subject-matter is similar to that of Djurdjević's *Mandaljena Pokornica*. Kanižlić portrays a young woman surrounded by luxury. All of a sudden she comes to her true self and goes out into the wilderness, where she devotes herself to worship and resists all temptations. Kanižlić dealt more deeply with the psychological emotions of his penitent. But he too gave more attention to his mode of expression than to his story. Like Djurdjević's work, his also contains many elegant, artificial elements. His poem, however, also contains artistic passages, especially descriptions of landscapes.

In his *Rožalija*, Kanižlić used the verse in vogue among many of the writers of Dubrovnik: double-rhyming twelve-syllable lines. Judging by the spirit of his writing and by his mode of expression, his work could have taken shape only in the Jesuit surroundings in which he lived, and by no means in contact with the life of his country, in which the foundations of cultural work had still to be laid.

Dalmatia and Dubrovnik, as well as Slavonia and inner Croatia, produced writers in the eighteenth century who continued the work of the preceding generations. They wrote lyric and epic poems, and plays; and they adapted and translated foreign works into Croatian; but they did not possess the strength to establish themselves fully as creators. The late eighteenth-century literature of Dubrovnik gradually came to be occasional literature. Aware of the decline of local conditions, the ruin of their native town, the better-educated and more prosperous *Dubrovčani* left their country and settled in Italy or France. An interesting instance in this connexion is the Frenchman who endeavoured to cultivate a sense of patriotism among the *Dubrovčani*.

Marko Bruerović (Lyons, 1774 — Cyprus, 1825), son of the French consul in Dubrovnik, and later consul himself (Bruère Desriveaux), learnt to love Dubrovnik and the *Dubrovčani*, and even chose a wife from among its people. He wrote a number of poems in the style of folk poetry. He described the folk customs of the region as far he was familiar with them. He warned the *Dubrovčani* not to leave their native town, not to be deluded by foreign countries; he aroused their interest in the beauty of their country and tongue.

Bruerović realized what the patricians of Dubrovnik had failed to realize: that their time was up and that the new conditions demanded new methods of public administration. Instead of understanding the inevitable march of social development, many of the better-educated and once prosperous *Dubrovčani* withdrew deeply hurt and with a feeling of profound contempt for the triumphant common people. This still aristocratic Dubrovnik was occupied by Napoleon's troops in 1806. After Napoleon's fall, the town went to Austria, and by degrees it deteriorated to the level of an ordinary provincial town.

Writers of a different kind in the eighteenth century were those cultural workers and men of letters, mostly from the ranks of the people, who purposely wrote for the most neglected part of the population, for the peasantry. Usually without any definite literary objective, but in keeping with the trends of their century, they wanted to be enlighteners. They were to be found also in Venetian Dalmatia, and in Slavonia, as well as in inner

Croatia. The most prominent among them were Filip Grabovac, Andrija Kačić Miošić, and Matija A. Reljković.

Filip Grabovac (1695—1750), from Vrlika, was a Franciscan friar in the military service of Venice. He was one of the first to perceive the social and educational conditions in Dalmatia, the backwardness of the peasantry, and the hankerings of the educated Croats after foreign models, the desuetude of folk customs, the difficult position of the Croatian people generally. He endeavoured to change these conditions through literature. His most important work, written in 1747, is *Cvit razgovora naroda iliričkoga aliti Hrvatskoga* [The flower of discourse of the Illyrian or Croatian people]. The work is not a solid whole, but rather a collection of various didactic and entertaining compositions in verse and in prose. They treat of religion, education and morality. In some of them, the writer is a severe religious fanatic. His style is spirited and easy. Some of his stories about the strange destinies of men in difficulty, who are always saved by their faith, are especially readable.

The work is notable for its Croatian patriotism. The writer reveals the miserable lot of the Croat, who is compelled to fight for foreigners, who also appropriate the fruit of his toil. Because of this book Grabovac was sentenced to long years of imprisonment. He died in prison.

Andrija Kačić Miošić (Brist, 1704 — Zaostrog, 1760) was also a Franciscan friar. He held various religious offices in Dalmatia and Bosnia. During his journeys, he became familiar with the backward conditions of the peasantry, with their ignorance of their history and of themselves. He also perceived that these masses had an art of their own, the epic poem, which was the repository of their knowledge of history and life. Much as he acknowledged the beauty of this poetry, he claimed that its subject-matter was not true. Accordingly, he published a book in 1756 which he called *Razgovor ugodni naroda Slovinskoga* [A pleasing account about the Slavs]. His next book was *Korabljica*, written in 1760. Both works are chronicles in the style customary for chronicles during that period. *Razgovor ugodni* is particularly important, as it is a complete history of the Yugoslav peoples, especially of their struggle with the Turks. Kačić rendered the best-known, or the most important events, in the ten-syllabled verse of the folk poem. In this manner he spoke a language comprehensible and close to the peasantry. His work was an unparalleled success. It rapidly spread in countless copies to almost all the Croatian regions, and to some parts of Serbia as well. It soon eclipsed the earlier Croatian literary works designated for the better-educated sections and most often written in imitation of West-European models. Its success was enhanced further by the fact that Kačić was deeply attached to democracy, that he regarded all men as equals, regardless of their station in life. In his work he firmly champions unification among the Yugoslavs, he finds inspiration in the history of the Croats and Serbs, he advises religious tolerance. *Razgovor ugodni* played no mean role in drawing the Yugoslav peoples together; in fact, his work is still popular.

Something similar was accomplished in another way in Slavonia by *Matija Antun Reljković* (Svinjar, 1732 — Vinkovci, 1798). His region, which had just been rid of Turkish domination, was invaded immediately by feudalists, and by various monastic orders each of which spread propaganda in behalf of its interests, but were incapable of approaching the people, who were unaccustomed to the European ways of life. In the first place, the people required to be rescued from their economic and cultural backwardness. Reljković had been an army officer. He was captured in 1757, during the Seven Years' War. As a prisoner of war in Frankfurt, he became familiar with the way of life in Western Europe. While in captivity, in Dresden in 1762, he wrote *Satir* [The satyr]. His objective was to be a teacher in the broader sense. Like Kačić in Dalmatia, he perceived the strength of versification among the peasant people. Accordingly he expounded his views regarding the backwardness of Slavonia, the baneful remnants of Turkish influence, in the ten-syllabled popular verse, offering advice on economy, the family, morality, knowledge, etc. While the work was a success among the peasants and advanced people, it was attacked by the conservatives and religious retrogrades.

Satir is an important cultural and historical picture of a transitional period. It is an attempt to extricate literature from the isolation of class confinement, and to make it popular in the broadest sense of the term. In addition to *Satir*, Reljković published a number of didactic works. They did not win the popularity of *Satir*.

For similar reasons — for religious propaganda or for educational purposes — an additional number of books were printed in Slavonia during the eighteenth century. The writers were *Antun Ivanošić, Vid Došen, Adam Tadija Blagojević*. Blagojević, a layman, had fixed views regarding the social relationships of his day, and voiced his protest against class discrimination. The best educated and most European of eighteenth-century Slavonian writers was *Matija Petar Katančić* (Valpovo, 1750 — Buda, 1825). He published a number of scientific works in Latin. One of his works of importance in Croatian literature is his collection of poems in Latin and Croatian, *Fructus Auctumnales* (1794), written in the old classical metre. Katančić is also the author of the first Croatian metrical rules.

During the eighteenth century, the central part of Croatia, in the vicinity of Zagreb, presented a heterogeneous social and cultural picture. The men of letters and cultural workers were mostly clerics or laymen, or members of various orders, especially the Jesuit and the Pauline. At the end of the seventeenth century, during the whole of the eighteenth century, and in the early years of the nineteenth century, several major works were published in this field which were important in the further development of political and national conditions in Croatia (*Jambrešić-Šušnik: Lexicon Latinum interpretatione Illyrica, Germanica et Hungarica;* 1742; *Mikoci: Otiorum Croatia liber unus;* 1806). They emphasized the significance of the Croatian people, the unity and consanguinity of the Yugoslavs.

The most outstanding Croatian writer of the latter half of the eighteenth century in *kajkavska* Croatia was *Tito Brezovački* (1757—1805), from Zagreb. He was at first a Pauline. When his order was dissolved, he turned layman. But, never able to agree with his superiors, he was continually persecuted. Being of a clear-sighted, frank nature, he refused to condone the corruption of the period, the superstitions and backwardness of a great part of the population, and the political position of the Croats. He recorded his observations in verse, Latin and Croatian. But the most important of all are his plays *Sveti Aleksij* [Saint Alexis], *Grabancijaš Dijak* [The sorcerer's apprentice], *Diogeneš* [Diogenes]. These plays establish him as the best Croatian dramatist of his period and as the most fruitful dramatist of the amateur drama company of Zagreb.

His first play merely elaborates the legend about the saint who lived for years among his kin as a beggar without being recognized. *Grabancijaš* and *Diogeneš* are in the style of the didactic plays of that period. They contain several scenes each which are joined together by the hero who appears in each of them, and after whom the plays are named. *Grabancijaš* is based on a folk tale: the hero is a pupil who has graduated from thirteen schools, the thirteenth giving him a command of sorcery. *Diogeneš*, on the other hand, is a servant employed simultaneously by two brothers who do not recognize each other.

Brezovački wrote his plays for educational purposes, to combat superstition, egoism, drunkenness and other vices. He demonstrated his ability to cast living characters typical of various classes: noblemen, government officials, merchants, pupils, etc. He was one of the first Croatian writers who, in his own, typical way, pointed to the decay of feudalism and to the absurdity of class privileges. His two dramas are still performed because of their lively character.

3. SERBIAN EIGHTEENTH - CENTURY LITERATURE

Having been arrested in its progress by the Turks, Serbian literature resumed its course in the eighteenth century, but in different regions and in economic and social conditions other than those of the Middle Ages. The literature of medieval Serbia was written and nurtured by the monks and by the members of the higher classes. The later Serbian literature was created by the Serbs who had fled to Hungary from the Turks.

The earlier and the later Serbian literatures were connected by the monks who had come from the thirteenth-century Rača Monastery on the river Drina. These monks were also engaged in copying old manuscripts. Taking their manuscripts and books with them during the migration of the Serbs under Arsenije Čarnojević, they moved to the new regions and resumed their work at Szentendre, near Budapest, assuming as their surname the name of their monastery. Two of them especially distinguished themselves: *Jerotej Račanin*, who wrote, among other things, a book describing his journey to Jerusalem (1704); and *Kiprijan Račanin*, who wrote the first dissertation on Serbian versification.

The position of the Serbian Orthodox Church in Austria compelled its representatives to ask the Russian Church for protection from being forced into union with the Catholic Church. Whenever they no longer required Serbs as soldiers, the Austrian authorities broke their promises regarding freedom of conscience, and endeavoured to convert them to Catholicism. In consequence, the Serbian Orthodox Church established connexions with the Russian Church. Young Serbian students of theology in Hungary, who sought higher education, went to the theological schools in Russia, especially to Kiev. As a result of this, many Russian words crept into the Serbian church language. Russian influence among the Serbs grew with the coming of Russian teachers to found schools in the Serbian towns (Sremski Karlovci) and to teach the Serbian children (1726–1729, 1733–1737). All this created a speech which was neither the Old Slavic of Cyril and Methodius nor popular Serbian, but a language containing elements from both, and also elements from the so-called Russo-Slavic. This artificial language now became the language of the Serbian Church and the speech of the educated Serbs. The Church and the intellectuals thus gradually became estranged from the masses, craftsmen and peasantry. By long usage the Russo-Slavic became, not only the literary language of the Serbs, but also the speech of the townsfolk.

The absolute authority of the Serbian Orthodox Church among the Serbian people in Austria had at least one advantage: it united the Serbs into a solid body and protected them from denationalization. On the other hand, its disadvantage was that the clerics and monks were the only national leaders. They often exploited the ignorance and credulity of the peasant masses to perpetuate their authority and to increase their estates. Medieval ideas continued to prevail in the Serbian areas even during the eighteenth century and at the beginning of the nineteenth, when progress in the natural sciences and philosophy had begun to check the influence of religion. The lives of the saints were still taken as an illustration of reality. Belief in miracles, in charms, in the power of the saints on earth, was taken for granted. Any attempt to spread advanced scientific ideas among the Serbs was pronounced by the conservatives as an attack on the faith and the Church.

The Serbian literature of the eighteenth century boasted a considerable number of writers, the majority of whom belonged to the Church, or were under its patronage. They were *Hristifor Žefarović, Vasilije Petrović, Aleksije Vezelić, Gligorije Trlajić, Jovan Rajić, Pavle Julinac, Djordje Branković*, etc. Some of them wrote didactic works (Trlajić), or historical works (Djordje Branković, Vasilije Petrović). Aleksije Vezelić also wrote verse; Jovan Rajić wrote, among other things, a history of the Serbs, Croats and Bulgars. Pavle Julinac published a translation of Marmontel's *Bélisaire*. But they wrote only for the educated who were practised in reading the artificial literary language; the broad masses continued illiterate.

The most distinguished writer in the middle of the eighteenth century who endeavoured to work for the people was the layman *Zaharije Orfelin* (1726—1785). Self-taught and educated at secular sources, Orfelin held various posts as a means of livelihood. He was a schoolmaster, the Metropolitan's clerk, a printer, engraver, a wine-grower, a proof-reader in a Vienna printing-office. He also moved frequently: to Sremski Karlovci, Novi Sad, Vienna, Venice, etc. What exactly his aim in life was, is hard to say; at any rate, during his lifetime he wrote and published didactic books: an abecedarium, a calendar, a manual on wine-growing, which were designated for the masses.

Orfelin's most extensive work is a biography of Peter the Great (1772), which was both a historical and a propaganda work. Orfelin also founded the first Yugoslav magazine — *Slavenoserbskij magazin* [The Slavo-Serb magazine] (Venice, 1768), which contained educational and other articles. From Orfelin, who was the foremost Serbian poet of the eighteenth century, comes the poem *Plač Serbiji* [The sobs of Serbia] (Venice, 1761), a touching picture of the destiny and trials of subjugated Serbia.

Orfelin published most of his works anonymously or under different pen names, owing to the danger which threatened him for writing books as a layman on affairs within the competence of ecclesiastics. Even the name Orfelin is his invention. In his mode of expression he digressed from the literary language of his time. He was not successful, for the Church was still a mighty force among the Serbs. Impoverished and ailing, he surrendered towards the close of his life. He died almost a beggar, on the farm of the Orthodox bishop of Novi Sad.

Orfelin was typical of the eighteenth century: a writer who believed in the omnipotence of knowledge. His primary objective was to spread education. He was the first opponent of conservatism, which was encouraged among the Serbian masses by the Church. Literary ambitions were for him of secondary importance. His work was continued in happier circumstances by Dositej Obradović.

Dositej Obradović (1742–1811), christened Dimitrije, was the son of a craftsman from Čakovo in Banat. His father died while Dositej was a child. Under the guardianship of his uncle, he also was expected to take up a craft. Having mastered the art of reading at an early age, he read books avidly. He was deeply impressed by the hagiographies. Influenced by them, he fled to Hopovo Monastery in Srem in order to become a saint, like his heroes. But in his new environments he soon realized that the life of the monks was not what he had anticipated. So he fled abroad to accumulate as much knowledge as possible. He passed almost his whole life in travelling, earning his way mostly as a tutor. He got to know Croatia, Dalmatia, Albania, Greece, Asia Minor. He lived in Constantinople, in Rumania, at Odessa. He spent a number of years in Vienna. He went as far as Germany, Italy, France and England. Thus he became acquainted with different environments, many people, and various customs. He had a good command of all the living tongues of Europe, and of Latin and Greek. He studied philosophy, the natural sciences and mathematics. He was familiar with the European literature of his period.

The fruit of Dositej's rich experience and endless study were his writings. He began to write in Dalmatia, for the practical purpose of teaching the illiterate. But it was later that he realized what the Serbs really required; and he began to publish more extensive works: *Život i priključenija* [Life and adventures] (1783), *Sovjeti zdravago razuma* [Counsel of sound reason] (1784), *Basne* [Fables] (1788), *Sobranie raznih naravoučiteljnih veščej* [A collection of various instructive devices] (1793), etc.

Often Dositej was not an original writer. He borrowed suitable material from various sources and rearranged it for his Serbian readers. His chief task was to educate the Serbs, and to eradicate superstition from among them. He especially combatted the fatal influence of the monasteries, whose ignorant monks deliberately perpetuated the ignorance of the peasant masses in order to continue their own leisurely way of life. Obradović regarded Joseph II, who had closed a number of monasteries, as one of the greatest men. He himself advocated religious tolerance, education for women, etc.

Dositej was almost a fanatic as regards his work. To an even greater extent than Zaharije Orfelin he had to combat the resistance of the Serbian Orthodox Church. It was his good fortune that he came on the scene at a time when a bourgeoisie, prosperous and craving for education, had already risen among the Serbs in Hungary. From this bourgeoisie he received both moral and material support.

Dositej's success was remarkable. His more important works were published in two editions during his lifetime. He spent the last years of his life in Serbia, in Belgrade, after the successful Serbian Insurrection, in the highest office that could be bestowed on him: he was made minister of education in a country in which everything had to be begun from the bottom. He died in Belgrade.

Although a cosmopolitan in his views, Dositej strongly influenced the development of the Serbian people. He was a protagonist of understanding and brotherhood among the Serbs, as well as between the Serbs and Croats. He particularly united the Serbs in the different regions by writing, not in the artifical literary language, but in the popular tongue as he knew it. His literary work in every respect marked the end of the Serbian literary tradition which had been conceived for a narrow circle of people.

Dositej rarely demonstrated pure literary tendencies. He did indeed write poems about the uprisings of the Serbs, but they were not art. Nevertheless he was a writer even when he had no intention of being one, when he held that he was only translating other peoples' thoughts into Serbian.

Knowing human nature as he did, and mature as he was in his views regarding life, Dositej impressed the seal of his personality on his works. His *Basne* is an original work: he borrowed the subject-matter and added his own observations. *Život i priključenija* is an autobiography. The work is important because of the manner in which the writer describes his experiences rather than for the experiences themselves. The work is so vivid and realistic that the characters he describes seem to be living portraits. His presentation of the subject on which he dwells is calm and in high relief.

Dositej's works radiate healthy optimism. Experience taught him that life is beautiful in essence; only, life should be lived wisely. He believed that men were in essence good; only, the good in them should be helped to emerge.

Dositej cultivated a style all his own. He was genial and kind, and he was of portly appearance; and his mode of expression seems to have taken on his portliness and warmth. And regardless of the didactic nature of his works, he is one of the foremost of Serbian writers. He was succeeded by a number of men among the Serbs who wished to continue his educational work. But they were not so successful, for they were not so skilled in writing as he was.

4. SLOVENE EIGHTEENTH - CENTURY LITERATURE

By suppressing the Slovene Protestant movement in the sixteenth century, the Catholic Church snuffed out the beginnings of Slovene literature. Whereas the Slovene Protestants had published fifty-odd books in the course of several decades, the Catholic clergy published just under one hundred in the course of the two hundred subsequent years. Besides this, as time passed, some of the lingual and orthographic attainments of Trubar's period were almost forgotten. Elements from the dialects of various Slovene regions began to filter into the literary language, and the orthography lost its uniformity.

A notable figure in the cultural history of Slovenia was *Ivan Weikhard Valvazor* (1641—1693). His great work *Die Ehre des Herzogtums Krains* (1689) is a detailed account of the geography, history and ethnography of Krain. But Valvazor was more German than anything else; hence his inability to engage directly in the cause of the national advancement of the Slovenes in Krain. An academy *(Academia Operosorum)* was founded at Ljubljana during his time; but it had no direct connexion with the Slovene national problem.

The very little literary work after the downfall of the Protestant movement was promoted among the Slovenes by the Catholic clergy for religious purposes. Scarcely anyone attempted in the course of the centuries to write a work with literary tendencies. Slovene poetry was developed and consolidated to some degree only in the sacred poems.

During the eighteenth century, the position of the Slovenes was more difficult than that of any of the other Yugoslavs in Austria. The composition of society in the Slovene regions continued to be such that the Slovenes themselves constituted a despised peasant majority. The population of the other nationalities regarded the Slovenes as one of the most backward nations in the world, and the Slovene tongue as incapable of conveying high intellectual ideas. The Slovenes with any education later wrote in German and pretended to be German, or at least of mixed German-Slovene origin.

New attempts to promote Slovene literacy and to create Slovene literature came during the latter half of the eighteenth century. They were associated with the cultural manifestations in Europe, and with the political strivings of Maria Theresa and Joseph II. But whereas the sword of enlightenment in Western Europe and among the Serbs was turned against the Church, among the Slovenes the clergy again set the course of cultural work.

The new development of Slovene literacy came in connexion with the work of the government authorities themselves, or in reaction to it. During the reign of Maria Theresa, the representatives of the State had their regulations translated into Slovene in order to popularize their plans. In substituting German for the Latin of the schools and administration, they occasionally allowed the Slovene language to be used temporarily in the schools so as to introduce German the more easily. The number of books in Slovene increased during the latter half of the eighteenth century. Not only religious works, but also works for practical use were printed in Slovene. There were individuals among the writers and publishers who were strong champions of Slovene nationalism and Slavdom. Affronted by the preference which the authorities gave the German language, they began to demonstrate their nationality in a special fashion. They wrote, not in order to satisfy the authorities, but in order to demonstrate that the Slovene people were also entitled to national and cultural independence. Although members of various religious organizations, they had a single goal: it was to raise the Slovene tongue to the level of a literary language.

The best-know among these was *Marko Pohlin* (1735–1801), who wrote a Krain grammar (1768), clearly emphasizing the tendency to use Slovene outside church as well as in it. No less conspicuous was *Juraj Japelj* (1744–1807), a Jesuit who translated the New Testament into Slovene, and wrote the text of hymns. *Leopold Volkmer* (1741–1816) composed lyric poems after the model of folk poetry. They gradually gained popularity among the people. The most prominent layman of this period was *Blaž Kumerdej* (1738–1805), a teacher at the Vienna Academy of Orientology. He drew up plans to establish popular education in Slovenia and Krain. He was imbued with Slovene and Slavic ideas. He endeavoured to supplant the inferiority complex under which the Slovenes laboured as a small nation with feelings of pride at being a member of the great family of the Slavs.

Cultural and educational incentive in Krain was evident in the eighteenth century also in the revival in 1779 of the *Academia Operosorum*, the task of which was to promote Slovene science and literature.

The period of enlightenment and rationalism was marked among the Slovenes by the publication of books for the peasantry. They include the praiseworthy attempts to reveal the past to the Slovenes through historical works. The writing of poetry in Slovene was frequent during that period; and a literary almanac, *Pisanice*, was published in 1779, 1780 and 1781, which included poems in the spirit of the day, chiefly in imitation of German models. Attempts were also made during this period to determine Slovene metrical rules. But neither the rules nor their application yielded any noteworthy results; nor did any writer of that period rise above well-intentioned poetic dilletantism, the cause, in addition to other things, being the social conditions: the feudal lords and the bourgeoisie were far removed from everything written in Slovene.

Changes in Slovene cultural life were introduced by a bourgeois group headed by Baron *Žiga Zois* (1747—1819). The son of a rich Italian manufacturer and of a Slovene mother, Zois suffered from ill health, which forced him to stay indoors. He had a European education, a keen taste for art, and a profound love for the Slovene people and for Slavdom. He read the Glagolitic and the Cyrillic scripts; he also wrote in Slovene, and accumulated a comprehensive Slavic library. He rallied a group of Slovene intellectuals with the purpose of advancing the cultural level of the Slovene people and of founding a Slovene literature. In Ljubljana they organized the performance of plays in Slovene, studied Slovene history, recorded folk poems and national customs. The most prominent among them were Anton Linhart and Valentin Vodnik.

Anton Linhart (1756—1795) was born at Radovljica. His mother was a Slovene, his father was a Czech immigrant. He studied theology for a time, but soon abandoned it, completed some courses in Vienna, and became a clerk. He took to literature by writing poems in German. Zois brought him into his circle, and drew his attention to his duty towards his people. Later Linhart wrote a history of Krain and the other Yugoslav regions in Austria, and two plays *(Županova Micka* — Župan's Micka; *Matiček se ženi* — Matiček marries). One would say at first sight that they were an imitation partly of a German and partly of a French comedy (Joseph Richter's *Feldmühle*, Beaumarchais's *Figaro).* Nonetheless, Linhart succeeded by this means in portraying Slovene characters of his day with the help of the subject-matter produced by other writers. He lashed the privileged nobility and extolled the revolutionary members of the subjugated classes as the protagonists of moral values and honour, and as the representatives of the future. He died in Ljubljana.

Valentin Vodnik (1758—1819) was a more complex character. Vodnik, who was born in the village of Zgornje Šiške, near Ljubljana, was a Franciscan friar. He wrote poetry for *Pisanice* from 1781. During the reign of Joseph II he left the Franciscan order and resided in various parishes as a layman. After Zois made his acquaintance, he engaged him in his literary undertakings. He appointed Vodnik editor of the calendar *Pratika*, which was published for the peasantry. Besides being the editor and publisher of the calendar, which contained articles on history, geography, and on other subjects, Vodnik was its chief contributor.

Of all his works, the most important were, however, his poems *Pesmi za pokušino* [Poetical attempts] (1806), *Pesmi za brambovce* [Poems to the defenders] (1809). Having dropped the rigid foreign metre of his earlier verses in *Pisanice*, Vodnik adopted the metre of Slovene folk poetry in his later poems. He described the character and mentality of the Slovene peasant in his stanzas; he praised his stalwartness, his virtues, his optimistic spirit. Towards the end of the eighteenth century his poems lacked the stronger, personal features; they did, however, portray the Slovene as he really was. Rarely, if ever, does Vodnik allow himself a personal note expressing the magnificence of the Slovene highlands, the magnificence of Slavdom and Yugoslavdom, or his loneliness in his clerical profession.

Inspired by his people and striving for their education, Vodnik enthusiastically welcomed Napoleon's reign, for during it a considerable part of the Yugoslav territories was united, the centre of administration being in Ljubljana. In addition to this, Napoleon introduced many educational reforms in favour of the Slovene people. In praise of Napoleon he wrote *Ilirija oživljena* [Illyria revived].

Vodnik held important offices in the educational development of his country during the five years of Napoleon's reign in Krain (1809—1813). After Austria regained Krain, he was deprived of office. He died in Ljubljana aware that he had roused his people during exceedingly hard times and that he had laid the foundations of modern Slovene poetry. Although he wrote few poems, and their motifs were one-sided, it was through Vodnik's poetry that the Slovene tongue spoke for the first time in a voice of its own in literature, and in it that the Slovene peasant discovered himself.

CHAPTER SIX

FOLK POETRY (NARODNA PESMA)

1. THE SOCIAL ORIGINS OF FOLK POETRY

The older Yugoslav literature was a product of the Church and feudal society. Most popular as the literature of the poor Croatian *Glagolashi* was, it appealed only to a relatively negligible part of the people — to the literate. The majority of the people — the peasantry — continued ignorant of literature. In the best event the peasantry came into contact with literature indirectly, through the educated classes. This relation towards literacy and literature, with the expansion of Turkish power, suffered deterioration, which affected all the Serbian regions and most of the Croatian. The entire population became a vast illiterate mass, which preserved and passed on its knowledge of events, its past, and its ideas about life and death by word of mouth.

Nevertheless this was not a period of cultural inertia. Where the written and printed word were missing, folk literature flourished profusely, and spread by tradition. Poems, epic and lyric, tales, riddles, sayings were composed. Through the centuries, from the earliest times down to the twentieth century, they were the direct expression of creativity among the part of the Yugoslav people who had no contact with written literature owing to their social status or to conditions under the Turks. Folk poetry flourished on a wide national territory: from Macedonia to Slovenia, and especially in the central regions — in Serbia, Bosnia and Herzegovina, Dalmatia and Montenegro. It was so forceful that it penetrated from the country into the towns, often against the will of their representatives.

Traces of folk poetry among the Yugoslavs are estimated to reach back to the sixth century, when some Yugoslavs followed Attila's camp in Pannonia. These records become more frequent from the twelfth century onwards, and its features may be determined more easily after that time. In the fifteenth century it is the subject of discussion by the humanists of Dalmatia, who either assailed it or defended it. In later centuries again, it was attacked by learned men and by the Church. It persisted stubbornly, however, and only in the nineteenth century, during the romantic period, did it gain recognition both at home and abroad.

2. LYRIC FOLK POETRY

Lyric poetry was cultivated by all the Yugoslav peoples, *epic poetry* mostly by the Serbs and Croats, though the Slovenes and Macedonians were also familiar with it.

The *lyric poem* reflects the entire public and private life of the Yugoslavs. Everywhere, on all occasions, the Yugoslav was accompanied by it. At work, in company, at weddings, funerals, at fairs it gave expression to feelings which seized both individuals and groups. It was an expression of happiness, despair, friendship, enthusiasm, esteem for the brave, parental feelings, brotherly love. The lyric poem expressed the most passionate sentiments of love, as well as the tenderest feelings of self-sacrifice. It was by turns profoundly sad, youthfully wanton, or full of bitter derision for human weaknesses and failings. Furthermore, while it gave a comprehensive picture both of private and of family life, it also expressed the beliefs and the philosophy of the nation as a whole.

As a reflection of national life in all its forms, Yugoslav lyric poetry displayed marked variations according to the part of the country in which it was created. The Slovene regions, chiefly mountainous, through which travelling was difficult, produced poems on the magnificence of nature, about solitude, defiance, and sorrow because of the unjust social position of the Slovenes. Fertile Slavonia produced poems expressing cheerfulness, wild gaiety, strength and forcefulness. At times this poetry was even obscene. Bosnia and Herzegovina, longest under Turkish power and longest exposed to Oriental customs, expressed melancholy, and produced sorrowful poems of love *(sevdalinka)*, full of unfulfilled yearning. Macedonian lyric poetry was the expression of rapture, irresoluteness, and regret for lost youth, and a picture of the difficult living conditions of the Macedonian migrating worker. From Dalmatia and Istria, associated partly with life at sea, sprang poems which hint at a yearning for foreign ports, and a longing for the people at home.

As the economic, political and cultural conditions altered, the division between the various geographical regions vanished, and the poetry of one region spread to others.

The lyric folk poem is set to a tune, and is sung by one or more voices. The text is not artistically perfect, and it might frequently be less pleasing were it not for its melody. Some Slovene poems, however, are an exception to this.

Set to a melody, the lyric folk poem makes every possible musical use of the Serbo-Croatian and Slovene language. It employs every possible type of verse, from the four-syllabled up to the sixteen-syllabled line. It thus laid the practical foundations of Yugoslav metrical rules.

3. EPIC FOLK POETRY

The source of the *epic poem* was its subject-matter. It was popularized by the bards, whose sole occupation often was to popularize the epic poem. They sang the poems to their own accompaniment, generally on the *gusla*, a rudimentary instrument with a round, concave body, a parchment soundboard, and one horsehair string. The music was a kind of wailing accompaniment to the words, it had no attraction in itself.

Although the lyric folk poem was significant in its subject-matter and in its musical elements as a reflection of national life, it was prone to changes, which followed those of life itself. Some of the poems are of great age; but it is evident that they primarily expressed the feelings and moods of different generations in their endless alternation. The epic folk poem, on the contrary, seems to have preserved its continuity and tradition. Having fashioned a style and language of its own, and adopted a series of motifs and personages, it was reluctant to give them up, although it too needed to be changed and modernized.

The first manuscript containing a detailed study of the subject-matter and technical elements in Serbo-Croatian epic poetry and the manner of its production goes back to 1531 (the travels of Benedikt Kuripešić). The first time epic poems were ever published was in 1568, when two epic folk poems were published in full in *Petar Hektorović's* work *Ribanje i ribarsko prigovaranje*. One of them mentions *Kraljević Marko*, the most popular figure in Serbo-Croatian epic poetry. Both poems are already so advanced in structure, and contain such clearly defined personages that they are indubitably the fruit of lengthy evolution. The epic folk poem is mentioned among the Slovenes in the sixteenth century, its heroes being *King Matjaš* and *Lambergar*.

The Yugoslav epic folk poem also dealt with the life of the people in all its phases and forms, some poems even containing traces of old Slavic pagan beliefs. It contains evidence of the first contacts of the Serbs and Croats with Christianity, the significance of the medieval state, traces of social and political life during earlier centuries. Serbian epic poetry has preserved data on the medieval Serbian State, starting with its earliest rulers (Stevan Nemanja), past its climax (Dušan the Mighty), down to its disintegration under the attacks of the Turks and dissension among the local lords. The Croatian folk poem reveals no traces of the medieval Croatian State, for it collapsed at a very early period. Nonetheless the Croatian folk poem also records historic figures from the fifteenth century onwards.

Most of the important epics both among the Serbs and among the Croats, and also to a certain extent among the Slovenes, were inspired by the clash between Islam and Christendom, which occurred on Yugoslav soil. The epic poems described both the external facts and the inner, deeper causes of this clash. The *Battle of Kosovo* (1389), in which the medieval Serbian State was defeated, was treated in the folk poems as the supreme historic event in Serbian life. The poems raise it to the height of a symbol of struggle between two worlds: between the world of good and the world of evil; between justice and oppression; between the conscious sacrifice for country and brutal selfishness. The main figures in the *Kosovo* cycle are given the stature of symbols, embodying unbounded heroism (Miloš Obilić, who killed the Turkish sultan), conscious sacrifice for the elevated ideal of justice (Knez Lazar, who was slain at Kosovo), treason (Vuk Branković, who survived the Battle). The folk poems also describe the events before and after the Battle: the departure to the field of the engagement, the misgivings regarding its outcome, the fate of the widows. Thanks to the folk poem, up to the early years of the twentieth century, the Serbs regarded *Kosovo* synonymous with the deepest patriotism, which does not shirk even the supreme sacrifice.

The battles of the Yugoslav peoples with the Turks, which persisted till the Balkan War in 1912, were described by the epic folk poem in various ways. The national bard had for several centuries extolled the fighters against the Turks as heroes, and he even included some foreigners among them (the Hungarians *Hunyadi János, Dojcsin Peter*) simply because they were in the Christian camp. He portrayed life under the Turks, recorded instances of opportunism, but primarily sang the praises of the champions of resistance. The epic folk poem glorified the Croatian feudalists who distinguished themselves in combat against the Turks (Zrinski, Karlović); it nurtured the cult of the *Hajduks*, the heroes who took to the woods in face of Turkish oppression and from there made sudden raids on the enemy (Starina Novak, Mijat Tomić); it referred to the soldiers who, as subjects of Venice or Austria, guarded the borders facing the Turkish empire (Ivo Senjanin, Ilija Smiljanić).

Nor did the epic folk poem deal only with the battles during the centuries of struggle: it presented its heroes also during their private moments. It described feasts, loves, marriages, misunderstandings, adbuctions, motherhood, struggles for justice and for a livelihood. In narrating historical events, chiefly with the feudalists as the wielders of power, the folk poem also criticized them, describing their behaviour towards widows and the destitute, their personal disputes, friendships and enmities.

Though it originated from the conflict between Christianity and Islam, and for the most part under the conditions of Turkish rule, Serbo-Croatian epic poetry also treated of relations between subjects and their overlords. It portrayed the Yugoslav people as the vassals of the Turks. Occasionally it demonstrates understanding for the Turkish sultan himself. It recorded the deeds of Turkish heroes as well as those of members of other races (the Arabs, for instance) in the Turkish host. Many Serbs and Croats, especially in Bosnia, having been converted to Islam, and considering themselves to be in part Turkish, a Moslem epic folk poem in Serbo-Croatian also came into being. Its verse and language are identical with that of the folk poem of the Christians, the only difference being that its heroes are Turks, and its severity is turned against the Christians. Consequently it appealed to Moslems only. Its heroes were also notable warriors (Mustajbeg of Lika, Djerzelez Alija, Budalina Tale). The bulk of the Christian epic poetry, on the contrary, reflecting resistance against Turkish oppression, became the property of all the Yugoslav peoples.

The most popular figure in the Serbo-Croatian epic folk poem is *Kraljević Marko*. A historic figure, the son of King Vukašin, who was the vassal of Emperor Dušan, the mightiest Serbian sovereign, he became king upon his father's death. He reigned during the period when the Serbian State was crumbling under the blows of the young Turkish empire. He recognized the Turkish power: he was even killed in a battle in which he fought on the Turkish side against the Christians. As described by the national epics, he was the ideal of physical strength. Apart from this, he is shown by the folk poem as a medieval feudalist, in the lists, as a Turkish vassal, and as an arbitrary tyrant; but also as a sufferer in a Turkish prison, as the champion of the weak, as a fighter for justice, equality and freedom.

The Slovenes, who were not so exposed to the attacks of the Turks, and had no political leaders of their own, never glorified figures of their own in poetry. But one of the most important figures in the Slovene epic is *Kralj Matjaž*, the Hungarian king Mátyás Korvin. Like *Kraljević Marko*, King Matjaž embodies the struggle for justice. Otherwise, Slovene epic poetry also contains lyrical elements *(Kralj Matjaž in Alenčica; Lepa Vida)*.

The Macedonian epic likewise extols the Macedonian opponents of alien rule.

The fundamental feature in the Yugoslav epic folk poem through the centuries has been its fighting spirit, its championship of freedom. The idea of Turkdom in it is, not so much one of nationality and religion, as it is a symbol of oppression, the exploitation of the weak. It still retained this feature as it entered the nineteenth century, when the power of the Turks was being broken by the insurgents in Montenegro and Serbia. In this struggle the folk poem both described events and inspired them. The national bard, depicting the position of the oppressed, also advanced plans of work and struggle in his verse. Evoking instances of sacrifice and heroism from the past, the folk poem sustained the longing for freedom as an integral part of Serbdom.

This was the period of its richest flowering. While keeping alive the history of the people, it still had sufficient creative strength to make heroes — types of bravery and manliness — out of its contemporaries. At the beginning of the nineteenth century, it portrayed the leaders of the Serbian uprisings for freedom, *Karadjordje* and *Miloš*, as well as many Montenegrin, Herzegovinian and Bosnian heroes, who distinguished themselves in countless engagements with the Turks.

Judging by some features, personages and motifs, most maintain that the Yugoslav epic of the earlier centuries originated in the feudal period. For the most part it describes the Serbian medieval lords, their way of life, their interests, and their conflicts; in the Croatian regions, it describes leading members of the Croatian feudal families. In addition to this, it contains distinct elements from Church life, obviously inserted under the influence of the monasteries and clerical sermons. At one time scholars were almost unanimous in the opinion that it originated in feudal surroundings.

With the downfall of the Serbian medieval State, and as the Church weakened under the Turks, the national epic lost its feudal features. Gradually it came to be the expression of the only class which was representative of the people — of the peasantry. During later centuries it became the opposite of what it had perhaps been during the feudal period: it became an opponent of the educated, of the upper classes. It remained for several centuries as the only possible mode of artistic expression of that part of society which was ignorant of schools, books, of the Central European type of culture. Even when the epic folk poem conjured up the way of life of feudal society, the picture it presented was like the one imagined by the poor man of the common people seeing the palaces and their occupants from a distance.

4. THE CREATORS OF FOLK POEMS

As the product of a part of society which was far removed from bourgeois civilization, the folk poem constituted a special type of culture for centuries. The verse, which was meant to be recited from memory and not read, reflected everything the people thought, desired, experienced. That is why the folk poem used subject-matter of many types, starting with historic events and the facts and personalities related to them, and ending with scenes from everyday life. Handed on from generation to generation, it preserved contact with the past; on the other hand, by recording current events, it gave its listeners information about many things of interest to them. Its function being such, it was in a state of perpetual creativity. New events called forth new poems, supplanted most of the old ones, or altered them according to the new conditions and requirements. Seeking for everything that might attract the listener, the folk poem recorded grave and ludicrous, important and unimportant events. Thousands of poems were composed in various regions, glorifying local heroes or ridiculing local events. But they most often experienced the fate of the newspaper of today: the majority of them soon vanished without a trace; only a few succeeded in spreading from their place of origin to regions in the vicinity, or even to more distant areas. Very few, however, survived the centuries, or indeed any considerable period of time, even in altered form.

The folk poem was popularized through the centuries by the bards, who competed with each other. They often envied each other their stock-in-trade, and as often they borrowed from one another. They usually endeavoured to suit the taste of their audience and, depending frequently for their living on the wealthy, they gave their poems a suitable turn in order to ingratiate themselves with their hosts. Among the Moslems in Bosnia, where feudalism endured till 1918, epic poetry retained some of the features of this system till recently, for the Moslem bard received gifts in plenty from his feudalist customer.

Like every other art, the epic folk poem was originally the product of particular individuals. The poems adopted by one poet or singer from another contain, in the main, the characteristics of the composer's art. *Filip Višnjić*, the singer of poems about the First Serbian Insurrection, took part in some of the battles himself, and gave encouragement to the fighters. The poems which *Vuk Stefanović Karadžić* took down from Višnjić's lips are distinctively his creation. He was an artist of remarkable calibre; he regarded the events of his day from exalted altitudes, from altitudes almost of outer space, as a part of the general world constellation. As he saw the Serbian Insurrection, which he described in the poem

Početak bune protiv dahija [The beginning of the rebellion against the dahie], it did not contain merely political and national features: he regarded it as a rebellion of the poor and oppressed against the oppressors and exploiters. *Milija*, another Serbian bard, studying men in their passions and personal conflicts, expressed fine irony in his poems.

The national bard wished to remain anonymous as an author, even when it was obvious that his stock of verse was chiefly of his own composition. The result was that, once created, the poem became general property. Whoever heard it, could pass it on; he could add to it his own views, alter it, deepen it, or spoil it. And the poem was the more easily spoilt as the national bard never committed it to memory but improvised it anew at each recitation. Thus the folk poem lost the original form given it by its creator, and became the expression of the whole nation.

Perpetually in creation, perpetually in motion, the folk poem reflected the spiritual restlessness of the masses in different regions and in different generations. Every generation might have brought something of its own into it. Originally associated with an event or an individual, some poems gradually lost their original features. They shed everything casual and ephemeral, keeping only that which was related to the listener even in the remotest regions.

Having originally sung about many figures of its period who had distinguished themselves in some special way, little by little the folk poem dropped most of the personages who were associated with passing events, centering its attention upon a few figures who towered above their time, or who evolved in the course of its own evolution into expressly literary characters who had scarcely any connexion with the historic figures whose name they bore. This process of development was one of many years' duration.

During the period when the folk poem became an object of study, the older poems were the best artistically, the poems about new events being the poorest. The poems describing the battles between the Montenegrins and the Turks at the beginning of the nineteenth century may be classed among the latter, for they are on the whole raw material overloaded with detail. They had not been through a process of crystallization and condensation. The only exception among poems of this type were those sung by bards of exceptional talent, like *Filip Višnjić*, the singer of the First Serbian Insurrection. His poems about the battles of this period are of superb depth.

The mode of expression, which had not been fully stabilized in the oldest written poems, passed during the centuries through the same phases as the subject-matter had. Burdened by verses of varying length and metre, the folk poem strove to create a distinctive mode of expression, clear in style and limited in length. At last, as the product of long evolution, came the *deseterac*, the ten-syllabled verse, which combines simplicity with the possibility of expressing extremely varied nuances.

5. THE SIGNIFICANCE OF THE FOLK POEM

With its best poems folk poetry has attained lofty heights of art. Its most successful examples have dealt with every theme in life and every problem which confronts the human being: with birth and death, love and fidelity, freedom and justice; with the individual and society, wealth and poverty, duty and egoism. Based on philosophic foundations, it is pervaded by the lofty ideas which inspired the greatest minds of mankind. It praises justice, self-sacrifice, the duties of the individual towards the community. Yet it is succinct, concise, calm: the purest realism, containing neither a word too much nor a word too little. The national bard frequently expressed every problem of his period in several ten-syllabled verses, and at the same time presented a multitude of characters and their conflicts, all from a single angle of vision: the superior type of man facing all these problems *(Uroš i Mrnjav-čevići)*, a wife's infidelity and her husband's magnanimous forgive-ness *(Banović Strahinja)*, mother love in all its magnificence *(Smrt Majke Jugovića)*, the mother country as the supreme value *(Car Lazar i Carica Milica)*, the endurance of pain with fortitude *(Stari Vujadin)*, strength of spirit in the struggle against physical super-iority *(Bolani Dojčin)*, disdain for those who value only wealth *(Kraljević Marko i beg Kostadin)*, the nation against oppression *(Početak bune protiv dahija)*, the calm acceptance of love and death *(Omer i Mejrima)*, the conflict of love and pride *(Hasan-aginica)*, the mother country and foreign parts *(Ženidba Maksima Crnojevića)*, etc. The bard dwelt upon all these subjects in his poems as if he were creating for eternity.

Many of the motifs in the Yugoslav national epic are inter-national. But its strength lay in the fact that it linked such motifs with the fate of the Yugoslavs, and expressed them in such a fashion that they acquired a national meaning.

The *folk tale*, which is freer in style, was never as important among the Yugoslavs as the epic poem. Nevertheless its best speci-mens reveal the same characteristics as the epic: simplicity, motifs of general human feeling, the creation of types.

Since it was created by the most numerous section of the people — by the socially oppressed — the peasantry, the folk poem was regarded with some contempt for centuries. The literature that was created by the Croatian bourgeoisie, who were beyond the reach of the Turkish authorities, in Dalmatia and inner Croatia, in the main assumed the forms of West-European literature. Considerable economic and social changes were to take place before this state of affairs could be remedied. Indeed, the folk poem had been infiltrating into this literature since its beginnings, as early as the period of *Ljetopis popa Dukljanina* (probably the twelfth century), but only sporadically, in isolated instances.

The first written collections of folk poems were compiled in the eighteenth century. The poems were written down both by Yugoslavs and by foreigners. The Italian traveller, Fortis, in his work *Viaggio in Dalmazia* (1774) took down the poem *Hasanaginica*, which created almost a sensation in European literature because of its uncommon beauty and classical idiom. An eighteenth-century manuscript, known by the name of the *Erlangen MS*, preserved in Germany, in the town of that name, is significant in this respect. It was written by a German soldier whom chance brought to the boundary of the Turkish empire.

Real interest in the folk poem was roused by the romantic movement in the nineteenth century. The first and foremost collector of Serbian folk poems was *Vuk Stefanović Karadžić*. His example was followed by many learned Serbs, Croats, Slovenes, who published the poems as Serbian, or as Croatian, or as Serbo-Croatian, or as Slovene folk poems. The most outstanding collectors and publishers were the poets *Sima Milutinović-Sarajlija*, *Petar Petrović-Njegoš*, and *Stanko Vraz*, *Kosta Hörmann*, *Božidar Petranović*, *Karel Štrekcej*, the society *Matica Hrvatska*, etc. Regardless of the names under which they were published, they are the common property of all the Yugoslav peoples, especially of the Serbs and Croats, because they are the echo of an identical destiny, of identical sorrows, of identical creative abilities; because they have been sung in identical verse and in the same language, and because they spread widely, regardless of religious bounds and national boundaries.

The Yugoslav national epic began to die out in the twentieth century. It was slowly strangled by the newspapers, by books, by schools, by easier communications. In the face of increasing literacy, the national epic withdrew to the backward regions, where the old economic and social relationships still prevailed. The national bard, once a creator, was now becoming merely the popularizer of someone else's store of verse. The romanticists, while esteeming the folk poem as of supreme artistic value, also regarded it as a form of civilization at a certain level of development, in the main primitive. That the folk poem would soon be extinct was believed to be a certainty by its greatest connoisseurs, including

Matija Murko, who considered this to be a sign of general progress, for with the extinction of the folk poem the Yugoslav people would be entering the sphere of European civilization.

However, these prophecies did not come true: *Murko* became personally convinced of the fact that the national epic flourished more strongly in 1918 than it did in 1913. The struggle for the national liberation of the Yugoslavs during the second world war again inspired the national singers to sound the praises of the heroes of their time, and to speed them onwards in the struggle against the enemy. In this way the modern folk poem is continuing the best traditions of the earlier periods.

CHAPTER SEVEN

THE NINETEENTH CENTURY

THE FOUNDATIONS OF MODERN YUGOSLAV LITERATURE

In the history of the Yugoslavs, the first half of the nineteenth century was a period of national progress, of relative political freedom and social emancipation; as well as a period in which they hazarded their first more definite and systematic plans for rapprochement and unification. In addition to this, the first half of the nineteenth century marked the period in which they laid the foundations of their modern literature.

1. SERBIAN LITERATURE DURING THE FIRST HALF OF THE NINETEENTH CENTURY

The Serbian people entered the nineteenth century still divided and still under an alien yoke, as they were in the eighteenth. But during the early years of the nineteenth century, considerable changes for the better were already discernible. Montenegro was gaining its independence. Serbia, however, was making the greatest strides forward. A Turkish pashalik up to the nineteenth century, Serbia defeated the Turks in the course of two insurrections, and became a principality — a principality still under Turkish sovereignty, to be sure, but absolutely autonomous in internal affairs. The small Serbian peasant nation, illiterate though it was, rose as one man, and headed by its leaders Karadjordje and later Knez Miloš Obrenović, freed itself during the insurrections of 1804 and 1815 from an incomparably stronger master, and founded a principality of its own.

It was necessary to set up such forms of government in liberated Serbia as would answer the requirements of the people. Land was distributed to the peasants, and a type of peasant democracy was established. Agriculture and livestock breeding were the basic industries; livestock exporting a very considerable source of revenue.

Retail trade and the crafts were town occupations only; the merchants and craftsmen were chiefly Greeks and Zinzars. The peasant people of Serbia followed a patriarchal way of life, in family cooperatives. Although the capitalistic system had penetrated into Serbia, and capital had attained a level of accumulation quite notable for a small country and for that period, the need for money in the country was not pressing; consequently, there were no marked social differences. The main political problem was how to regulate relations with the Turks and with the Knez. With his wonted cunning the first Knez of Serbia, Miloš Obrenović, had consolidated the independence of the country; he had also succeeded in making power hereditary in his family. Finally he strengthened his autocratic regime. As the Turkish pashas had once done, he also wished to dispense with all control over his rule. Being himself a pig-breeder, he put a stop to competition unfavourable to him, and became the wealthiest man in the country. The political struggles which had originally been waged by the illiterate though cunning peasant tribunes, by degrees became a struggle between the people and the Knez. In the end, in 1842, Knez Miloš was forced to leave Serbia, and Aleksandar Karadjordjević, Karadjordje's descendant, came to the throne.

Cultural life flourished rapidly in liberated Serbia. A high school (Velika škola), in which government employees were trained, was founded in Belgrade immediately after the termination of the insurrection; a scientific society (Srpsko učeno društvo) and a theatre were founded in 1844. Schools were also opened in the interior of the country. But their number being small, and having no traditions to fall back on, they were insufficient to train the necessary personnel for the administration.

Owing to the lack of intellectuals in Serbia, educated Serbs from Austria were encouraged to come to the country. They occupied important offices both in Belgrade and in the interior. They were administrators, doctors, teachers; there were some noble natures and far-seeing men among them, capable of grasping the psychology of the Serbs, and their own tasks, at the right moment. On the other hand, there were also some adventurers and spies among them, as well as various self-opinionated men who regarded the primitive Serbian peasantry as a backward and worthless mass, and affected a superior attitude towards them as regards dress and manners. They strove to introduce the Austrian way of life in Serbia at all costs.

The Serbs in Austria had also made remarkable progress. The Serbian townsfolk, who were growing ever more prosperous, endeavoured to equal the townsfolk in Austria in education and way of life. A newspaper (Novine srpske) was founded in Vienna in 1813; a literary society *(Matica srpska)* was founded in Buda-pest in 1826, which started a literary magazine *(Ljetopis matice srpske)* in the same year; a teachers' school was established at Szentendre, and a gymnasium was opened at Novi Sad in 1816; Serbian libraries and printing-presses were also opened.

The Serbian Orthodox Church and the Metropolitan of Srem-ski Karlovci continued to be the main cultural and political pivot among the Serbs in Austria. The nineteenth century differed from the eighteenth among the Serbs in Austria, for in the nineteenth century a number of intellectuals came from the ranks of the bourgeoisie. They studied at secular schools in Austria and took up secular occupations: they were teachers, lawyers, administrative officials. However, they also depended more or less on the Church owing to its prestige and significance for Serbdom in Austria.

In the cultural life of the Serbs in Austria the strength of the Orthodox Church was conspicuous in two ways: nothing could be printed unless the Church gave its approval; the artificial Slavo-Serb language had to be employed in the literature, because it was used by the Church, which regarded it as sacrosanct and characteristic of Serbdom and the Orthodox creed.

The growing number of lay intellectuals who were educated in Austria helped to create a flourishing literature in Serbian. They were poets, playwrights, travel writers, historians, etc. A feature which they had in common was that they all wrote in Slavo-Serb, which the masses were unable to understand. This tongue contain-ed no recognized rules, and it frequently sounded artificial. Besides this, the writers used a number of redundant letters which represented no sound in the spoken language, and this only made it still more difficult to read printed matter.

This language, however, such as it was, was almost generally accepted through long usage.

Having been pupils in the gymnasia and high schools of Austria, the educated Serbs accepted such views in literature as were taught in their schools. The classics as the chief gymnasium subjects, as well as classicism and pseudo-classicism, produced a type of intel-lectual among the Serbs in Austria towards the end of the eighteenth century and early in the nineteenth who resembled the educated Austrian and German. His literary models were Horace and his German disciples *(Klopstock, Rammler)*. During the period of European romanticism, when the fetters of art were being broken and the divisions between literary categories brushed aside, the most distinguished Serbian writers were composing odes after class-ical models, invoking Greek gods and goddesses, using antique classical terms, etc. Among the many names in Serbian literature which shone out at the beginning of the nineteenth century, three shone the brightest: Lukijan Mušicki, Sima Milutinović-Sarajlija, and Milovan Vidaković.

Lukijan Mušicki (Temerin, 1777 — Gornji Karlovci, 1837), a monk, became the head of a monastery, and a bishop in his later years. He was the most cultured Serb of his time. He was often the victim of persecution and humiliation owing to disagreement with the heads of the Church. He distinguished himself most as a writer, and wrote numerous odes in eulogy of Serbdom and its past, freedom, knowledge and virtue. Owing to his employment of various classical metrical rules, he gives an impression of coldness; but from the hard crust of his mode of expression, there emerges occasionally the sincere feeling of a noble and suffering spirit. Especially in his poems there breathes a feeling for Serbdom, a pride in the splendour of its past, and a belief in its future. Mušicki was fully aware of the lingual shortcomings of his poems and, while admitting the advantages of the popular tongue, he contended that there need be no differences between it and Slavo-Serb. He was of the opinion that the two speeches represented two roads to the same goal.

Sima Milutinović-Sarajlija (Sarajevo, 1791 — Belgrade, 1847) was a self-taught eccentric, who lived a restless life. During the rebellions and disturbances at the beginning of the nineteenth century, he was a typical tramp, living first in Bosnia, then in Serbia, and later in Bulgaria. He studied at Leipzig; he was a gardener at Vidin; he was tutor to the Montenegrin poet and bishop, Petar Petrović-Njegoš, at Cetinje. He wrote lyric and epic poems, plays and historical works, in which he exalted the Serbian people, their sufferings, struggle and glory. He violated every traditional literary form: he mixed mysticism with reality, dreams with wakefulness, purely lyric forms with dramatic and epic passages, romantic hotchpotch with classic elements, the popular tongue with expressions from antique classical mythology. His best-known work is *Srbijanka* (1826), which should have been an epic about the First Serbian Insurrection, and abounded in imaginary historical details. Written in a difficult style, in an idiom clipped and curt, it made an impression of unusual beauty on the readers of his time. It is even said to have appealed to Goethe. Milutinović was soon forgotten after his death, although he had been very popular in his earlier years.

Milovan Vidaković (1780—1841) enjoyed a popularity of greater duration. He was the first writer of the later Serbian literature to be born in Serbia (Nemenikuće, near Belgrade). While he was a child his family moved to Austria, where he finished his schooling. Then he earned a meagre living as a private tutor. He died in Budapest. He published several epic poems and a number of novels: *Usamljeni Junoša* [The lonely youth] (1810), *Ljubomir u Elisiumu* [Ljubomir in Elysium] (1814), *Karija carica* [The empress Karija] (1827), etc. Serbian history formed the theme of most of them. Without exception they abound in strange events: the sufferings of the innocent, clashes between chivalrous figures and villains, salvation at the last moment, miracles, charms, sentimental love, etc. Far removed from psychology and reality though they were, Vidaković's novels, nevertheless, gratified the taste of the Serbian petty-bourgois public, and induced them to read books in Serbian. Although these works are devoid of artistic value, they have endured on the bookshelves. Vidaković also wrote in Slavo-Serb.

Almost all the younger Serbian writers up to the forties of the past century followed in the footsteps of Mušicki, Milutinović and Vidaković. Serbian literature was pervaded up to the middle of the century by a school of objective lyricism, as it was called, the principle of which was to reveal, not sentiments, but thoughts.

This Serbian literature, except for Vidaković's novels, was inaccessible to the peasantry, who constituted the majority of the people, and to some extent also to the townsfolk, who were unable to assimilate it, although they were able to understand it to some degree. The flourishing folk poem continued to thrive among the peasant masses. The townsfolk, on the other hand, composed their lyric poems in their everyday speech. The folk poem was popularized orally, the lyric poems in printed booklets. The bourgeois lyrics had a reading public among apprentices, merchants, clerks and women of every age. It was not erudite; rather it was direct and gave a sense of reality.

Inaccessible to the masses though it was, its language and orthography, from the beginning of the nineteenth century, were distinguished by a common feature: they were inspired by a strong feeling for Serbdom, a love of the Serbian past, a pride in the medieval Serbian State, and a fanatical hatred of the enemies of Serbia, particularly of the Turks. These sentiments pervade the more important Serbian literary works of that period: the novels of Milovan Vidaković, the poems and plays of Sima Milutinović-Sarajlija, the odes of Lukijan Mušicki, as well as the products of minor writers.

The problem of language faced Serbian literature from the very beginning of its revival. Every more perspicacious writer was aware of this problem, and endeavoured to solve it. There were writers, independent of the majority, who even used the popular speech as their medium. What is more, the conservative writers now and then ventured the opinion that the literary language should be brought closer to the speech of the people. But because of literary tradition and the prestige of the Serbian Orthodox Church, they were forced to halt midway.

A complete break with later Serbian literary traditions was made by writers who were dependent neither for their social standing nor for their spiritual associations on the Serbian Orthodox Church, and who had no connexions with the spirit of the Serbian bourgeois intellectuals. They were Vuk Stefanović Karadžić in Serbia and Petar Petrović-Njegoš in Montenegro. It is true, Njegoš used the old orthography; but he wrote in the language of Montenegro. He was disinclined to involve himself in literary controversy owing to his position in the Church; but he espoused the cause of those who endeavoured to discard the obsolete. Vuk Stefanović Karadžić, on the other hand, was a conscious fighter for the victory of the popular spirit and speech in literature, against whatever was archaic, artificial, unnatural.

The Serbian literature of the first half of the nineteenth century was, after the appearance of Vuk Stefanović Karadžić, marked more or less by this struggle between the old-fashioned and the modern. It was not a struggle only for the language and orthography: the root of the problem lay in whether the church hierarchy, and the bourgeoisie as it had developed in Austria, would continue to dominate the Serbian people, or whether the Serbian peasant element in Serbia would come into its own.

Vuk Stefanović Karadžić was the first writer in Serbia to endeavour to bring the thought and mode of expression of the Serbian peasantry to triumph, contending that it was the Serbian peasantry alone that had preserved the pure Serbian popular spirit. His struggle lasted about half a century, during which he often had to fight a solitary battle. He was opposed both by the official church and by the Serbian intellectuals, and finally by the government in Serbia. However, his prospects steadily improved with the coming of the young intellectuals to his support.

The year 1847 is especially memorable in Serbian literature, for the greatest work in Serbian literature, *Gorski vijenac* [The Mountain Wreath] by Petar Petrović-Njegoš, *Pjesme* [Poems] by Branko Radičević, and *Rat za srpski jezik i pravopis* [The battle for the Serbian tongue and orthography] by the young linguist Djura Daničić, were published in that year. *Gorski vijenac* and *Pjesme* were written in the popular tongue; *Rat za srpski jezik i pravopis* is a scientific defence of Vuk Stefanović Karadžić's principles. The battle continued for a time; but there was no doubt by the middle of the nineteenth century that the artificial Slavo-Serb was dead as far as literature was concerned, and so was its orthography; and that the popular tongue, with its simplified spelling, was triumphing in every respect.

Vuk Stefanović Karadžić was the most prolific and the most influential Serbian writer of the nineteenth century, and one of the most prominent Serbs of the century generally. He founded the modern Serbian literary language, and reformed Serbian orthography; he was the foremost collector and connoisseur of the folk poem, an ethnographer, historian, literary critic, polemicist. His work was so important that he transcended the bounds of literature, for in a fashion he was also the creator of modern Serbian nationalism.

Vuk Stefanović Karadžić was the son of a Serbian peasant (he was born at Tršić in 1787). During his childhood he was physically weak and unfit to work on the family farm. Having learnt to write, he went to school in Belgrade and Sremski Karlovci. But owing to recurrent upheavals and general unrest in Serbia, his schooling was irregular. He took part in the First Serbian Insurrection as a scribe, and held various offices after the Insurrection. He fled to Vienna with many other refugees after the reoccupation of Serbia by the Turks in 1813; and there he made the acquaintance of Bartolomej Kopitar, the Slavonic scholar from Slovenia, who was a censor of books in Slavic languages at that time. Under his guidance and instruction, Karadžić soon mastered problems of language and literature, and lived after that only for science and letters. He died in Vienna in 1864.

Karadžić's first book was *Mala prostonarodna slavenosrpska pjesmarica* [A little Slavo-Serb book of folk poems] (1814), an edition of folk poems containing songs which he had noted down from memory. He then began to collect the folk poems systematically, both personally and with the assistance of his acquaintances and friends. Lame and ailing though he was, he went wherever he heard there was a good bard, his travels taking him from one end of the country to the other. In this way he collected sufficient material for the publication of four extensive volumes of Serbian folk poems (1823–1833). He completed his collection with a total of six volumes (1841–1866). His folk poems made a profound impression both at home and among European scholars: Karadžić became famous; he was elected a member of many learned societies; while the Serbian folk poem was the object of translation and study.

Karadžić also collected and published folk tales, proverbs, and riddles. He described Serbian customs, and wrote historical works on Montenegro. In order to publish his manuscripts, he founded magazines and almanacs *(Danica* — Aurora; *Kovčežić* — The coffer). Translating the New Testament into Serbian, he published it without the approval of the ecclesiastical authorities. He advanced his views in the prefaces to some volumes of folk poems, or in special articles, on the national bards and on the conditions under which the folk poem flourished. In this way he offered valuable material for its further study.

87

Karadžić also occupied himself with problems of language. At the beginning of his work in 1814 he published a brief grammar of the Serbian popular tongue. In 1818 he published a detailed Serbian dictionary. In both works he dropped the forms and orthography of the Serbian literary language and, without precursors or teachers, he began to write in the language which he spoke at home and which was spoken by the peasantry of the western parts of Serbia. He simplified the spelling by dispensing with the signs which were unnecessary to the Serbian Cyrillic script. His principle in language and orthography was: one should write as the Serbian peasant speaks, and one should write the words down exactly as they sound.

At first Karadžić was not aware of the extensiveness of his reforms, and on some points he later became doubtful. Nevertheless he adhered to the main idea of doing away with the artificial Slavo-Serb language of the Serbian writers, and of introducing a phonetic orthography.

Karadžić's language and orthography roused the ire of the majority of the educated Serbs in Hungary. They held that the Serbian literary language was so highly advanced that it was capable of expressing any idea, whereas the peasant tongue was deficient in this respect. He was also opposed by the representatives of the Serbian Orthodox Church, who maintained that the language, as it was, was the distinguishing mark of Serbdom and of the Orthodox creed.

His initial success with the editions of his folk poems and dictionary were followed by years of poverty and struggle. He was opposed by power and money. Burdened with a large family, with ailing children, he often suffered from actual want. On a number of occasions he went to Serbia, where he accepted various offices in the administration. But he never remained long, for Knez Miloš's backward camarilla were unable to grasp the importance of his work. Only during the closing years of his life, as the younger generation began to understand him, was Vuk Karadžić able to live in a certain degree of comfort.

In its consequences Karadžić's work far transcended the bounds of folklore and linguistics: it was of literary, social, and national importance as well.

Classifying the collected folk poems, Karadžić demonstrated that he was no average collector, but a man of taste. Out of the mass of material he gathered, he published only what was of artistic value. It is true that he was fortunate in beginning to collect the folk poems during their best period, and was in a position to choose what most appealed to him. But only he was capable of separating the grain from the chaff. His six volumes of folk poems contain more poetry than the entire Serbian literature of his period, and more than any other collection of Yugoslav folk poems.

Karadžić was the first to understand properly the fundamental characteristics of the Serbian folk poem: its simplicity and its profundity as the essential traits of national expression. Accordingly he held it up as a model for Serbian writers who had been seeking a pattern to follow in the classics and pseudo-classics, in Horace and in his German imitators. He was, besides, an excellent writer, and whatever he wrote about, he expressed himself as a man of letters. He was aware of the power of words, he was conscious of the rhythm of a sentence, the value of the nuances of syntax. In addition to this, he had a keen vision, and could convey his observations with subtlety and accuracy. During the romantic period, he was definitely realistic, a sober spirit; consequently his works are distinguished by realism and balance. His style is both popular and personal. In his work the Serbian speech found its place in the literature of the nineteenth century. He knew how to take the traits of the folk poem and of the folk tale, and make them his own idiom.

During the period in which he lived, — a period of great economic, social and political changes — Karadžić accomplished a mighty transformation in Serbia. He helped the peasant element to rise to the surface in Serbia and in the areas under Austria by discarding everything that was a mere fashion, artificial, affected, introduced into the Serbian way of life by some educated people.

Both intentionally and unwittingly, Karadžić exercised powerful influence on the development of the Serbian people in the nineteenth century. His collections of Serbian folk poems are not impersonal classification. They reflect the ideals of the two Serbian insurrections: the striving for national freedom, the tradition of cherishing the memory of the Serbian past, Serbian pride, the strivings for the unification of all the Serbian regions. These ideas sustained the fighting spirit of the Serbian youth and Serbian people through the nineteenth century and at the beginning of the twentieth. The Kosovo legend, the *Hajduk* and *Uskok* cycles, became components of nationalism; and Karadžić consciously laid stress on this nationalism and its political implications. Its core was democratic, it promised complete freedom and the participation of the masses in goverment. Karadžić frequently had severe differences with the regime of Knez Miloš. But the generation that immediately preceded Karadžić's death introduced views into Serbian political and literary life which it had evolved from a study of his writings.

Owing to the individuality of his principles, the vastness and significance of his works and the boldness of his views, Karadžić soon gained recognition and influence, in spite of the obstacles which the Serbs themselves put in his path. His work played an especially important part in drawing the Yugoslav peoples together. The Croatian writers printed poems from his collections, and fragments from his prose works; he was the mentor of many of them in the early thirties. In 1850 there took place in Vienna a meeting of the most outstanding Serbian, Croatian and Slovene writers. It ended with the adoption of the principle that one nation should have one literature. Its purpose was to urge all the Yugoslavs to adopt a single literary language, similar to Karadžić's.

The meeting failed in its object, for only the Croats wrote in the southern speech *(ijekavski)*, which Karadžić also used. *Ekavski*, or the eastern dialect spoken in Hungary and in Belgrade, prevailed among the Serbs. Nevertheless Karadžić's manuscripts were the foundation of the first scientific grammar of the Serbian or Croatian language, written in 1899 by *Tomo Maretić*, a Croat. Since then the Croatian and Serbian literary languages have been identical.

Petar Petrović-Njegoš (1813—1851) was one of the first writers of his native country, Montenegro, and the greatest Serbian writer of the period. He was also one of those rare artists who knew how to appeal to the people, to keep abreast of the times, and to be deeply human. Besides this, as a ruler, Njegoš endeavoured to render Montenegro completely independent, and to turn it into a modern State.

The independence of Montenegro was destroyed by the Turks in the fifteenth century; but they never took over the whole country. When they occupied the plains and valleys, the people fled to the impenetrable forests, from which they made raids on the enemy, while during better times they returned to their homes. Thus the Montenegrins assumed a special, warlike way of life. Every male was a soldier, and ready for action at a moment's notice. For centuries Montenegro had lived a patriarchal life, without taxation or legislation, divided into clans and communities, each member of which had fixed military duties. The head of the Church at Cetinje, the bishop, as the supreme spiritual authority, was held by the people in the highest esteem.

The decline of the Turkish power, which began towards the end of the seventeenth and at the beginning of the eighteenth century, had its effect also in Montenegro. Although neither the Turkish government nor the European states recognized Montenegro as a separate state, it steadily plodded on towards complete independence. It began to win this with the coming of the members of the Petrović-Njegoš family, from the village of Njeguši, as bishops and as the secular heads of the State.

At the beginning of the nineteenth century, the religious head of Montenegro was Petar Petrović-Njegoš. He succeeded in uniting the Montenegrin clans, and they swore allegiance to him. With very few literate men, without any government employees, with no trade, books or newspapers, Montenegro was at that time an exotic land which only the daring traveller and adventurer was eager to visit. It was not able to boast of the organization of the orderly states of the capitalistic world, with their efficient administrations and trained armies. Petar I was succeeded in 1830 by his nephew Rade, who took the name of Petar at his consecration. Very strong in mind and body, Petar II Petrović-Njegoš received an indifferent education, partly in the Topla Monastery in Boka Kotorska and partly under the tutoring of Sima Milutinović-Sarajlija, who had been the old bishop's amenuensis at Cetinje for several years. Njegoš was only seventeen years of age, and without thorough theological training when he assumed secular and spiritual power, as was customary in Montenegro. Extremely difficult problems faced the young bishop: the Turks were preying upon Montenegro, and so were Austria and Venice; the local chieftains strove to make themselves as independent of the central government as possible.

Njegoš's first task on coming to power was to consolidate his own dignity, to maintain peace in the country, to substitute modern administration for the patriarchal clan system. He strove, besides, to advance education, to make the borders safe against Turkey and Austria, and to gain formal recognition of independence.

In the course of several years of fruitful work, and with the help of Russia, Njegoš carried through his plans. The difficulties were enormous: often he had to wage war, to repulse the attacks of the border Turks; often he had to overcome by harsh methods the resistance of the clan chieftains, who regarded the strengthening of the central government as an attack on their freedom. Taxation, as a means of setting the State upon modern foundations, was attacked by the Montenegrins as being identical with the Turkish imposts, and as an infringement of their rights.

While bringing order into his tiny State, Njegoš realized that it was but a part of Serbdom and of Yugoslavdom; in the final analysis, a part of Slavdom, which was broken up into a number of states, almost all of which were in a position of subjection. It was his dream to see Serbdom free and united. In his time he was a steadfast and almost fanatical champion of Slavdom; he was conscious of all the hardships and humiliations which, owing to their position, the Slavs were enduring. While he discharged his affairs of State, Njegoš also concentrated on his education. He studied foreign languages; when he went on official journeys abroad (in Vienna, to Russia and Italy), he purchased books and instructed himself in the literature of Europe. Strong as his constitution was from childhood, the strenuous, restless life he lived soon ruined his health: consumption set in, and he sought a cure in Italy, but in vain. He died at Cetinje, and was buried on the summit of Mount Lovćen.

Njegoš's literary propensities began to develop under the influence of the folk poem, and through the encouragement of his tutor, Sima Milutinović. Living in a country in which every event was a theme of the folk poem for want of newspapers, Njegoš himself formed the habit of composing poems in ten-syllabled verse about the clashes between the Montenegrins and Turks, about comic mishaps at weddings, etc. Sima Milutinović also made him acquainted with conditions in Serbian literature and with his own works.

From the folk poem Njegoš gradually advanced to poems with a more personal note. His first more extensive work was *Svobodijada* [Song of freedom], a rather amateurish description of the battles of the Montenegrins for freedom which began in the eighteenth century. It was not published during the poet's lifetime.

As he gained experience, Njegoš proceeded to philosophical and general human topics. He published shorter poems, either separately or in *Grlica* [The dove], an almanac which he founded at Cetinje after setting up a printing-press. His principal works are *Luča mikrokozma* [The light of the microcosm] (1815), *Gorski vijenac* [The Mountain Wreath] (1847), *Šćepan mali* [Šćepan the small] (1851).

Luča mikrokozma signifies the light, or souls of the miniature cosmos, man. It is in the nature of a philosophical epic; and in it Njegoš endeavoured to solve the problem of man's fate on earth. His point of departure was the observation that human life is mere misery, and that at first sight it is meaningless. In view of this, man's aspirations, all his endeavours on earth are utterly ridiculous. Njegoš found the answer to this problem in the pre-existence of the soul: man is one of the angels who mutinied with Satan against God. He repented during the conflict, and was sent to earth to live there in desolation and to remember his days of happiness instead of being banished to Tartarus. His body is condemned to suffer the fate of all things earthly, his soul being his link with immortality. The epic describes the mutiny against God, and its outcome.

Gorski vijenac — a wreath of glory for the heroes of Montenegro — is a dramatic poem. It is a description of an event supposed to have occurred at the beginning of the eighteenth century, when the Montenegrin chieftains, with Bishop Danilo at their head, decided to banish the native Moslems from the country in order to restore unity in it. An attempt to reach a peaceful understanding with them, and to persuade them to return to the fold of Christianity having failed, the Montenegrins take the Moslems by surprise, kill many, and drive out the survivors. Njegoš built a number of scenes around the central event: the deliberations of the Montenegrin chieftains, a wedding, an abduction, a funeral, witchcraft, cultural conditions in Montenegro, folk customs. Thus *Gorski vijenac* is a mirror of life in Montenegro.

Njegoš's last work is his drama *Šćepan mali*. It describes an event from the eighteenth century, when an adventurer called Šćepan, who pretended to be Czar Peter of Russia, came to Montenegro. The Montenegrins welcomed him and made him their ruler. No assurances of the wise men, nor the coming of some Russians, were able to convince them of the opposite, or to persuade them to drive the imposter out of the country. Incidentally, he proved to be a good ruler. He was killed by a Turkish mercenary.

Njegoš's works, apparently varied in matter, are linked together by two essential features: they all derive from his patriotism, his love of Serbdom, Slavdom, his love of freedom; and from his striving to understand human life. Both features are discernible in all his more important poems. His principal work, however, is *Gorski vijenac*, for it contains all the perfection of his work. On the other hand, *Luča mikrokozma* in a fashion escapes reality and is unsubstantial. *Šćepan mali*, again, contains some excellent realistic scenes, typical of the Montenegrin character; but it is obviously the work of a tired, ailing man. In *Gorski vijenac*, on the contrary, Njegoš gave free rein to his extraordinary creative powers. It is expressive equally of the writer's philosophy and of his human and popular qualities; and in it he attained the height of his powers of expression.

In observing life and discharging his arduous duties as a ruler, Njegoš lost all his illusions about happiness on earth, about human kindness, about justice. He was aware of the world's unending struggle, in which the best are often defeated. During his frequent moments of trial, he lost all faith in man and in himself; any striving towards improvement was futile. *Luča mikrokozma* is the expression of his profound pessimism; *Gorski vijenac* also is by no means devoid of it. But Njegoš realized in time that during his constant struggle on earth, man's duty is to combat evil and to stamp it out wherever he can. This realization is manifested to a certain extent in *Luča mikrokozma*, but even more so in *Gorski vijenac*.

Gorski vijenac, as a whole, is a poem of struggle for freedom. The historic event which the poet depicts is regarded as the beginning of the work for the liberation of Serbdom. The poet, accordingly, dedicated his work to Karadjordje, the leader of the First Serbian Insurrection. In almost every scene the poet adjures the Montenegrins to rise against the Turks, and curses deserters and traitors. Throughout the work the reader discerns the history of Montenegro, with its struggle and its sufferings; but also with its pride and its faith in final victory. Out of every verse emerges the conviction that freedom is earned and pride and independence saved, not by compromises and servility but through heroism.

While he was writing *Gorski vijenac*, Njegoš never ceased to keep his own period in mind. He described what he hoped for and what he saw; and he portrayed the men of the eighteenth century against the background of his day. But while he dwelt within the circle of his times and of contemporary reality, Njegoš's work embraced general human vistas. He dealt with an apparently trivial event in the endless chain of strife between Christendom and Islam in such a fashion that his work echoes the perpetual, universal struggle between Good and Evil, Light and Darkness, Progress and Violence. In this struggle Njegoš is resolutely on the side of Good.

Gorski vijenac though relatively short, demonstrates the writer's remarkable creative powers. He depicted a multitude of characters: Montenegrins and Turks, men and women, the old and the young, individuals and crowds. In some scenes he seems to describe with photographic precision the life of the Montenegrins, dialogues, beliefs; but he also pictures the individual in his perpetual relationship to the problems of life, love, death. He drew his fellow Montenegrins as they really were — primitive, half *Hajduks*, but devoted to their country. In the countenance of his chief character, Bishop Danilo, he described his own lot: the lot of a lonely superior man who sees more than anyone else, and as a consequence feels more strongly the bitterness of his time. With remarkable conciseness Njegoš described his characters in their primitive crudeness, in their relation to the enemy, as well as in their moments of the most delicate ecstasy of love. He also set forth the position of his country towards the cultured West, and towards the sensuous and overbearing East.

In describing scenes, feelings and thoughts, Njegoš expressed himself concisely and forcefully. His poem appears to be hewn out of the rock of his own Montenegro. Every sentence in his dialogues and monologues seems to be pervaded by the views and moods of his people, to delve deeply into the mystery of general human relationships. The sentences, like wisdom which is the fruit of long ripening, are irrefutable. Some of them seem to contain the essence of the philosophy of life, to be the fruit of painful experience and of dreary solitude:

94

"Zemlja stenje, a nebesa ćute".
("The earth doth groan, the heavens silence keep").

Njegoš took many phrases from the people; but under his pen they received a new, individual meaning. His verse, apparently the usual popular ten-syllabled verse, has in his work a different, more personal touch; and there is something painful and deeply melancholy in it, just as Njegoš's whole countenance was deeply sad.

In some respects *Gorski vijenac* can be related with other contemporary Serbian literary works. But in artistic quality it soars above its time, as if magically inspired. Derived from the people, from contemporary conditions prevailing in Montenegro and in Serbdom, it is at the same time the broadest, the most human of works in Serbian literature. During the period in which the foundations of the new Serbian literature were being laid in the struggle for a new language and new spirit upon the traditions of the older Serbian literature and upon elements of folk poetry, *Gorski vijenac* is its first great accomplishment. It is a blend of perfect simplicity, precision and profundity, with elements taken from the people; and it is personal from beginning to end.

Branko Radičević (1824—1853) emerged as the first reformer of Serbian lyricism, at a time when Serbian poets were still following *Lukijan Mušicki* as a model — employing modes effete, sententious, inflexible. The son of a clerk, born at Brod na Savi, Radičević graduated from the Serbian gymnasium at Sremski Karlovci and studied law in Vienna. He published his first book of poems in 1847, at the height of the tension between Vuk Karadžić and his opponents. His book was in the popular tongue with Karadžić's orthography; and it was gay, youthful, carefree.

Radičević was scarcely twenty-four years old, yet he was a mature poet, whose work differed from the lyrics hitherto produced by other Serbian poets. His poems contain nothing out of the text-books. They describe the sentiments of a young man who wants to sing, to enjoy the inexhaustible ecstasy of beauty and song. The motifs of his lyrics are not numerous. He sings about the morning, flowers, the dew, about lovesickness, youthful exuberance, about school life; and on the surface his perceptions are very simple. His love poetry is clearly sensual, physical; but it is expressed in such sincere and happy terms that it cannot but impress as being something rare and fresh, thus parrying objections that it was obscene. For youthful though it is, this poetry exudes a feeling of transitoriness, sickness, and early death.

Radičević expressed his feelings in an apparently simple verse-form — that of the folk poem. Its simplicity should not be ascribed to his having adopted blindly the form of the folk poem, but to

95

his being able to find the most direct and precise expression for an emotion. He is therefore doubly important in the Serbian literature of his period: both to the nation and to its literature. In his works Serbian lyrics for the first time give full significance to the popular speech and style. In addition to this, with Radičević's poems the Serbian poet won the right to sing about his own feelings.

Radičević was aware of his place in Serbian cultural life. His poetry was not merely literature: it represented a definite outlook upon life. In his poem *Put* [The road] he attacked the conservatives who opposed Vuk Karadžić in Serbia. In 1848 and 1849, he was one of the leaders of the Hungarian revolution, although he did not take part in the actual fighting. He was forced by the Serbian authorities to leave Belgrade. In his poems, like Karadžić in his articles, he fought against everything coming to Serbia from Austria as a fashion, artificial, imitative, supposedly progressive while actually being a sign of vitiation and decay.

After the revolution he returned to Vienna to study medicine. He published a second book of verse — epic poems — some of which contained elements borrowed from Byron. At this time he was seriously ill, and the poems of this period are of an inferior quality. Shortly afterwards he died in Vienna. Some ten years after his death he became the idol of the younger romantic generation.

Jovan Sterija Popović (1806—1856) stood detached from the literary controversies of his time. He was older than Njegoš and Radičević, and preceded them as a writer. He died shortly after they did, of the same illness which had caused their early death — of consumption.

Popović came of a bourgeois family, from Vršac in Hungary. His father, a merchant, was Greek; his mother was a Serb, a cultured and sensitive woman with a taste for art. His father directed him to money-earning as the main object in life; from his mother he inherited his love of literature and learning. Notwithstanding many inconveniences and interruptions, he succeeded in obtaining a degree in law. He was first a gymnasium teacher and later a lawyer in his home town. He eventually moved to Belgrade, where he was first a professor at the Lyceum, and then the head of a ministry department. In the ministry he showed immense activity: he founded the theatre, a Serbian society of learning *(Društvo srpske slovesnosti)*, and he wrote school books. Owing to disagreements with his superiors in Serbia, he returned to his birthplace, where he died.

Popović was weak constitutionally, and a sensitive and retiring man. Attracted to literary work in his boyhood, he gave vent, as was the literary fashion, to his hatred for the Turks as the oppressors of Christendom. At first he wrote in Slavo-Serb, but later he adopted Vuk Stefanović Karadžić's popular language. He wrote a novel, *Boj na Kosovu* [The battle of Kosovo] (1828), and several plays on Serbian history and the national epics *(Svetislav i Mileva; Miloš Obilić; Nahod Simeon* — Simeon the Foundling), in which he eulogized the Serbian past and the great men of medieval Serbia, expressed his horror of the Turks, and sang about Kosovo. These works contain scarcely anything from actual history. The characters resemble knights in sentimental novels; the events are unexplained, often very strange, abounding in unexpected turns; the style is stilted and full of pathos.

Popović, however, developed steadily. He was well-versed in European literature. He also interested himself in the theory of literature. The first pseudo-historical plays were followed by other more serious dramas *(Smrt Stefana Dečanskog* — The death of Stefan Dečanski; *Skenderbeg; Ajduci* — The Hajduks; *Lahan)*. In these he also dealt with the Serbian past, or with motifs from folk poetry. With them he sought to deal dramatically with perpetual human passions and conflicts: intrigue, the influence of a woman on the relations between a father and his son *(Smrt Stefana Dečanskog)*, the idealism of the individual and the scheming of the mob *(Lahan)*, the deceptiveness of the romantic conception of the Hajduks *(Ajduci)*.

Popović's historical dramas are in the main an expression of the aspirations of the young Serbian bourgeoisie, which was building up Serbian nationalism on the foundations of the Serbian past, of the magnificence of the old Serbian State, and of the Kosovo myth. He also had a keen eye for the weaknesses of the bourgeoisie; and as the first comic writer in Serbian literature, he did not spare it his satire.

In a number of comedies *(Laža i paralaža* — Liar and superliar; *Tvrdica* — The miser; *Pokondirena tikva* — The upstart; *Ženidba i udadba* — Marrying and giving in marriage; *Zla žena* — The bad woman; *Beograd nekad i sad* — Belgrade past and present; *Rodoljupci* — The patriots), Popović presented realistic pictures of the social life of his period, directing his taunts especially at the bourgeoisie and petty bourgeoisie. He was the first Serbian writer to introduce the ordinary, everyday man into literature. He stigmatized the members of the young Serbian bourgeoisie and their craving for wealth, the silly adoption of foreign mannerisms, sham scholars. He potrayed the wives and daughters of tradesmen who wanted to live at all costs like the upper-class bourgeoisie. He depicted the local Greeks in their miserliness and cupidity. He lashed at the false patriotism of his contemporaries, whose only objective was money, and in order to get it were always going over to the winning side, and demanding immediate payment for having done so. His *Roman bez romana* [A novel without a story] satirizes romanticism.

As far as his own ambitions went, and according to his own declaration, Popović was not a true creative artist. He might have been an eighteenth-century writer living in the nineteenth who primarily wanted to teach the people something and be useful to them. This being the case, it is easy to understand that it is possible to discern passages which he borrowed from the works of European writers (Shakespeare, Rabener, Molière, Kotzebue). He failed to round off a considerable number of his dramas, the characters of which he merely sketched.

But as he became a more earnest student of life, through which he went alone and embittered, his powers of observation grew keener. He perceived the vast difference between men's utterances and their deeds; he realized of what very little value uprightness, knowledge, nobility of character, were in the perpetual race of the society of his day for money. And he revealed his observations in his works, which sank into deeper pessimism as they multiplied. Accordingly, he was at his strongest in those works which contained bitter observations on the perverseness of men and life. Probably his most personal works are his tragedy *Lahan* and his comedy *Rodoljupci*. The former describes a man who sacrifices himself to the utmost for the liberation of his people; but when he seeks personal happiness, his associates slay him. The latter is a record of his disappointment with the year 1848, when lofty phrases about freedom and nationality were misapplied by scoundrels and egoists for the sake of career and money.

Popović entered literature as a lyric poet, and as a lyric poet he died. His final book *(Davorje)* is a book of poems expressing the poet's complete exhaustion, skepticism, and complete distrust of men. It turns to death as the solution of all hardships and injustices.

Popular and esteemed, during the forties, as the greatest Serbian playwright, Jovan Sterija Popović refused to bow before the vigorous romantic generation which was appearing on the horizon in 1848. He died forgotten and unrecognized; and he was rediscovered only towards the end of the nineteenth century.

2. SLOVENE LITERATURE DURING THE FIRST HALF OF THE NINETEENTH CENTURY

The priesthood had for centuries enjoyed a special position among the Slovenes, owing to social and political conditions. Since it alone of the educated sections remained in touch with the people, the priesthood assumed leadership, and jealously endeavoured to ward off all interference with its status. The clergy supported elements of cultural life in the Slovene areas, thus sustaining its national existence; but it was instrumental in preventing the literature of the Slovenes from evolving into a literature of European standards, and it perpetuated its pious and didactic character. Any bolder demonstration of feelings was stifled by the clergy as being sinful and dangerous. The Slovenes were in a position to gain full literary freedom only at the beginning of the nineteenth century, when the Slovene bourgeoisie began to rise, and when laymen took to writing.

Radical political and social changes occurred among the Slovenes at the beginning of the nineteenth century. The causes were the Napoleonic wars, the changes in Austria, and European, particularly German, romanticism, the centre of which for a time was Vienna.

Of all the states of Europe, Austria resisted Napoleon the longest. All the nations in Austria, including the Slovenes, fought against him. In 1809 Austria was defeated, and Napoleon occupied a considerable part of Austrian territory, including the Slovene areas. Ljubljana became the centre of Napoleon's Illyrian Provinces. The continual wars, the influence of the French, their views of society and religion, the conservatism of the older generations, brought a period of restlessness among the Slovenes. Although they regarded French supremacy with hostility, they soon realized that it had some good points: it concerned itself with the welfare of the peasantry, it promoted economy in the conquered areas, it allowed the use of the Slovene language. Slovene became a subject in the Ljubljana gymnasium in 1811. Austria respected this change after Napoleon's defeat; moreover a Chair of the Slovene language was founded at Graz.

During the early decades of the nineteenth century, there were a number of young Slovene intellectuals of bourgeois descent who had been preparing for the priesthood, but had changed their minds. They became clerks, teachers, journalists and lawyers instead. Having studied at Graz and Vienna in German, some of them gained an excellent command of European languages and a knowledge of European literature. Unlike the preceding generations, they did not succumb to German influence: they remained Slovenes, and consciously endeavoured to strengthen their nation and raise it to the level of the other European nations. Some of them spent years in German surroundings, at Graz and Vienna, which were centres of government, and from thence they influenced their fellow countrymen. Others returned to their country, practised their professions in the Germanized towns, and grouped themselves into what became a distinctively Slovene bourgeoisie.

Two Slovenes, Bartolomej Kopitar and Dr. Matija Čop, especially distinguished themselves during the first half of the nineteenth century.

Bartolomej Kopitar (Raprije na Gorenjsko, 1780 — Vienna, 1844) became a consummate Slavonic scholar in Zois's circle, being second in importance, in level of scientific training and in scientific connexions only to the Czech, Josef Dobrovsky. He published old Slavic manuscripts, wrote a scientific grammar of the Slovene language in German, and tried to solve the problem of Slovene orthography. For many years he was official censor of Slovene books in Vienna. He enjoyed an excellent name among the Slovenes, although as censor he could ban any book which was not to his liking, which he frequently did.

Matija Čop (Žirovnica, 1797 — Ljubljana, 1835) was a gymnasium teacher (at Rijeka and Lvov), and later a librarian (at Ljubljana). He acquired a vast knowledge of literature, had at his command almost all the living and extinct languages of Europe, and read in the original all the more important works of world and Slavic literature. He wrote little; rather he exercised his influence by means of the spoken word, revealing to his fellow countrymen the wealth of the literature of the world. He was drowned in the river Sava.

Owing to the political and social conditions of the time, German romanticism, with its centre in Vienna, spread to the German bourgeois people in the Slovene areas: in Ljubljana there were newspapers and literary reviews in German. Consequently German romanticism also affected the Slovenes. As a result, they began to give more attention to their own past, their own language, and to the life of their peasantry. Attempts were made to continue the work of *Valentin Vodnik*, and to advance Slovene poetry; but to this there were many obstacles, such as the political fragmentation of the Slovene people into several districts, the want of a literary centre, the several orthographies. Some intellectuals endeavoured to resolve the problem of the Slovene literary language and script, as *Vuk Stefanović Karadžić* had for the Serbs, but their attempts failed. During the thirties of the century the Illyrian movement began to spread from Croatia to the Slovene regions, the idea being that the Yugoslavs should unite under the name of Illyrians and that they should have one speech and one orthography.

The problem of the Slovene literary language was solved in the main with the coming of a new name, Francè Prešern, a poetic genius, and with the foundation of the first Slovene literary almanac, *Kranjska Čbelica* [The Krain bee] (1830—1834).

The Ljubljana newspaper in German, *Illyrisches Blatt*, also published articles in Slovene. Plans were also made to found a separate newspaper in Slovene in that city. The authorities, however, refused to grant permission for this, evidently considering that it was sufficient if the publication in German occasionally printed something for the inferior Slovene nation in their own language.

In 1830 a small group of Slovene bourgeois intellectuals succeeded in founding *Kranjska čbelica*. The publisher and editor was *Miha Kastelic*, a librarian, the spiritual head was Matija Čop, and the principal poet Francè Prešern. Some numbers of the almanac also contained articles by older or younger writers of minor importance. However, *Kranjska čbelica* throve on Prešern's poems, for he was the most notable poetic figure among the Slovenes, not only during his time, but generally — a figure whose significance stepped beyond the bounds of literature.

Francè Prešern (1800—1849) was the son of a well-to-do peasant, born at Vrba near Bled. Several priests also came from his family. He had intended originally to take orders, as his two brothers had done; but having no inclination for that profession, he went to Vienna after graduating from gymnasium, to study law, ending up by taking his doctorate. He was unable, however, to find permanent employment. He even worked as a beginner without pay, and then as a lawyer's clerk in Ljubljana; and it was only towards the end of his life that he managed to acquire an independent practice in Krain. In Krain he also died.

Prešern belongs to the first generation of Slovene intellectuals from the countryside who entered life as laymen instead of following the well-worn path of the priesthood, as the educated Slovenes who came from the common people had always done before him. The son of a peasant, liberal-minded, an opponent of religious fanaticism and superstition, he was unsuccessful in obtaining a government post, for the civil service was the heritage of the children of bureaucrats. Nor was he able to practise law for a lengthy period of time, for the legal profession was exclusive, and marked primarily for the members of the bourgeoisie in the Slovene areas, chiefly for the Germans. Highly strung and temperamental, he was in conflict either with petty-bourgeois selfishness or with vulgarity; or he met with misunderstanding on the part of those whom he loved. His deep love for a wealthy bourgeois girl called Julija Primicova was his downfall. His love affair with the uneducated Ana Jelošek brought him a number of children, as well as material cares and spiritual strife. He died relatively young, broken in spirit, disappointed and poor.

The conditions under which Prešern lived and worked were dreadfully cramped. The small number of Slovene intellectuals who followed literary pursuits were torn by controversies over the literary language and the question of orthography; besides this, some of them were narrow-minded and bigoted in literary matters. The number of the reading public which might have accepted literature in Slovene was still inconsiderable; the bourgeoisie spoke and wrote German, and chiefly demanded books written in this language.

Prešern was endowed with a rich gift for language and literature. In Vienna he increased his knowledge by reading works of world literature, particularly the German romanticists. His knowledge of literature became still more profound under the influence of Matija Čop, his most faithful friend and trusted adviser.

Prešern began to write verse in Vienna; he began to publish his poems in 1827 in the German newspaper of Ljubljana. In 1831 his contributions to *Kranjska čbelica* brought him popularity and renown.

Prešern's goal as a writer was to create a literature in Slovene for the educated bourgeoisie which would compare favourably with the bourgeois literature of Europe. To this end it was necessary to cut himself off from the traditions of the didactic and pious Slovene literature, designed for the peasantry, and to express life itself in all its richness in his literary work.

Prešern's first poems in *Kranjska čbelica* were perfect works of art, and of European stature. They revealed the sentiments of a man who felt himself a part of his small nation; of a man who had something to say about the profoundest things of the heart and the mind: of love, of the transitoriness of life, of the beauty and briefness of youth, as well as of the frictions and inconveniences under which he lived. Owing to the forcefulness of the feelings which they displayed, to the depth of his ideas, and to the precision of his expression, Prešern's poems in *Kranjska čbelica* aroused the enthusiasm of those who knew what art was. In his poems he showed himself to be a bourgeois intellectual who rose against the narrowness, rigidity and shallowness of Slovene cultural life.

Modern Slovene literature from its very inception had a poet of the first order in Prešern. His poems, however, caused alarm among those Slovene public figures who led the way in cultural life, especially among the clergy. The malcontents were joined by Kopitar, who had been considered the most outstanding Slovene till then, because Prešern and his group refused to accept Kopitar's tutelage. They attacked Prešern for what was supposed to be the immorality of his love poems. Permission for the appearance of the fourth number of *Kranjska čbelica* was withheld, and publication ceased in 1834.

This was the first blow. Prešern had nowhere else to publish his poems. The unexpected death of his friend Matija Čop, the only man who fully understood him, was the second blow.

Unhappy in life, without a sure existence, unhappy in love, he felt tired and lonely. Consequently his great plans to write a tragedy, a novel and other things failed to materialize: almost all his life-work is contained in his little volume of poems, *Poezija* (1847).

Prešern was an artist of the highest order. He created only when the mood was on him. He did not record superficial emotions, but only that which had already settled in him and crystallized completely; and it was only then that his feelings and views found full expression in his poems. There are no poor, amateurish or uninspired poems among his works. Each of his works is perfect and compact.

In his poems Prešern revealed his love dreams, his disappointment at the infidelity of women; and his personal, painful revelation of the blows and miseries he endured during his life as a penniless intellectual away from his village. In verse he also described the dismal moments of weariness which came over him when he contemplated what he regarded as his failure in life. But he did not lack courage to censure the literary conditions among the Slovenes, the folly and narrow-mindedness of those who were supposed to be in authority. His poetry nevertheless breathes deep faith in his people, faith in Slavdom, in humanity, and in the meaning of art.

Prešern's central work is *Sonetni venec* [A sonnet sequence] on his unhappy love for Julija Primicova. In perfect harmony of subject and form the poet revealed his love and suffering; and at the same time he defined his position in relation to the Slovene nation, and its position in relation to Slavdom.

In his poetry Prešern united several elements: sincere, intense feeling, perfect Slovene, absolute simplicity of expression, the forms of European romanticism which connected him with the European literature of his period. But most fundamental in his poetry are those traits which bind him closely to the Slovenes, to his own peasant people, as the most distinctive Slovene section. For the first time in history, the Slovene language as he wrote it spoke in its melodious, unique voice. And Prešern was the first of all the Slovene writers to display both the affliction of his nation and its lyrical gentleness, as well as its steadfastness.

Late in the thirties Prešern felt defeated and almost old. This feeling was intensified as he became aware of the unfavourable reception that his poems met with among the conservative Slovenes, who formed the bulk of the educated people. His condition was aggravated by the death of his friend Čop, whose loss made him feel quite alone in the world. In memory of his friend he wrote the epic poem *Krst pri Savici* [The christening on the

103

Savica]. This work in a way marked a turning point in his life and creativeness.

Krst pri Savici describes the closing struggle of the pagan Slovenes with victorious Christianity. Their young leader Črtomir seeks his betrothed after his defeat, and finds that she too has accepted Christianity. She persuades him to accept the new faith and to become its missionary. They will part for ever in this life, but after death they will come together again in the world beyond.

The work is a masterpiece. It is an acknowledgment of his own defeat, a realization of the futility of struggle, a renunciation of personal happiness in this world.

The Slovene conservatives, having also taken cognizance of Prešern's surrender, spoke more genially about him. But he wrote less and less, particularly after the general conditions changed among the Slovenes.

During the forties of the nineteenth century, a new generation, headed by Dr. Janez Bleiweiss, a physician and veterinary surgeon, made its appearance among the Slovenes. Having become the editor of the first popular newspaper, *Kmetijske in rokodelske novice* [Farm and handicraft news] (1848), Bleiweiss sought to revive the earlier traditions in Slovene literature. In his opinion the Slovenes had no special need for a bourgeois literature, because the Slovene bourgeoisie was small. On the contrary, it was for the peasantry and craftsmen that literature should be written, for they constituted the core of the Slovene people. The idea was justified on the whole, for the prime necessity was to save the Slovene countryside for the Slovene nation, and gradually to raise its cultural level. Bleiweiss and his group not only disdained Prešern's type of literature, but even deliberately neglected it, considering it to be absolutely unnecessary and useless. Bleiweiss was joined by the conservatives, notably by the clergy.

There is no doubt that *Kmetijske in rokodelske novice* contributed much to the enlightenment of the Slovene peasantry. Its readers realized that the Slovene language was capable of expressing anything appertaining to economic and cultural life. It published literary pieces, especially tendentious poems and pious verse. Prešern also occasionally had something published by this periodical. It was not Prešern, however, but *Ivan Vesel Koseski* who was the first poet to contribute to it. He wrote patriotic odes in the style of Schiller, full of pathos and prolixity. This style appealed to the reading public, and Prešern was almost overshadowed by Koseski. Prešern, however, came forth again more openly in 1848, when the censorship was abolished in Austria during the revolutionary upheavals.

104

Apart from his literary merits, Prešern was of national significance among the Slovenes. He was the first to demonstrate that the Slovene language, till then almost inarticulate and known only in books for the common people, was a suitable vehicle for the creation of great literary works. Prešern was a champion of Slavdom and of the Yugoslav idea. But he refused to allow the Slovene tongue to disappear as a literary language. In this respect he purposely resisted the reformatory attempts of the Croatian Illyrians. He proved with his works that the Slovene language should be kept alive in literature. After these works, no serious attempts were ever made again to impose a single language on the Yugoslavs. After brief resistance, *Kmetijske in rokodelske novice* did introduce the Croatian orthography, according to the principles laid down by Ljudevit Gaj, although in 1848 many Slovenes were seized by a wave of Illyrianism, and even wrote in the language of the writers of Zagreb. But the idea of the Illyrians that all the Yugoslavs should unite in a single literary language was unrealizable. The Slovenes were for preserving their linguistic individuality, for they now had a poet of their own.

3. THE LITERATURE OF THE ILLYRIAN MOVEMENT

The Croatian people entered the nineteenth century territorially and socially fragmented, nationally and culturally weak. Towards the end of the first ten years of the century, political Croatia had been reduced to the regions between the rivers Sava and Drava, for Napoleon had taken the regions to the south and incorporated them into his Illyrian Provinces. These regions were retaken by Austria after Napoleon's fall; but they were joined to Croatia only in 1888. Dalmatia remained under the direct administration of Vienna till Austria-Hungary was defeated in 1918.

All political power in Croatia continued to be dispensed by the nobility and the high clergy, who were numerically an insignificant minority in the country. But as a select group, they were trained in the principles of state organization, and jealous of their class privileges. Up to 1848 Croatia was a feudal territory, the bulk of the peasantry being bound in serfdom. The official language was Latin, which was used in writing and speaking by the nobility, who, by so doing, deliberately estranged themselves from the masses. Most of the bourgeoisie spoke German. The Croatian speech of the overwhelming majority of the people was neglected in its own country, and almost scorned.

After the death of Joseph II, the ruling class of the Hungarian feudalists demanded the introduction of Hungarian instead of Latin on the whole territory of Hungary, which included Croatia. The political representatives of Croatia realized that this was an attempt to Magyarize their country. While Latin, as the official language, linked the several nations of Hungary, there was no danger to these nations. But if one of the tongues of Hungary were forced upon the others as the official language, it would become a dominating factor over the other nations. These endeavours on the part of the Hungarians stirred up resistance. The Hungarians, however, persisted: they even requested that Hungarian be introduced as the language of instruction in schools. They proposed that no one in Croatia should be allowed to become a teacher or government employee unless he knew Hungarian.

For several decades the Croatian nobility defended the use of Latin as the official language, for by so doing they were defending their social positions, which were associated with the old constitutional system. But as time passed, their resistance flagged. At the beginning of the thirties of the past century, the various representative bodies of Croatia, including the Croatian Sabor, were prepared to fall in with the Hungarian plans. The Croatian writer, *Pavao Štoos*, described the position of Croatia in 1831 in an allegorical way as resembling the countenance of a woman who has been forsaken by everyone, declaring sorrowfully that,

> "Vre i svoj jezik zabit Horvati
> „Hote ter drugi narod postati."
>
> ("The Croats will forget their language even,
> "And become another nation.")

It is true that there were those who endeavoured to prove historically that Croatia had joined Hungary of its own free will; accordingly Hungary had no right to force its tongue upon Croatia. Others, more radical, such as *Antun Mihanović*, the writer of *Reč domovini o basnovitosti pisanja vu domorodnom jeziku* [A word to my country about the benefits of writing in one's native language] (1815), advanced a broad Croatian political, economic and cultural programme in order to strengthen the position of their homeland. These solitary efforts would have been futile, however, but for the birth of a new cultural and literary, political and social movement in the ranks of youth known as the Illyrian movement.

The representatives of the Illyrian movement were all young men, born about 1810. They were the children of peasants, of noble families without property, and of bourgeois families. In their work they imitated some of the earlier Croatian writers (Gundulić, Vitezović) who wrote about Slavdom, Yugoslavdom, or Croatism. They took as their model the contemporary Czech cultural workers (Šafarik, Kollár) with their broad Slavic outlook.

106

In their plans and work the Illyrians ignored the struggle of the preceding feudal generations for the principles of polity, for they regarded the situation as it really was. Their point of departure being the numerical value and significance of Slavdom, the founders of the Illyrian movement in Croatia embraced the idea of Slavic solidarity expounded by the Czech writer Kollár. According to this teaching, the Slavs were one people with four dialects: Russian, Czech, Polish, and Illyrian. The Yugoslavs were Illyrians, according to Kollár. The Illyrians from Croatia, accordingly, sought to apply the name "Illyrians" to all the Yugoslavs, for they regarded them as the descendants of the ancient race. They planned to carry their idea through primarily with literature. Accordingly they advised that all the Yugoslavs should recognize one literary language: the *štokavski* dialect, which was used by the Dubrovnik writers — the language of the most beautiful folk poems for which *Vuk Stefanović Karadžić* was fighting among the Serbs.

In addition to its literary aspect, the Illyrian movement also possessed distinctive social and political features. Its non-feudalist representatives were supplanting the official Latin of the privileged classes primarily with the tongue of the despised peasant masses. The political consequences of the Illyrian movement, however, were far-reaching, for the whole movement was a mighty counterpoise to the endeavours of the Hungarians to impose their supremacy. Unlike the weak resistance which the Croatian feudalists put up against the Hungarian onslaughts, the initiators of the Illyrian movement inspired the Croatian people with faith in the magnificence of their nation, which was a part of Yugoslavdom and Slavdom.

The Illyrian movement in Croatia was soon joined by the young educated and enthusiastic people who were not of feudal origin. Even some of the nobility, realizing that the feudal system was already effete, joined the movement. The foremost leaders of the movement were Ljudevit Gaj and Count Janko Drašković.

Ljudevit Gaj (1809—1872) was the son of a doctor from Krapina. Having taken his doctorate at the Faculty of Philosophy at Leipzig, he concentrated on literary and political work instead of seeking a profession. He simplified the Croatian orthography *(Kratka osnova hrvatsko-slavenskega pravopisanja* — The elements of Croato-Slovene orthography in brief), founded in Zagreb the newspaper *Narodne novine*, and its literary supplement *(Danica)*, established a printing-press, agitated, travelled. He was an efficient organizer. With untiring work and the charm of his personality he mobilized the progressive young men of his period. He was the undisputed leader of the whole movement till 1848, when, under the altered conditions, he was compelled to withdraw from public life. He died in Zagreb.

Count Janko Drašković (Zagreb, 1770 — Radgona, 1856), a member of one of the most distinguished Croatian feudal families, perceiving the spirit of the times, joined the cause of the young generation. He wrote some poems and two small books, one in Croatian *(Disertacija;* 1832), and one in German *(Ein Wort an Illyriens Hochherzige Töchter;* 1838). *Disertacija* is the economic and political programme of Croatia; *Ein Wort* is his endeavour to enlist support for the Illyrians among the Croatian women who were under German influence. Since Gaj was not a feudalist, and therefore unenfranchised, the strivings of the Illyrians were represented in public by Count Drašković. He was at the head of every important cultural action; he represented the movement before the authorities and before the higher classes of society.

The movement soon roused the whole of Croatia. It even spread into Serbia, Krain and Styria. Aware of its significance, the Hungarian authorities tried to crush it directly by police action, and indirectly by describing it to the emperor in Vienna as rebellious. There came a period of persecution, imprisonment for its members, severe censorship of its publications. A section of the Croatian nobility openly sided with the Hungarians for the sake of preserving their class privileges. Open clashes occurred between the Illyrians and their Magyarophile countrymen. In 1843 the authorities ostracized the very name of the movement. Because of the severe censorship in Zagreb, in 1844 the Illyrians started a new newspaper in Belgrade, which they called *Branislav.* It was impossible to stamp out the movement itself: it hardened the Croatian people in resistance and further struggle, preparing them for the year 1848. The social side of the movement succeeded in bringing the feudal system into such disrepute in 1848 that it dissolved of its own accord.

The Illyrian movement was most successful in literature. During the early decades of the nineteenth century, Croatian literature was confined in the main to political Croatia, that is, to Zagreb and its neighbourhood, where, having few writers and few readers, it barely subsisted in the rarely used *kajkavski* dialect. Indeed, endeavours were made to revive it; but social and political conditions in Croatia were such that no attempt of this kind was successful.

Croatian literature, however, received new impetus from the members of the Illyrian movement.

The first works of the young generation of writers, which were published in the thirties, were plays, poems, political and literary brochures with a nationalistic trend. Foremost among them was a work on orthography by *Ljudevit Gaj* (1830). However, the first notable success of the movement came in 1835, when the magazine *Danica* began publication as a supplement to *Narodne novine,* thanks to Ljudevit Gaj.

The writers of the Illyrian movement being mostly from Croatia proper, they wrote in the *kajkavski* dialect; but they were soon joined by their fellow writers from other regions. Aware that Croatian literature could not develop within the narrow orbit of the dialects, and hampered by the several orthographies, the Illyrians first tried to solve the problem of the literary language and orthography. They solved it smoothly and quickly; and less than a year later, in 1836, they were all writing in the *štokavski* dialect, the most popular dialect of the Croatian and the Serbian tongue. They simultaneously adopted the orthography proposed by Ljudevit Gaj: for each sound a separate letter, with marks added over some Roman letters for the distinctive Slav sounds (after the Czech orthography).

Having solved the problem of language and orthography, the Illyrians went forward. Croatian literature had till then been developing under different political and social environments and influences. It now required a single direction and meaning. To this end the Illyrians popularized the literatures of Dubrovnik and Dalmatia in order to demonstrate how old Croatian culture was; they drew attention to the beauty and profundity of the Serbo-Croatian folk poetry, which accorded with their romantic views; they pointed to specimens of the most developed Slavic literatures, notably that of Russia and Poland, with the idea that by contemplating Pushkin and Mickiewicz Croatian literature would become distinctively national.

Evolving from the severe social and political differences of those times, the literature of the Illyrian movement was distinctly militant. It should have been the artistic expression of those classes which constituted the majority of the people; these, however, had neither the power nor the property (it consisted of the peasantry, a section of the petty bourgeoisie, the unpropertied nobility). Hence its fundamental characteristics: militancy and tendentiousness; hence also the fact that it cultivated lyricism, both patriotic and amatory, as its principal literary form, and the drama and novel as a secondary one.

The literature of the Illyrian movement must not be regarded as distinct from the European literature of that time. The writers of the movement were conversant with contemporary West-European literature. Some coincidental similarities between their own and the Italian, German and French literatures are perfectly obvious. Although the Illyrian literature evolved during the romantic period, it was spared some of the typical qualities of romanticism in Western Europe: it did not suffer from weak individualism, sentimentality or mysticism. Having grown out of the soil of reality, from the struggle of a people for existence, it was imbued with a feeling of strength and faith in the people and their future. The writers of the Illyrian movement regarded their work as a national and political duty.

Faced by a multitude of problems, the writers of the Illyrian movement hesitated between domestic and alien models. Only the strongest among them surmounted the many hardships and obstacles which they encountered. They not only created successful works, but also set the course for the entire subsequent development of Croatian literature.

During the fifteen years of their work, the writers of the Illyrian movement supported the first Croatian literary magazine and founded new literary publications: the miscellany *Kolo* [The reel] (from 1842 onwards), the almanac *Iskra* [The spark] (1815); they organized literary societies *(Matica Ilirska;* 1842), the performance of plays in Croatian; they engaged in dramatic work, wrote criticisms, feuilletons, stories, novels; they began to publish works of the old writers of Dubrovnik (Gundulić), folk poems, etc.

The writers of the Illyrian movement failed to unite the Yugoslavs under one name: the Serbs already had a firmer literary tradition and a better political position; the Slovenes had their poet Prešern, and refused to forsake their literary language. Only a few Serbs and Slovenes joined the Illyrian movement, Stanko Vraz being one of the more outstanding Slovenes to do so. But the Illyrians succeeded in uniting the Croats in a single literary language, and laid the foundations of modern Croatian literature. Their having adopted the most popular Serbo-Croatian dialect as their literary language marked their unification with the literary language of the Serbs. In orthography, on the other hand, the Slovenes adopted Gaj's reforms, naming their orthography *Gajica* after him.

The most important writers of the Illyrian movement were Ivan Mažuranić, Stanko Vraz and Petar Preradović. Dimitrije Demetar and Antun Nemčić were also prominent.

Ivan Mažuranić (1814–1890) came of a peasant family from Novi in the Croatian Littoral. He graduated from gymnasium and gained a degree in law in Zagreb. Though a poor boy, he managed to make his way through school by sheer industriousness. While he was still at school, he learnt Italian, Latin and Hungarian, and studied French, English and Slavic languages. After finishing school he became a part-time teacher at the gymnasium in Zagreb, and later practised as a lawyer at Karlovac. After the feudal system collapsed in 1848, he became a national deputy in the Croatian Sabor (the Assembly), in which he immediately distinguished himself. He climbed the ladder rapidly, and in 1873 became Ban of Croatia, the first bourgeois to receive this high office. In politics he was one of the first representatives of the young progressive

Croatian bourgeoisie who were striving to organize the country along West-European lines. During his term of office (1873—1880) he organized the school system and an administrative apparatus.

Mažuranić was a man with an education of the highest order. He was an excellent jurist and mathematician. He was interested both in philosophy and astronomy. He was of a retiring nature, taciturn and meditative. He was actively engaged in literature only during his younger years, before he devoted himself to politics.

Mažuranić, who, like Kačić, was homesick for his birthplace, wrote his first verses while he was a gymnasium pupil at Rijeka. After the foundation of *Danica* he became one of its most esteemed associates. In it he published a number of lyric poems, aphorisms, articles, commentaries and translations between 1835 and 1848. He added two concordant stanzas to Gundulić's *Osman* (1844). However, his most important work is the poem *Smrt Smail-age Čengića* [The death of Smail Aga Čengić] (Iskra, 1846), one of the most remarkable productions of Croatian literature.

Mažuranić voiced the dynamic ideas of the Illyrian movement in his poems. He emphasized the importance of unity among the Yugoslavs. He extolled the past martial fame of the Slavic nations, but declared that they should now gain fame in cultural work. He lauded the leaders of the Illyrian movement, and described the evils caused the Yugoslav peoples by their enemies. He endeavoured to give utterance to the philosophy of the Illyrian movement, and to the Messianic role of Slavdom. He wrote a number of love poems in addition to his patriotic verse, in which he exalted the power of love and the rights of youth. He also distinguished himself as a writer of occasional poetry in honour of men who had in some way affected the life of his people.

The most remarkable of Mažuranić's poems were those which he dared not publish during his lifetime. They express the sentiments of a man whom the members of the privileged classes strove to suppress; he himself, however, was confident of his superiority.

Although Mažuranić's shorter poems constitute an ideal whole, they are extremely varied in expression. The first among them approximate to the classical in metre; but later he followed the poets of Dubrovnik both in language and in metre. For a time he imitated either the Italian lyrists or the folk poem. He evinces traces of Monti, Foscolo, Lamartine, and Byron. His changes of style are not characteristic of him alone: they are common to Croatian literature as a whole, which had as yet not taken a definite direction.

After ten years of vaccilation, Mažuranić discovered his proper style in the simplicity of the folk poem. He attained the peak of his creativeness and his idiom in *Smrt Smail-age Čengića*.

Mažuranić wrote his most important work in connexion with an event which occurred in 1840. The Montenegrins had killed one of their worst enemies, who had done them much harm in the border areas. The event was given extensive publicity in the Serbian and Croatian papers. Several years later, in 1845, Mažuranić referred to this event in his Illyrian and Slavic enthusiasm, in his desire to express his admiration for the Montenegrin fighters and to give vent to his aspirations for national freedom, and to his hatred for the oppressors. He was concerned, not so much with presenting the incident in detail, as he was with taking the case of Smail Aga as a pretext to describe the sufferings of his people under the centuries-long Turkish yoke, their heroic behaviour in their sufferings, and their faith in victory over the tyrant. In five scenes *(Agovanje, Noćnik, Četa, Harač, Kob)* he described the crimes Smail Aga had committed against captive Montenegrins; the preparations of the Montenegrins for revenge; the assembling of the reprisal group; the attack on the criminal and his death; his posthumous fate.

The magnificence of Mažuranić's poem lies in its conciseness, fullness and plasticity. His expression is reduced to the essential: not a single word could be omitted from the poem without detracting from its clarity. The personages are delineated in a few clear lines, with all their individual qualities, propensities, desires. The poem is a concise history of the Croats and Yugoslavs during centuries of struggle with the Turks. In vigorous, telling strokes Mažuranić presents scenes of unparalleled suffering, pride, poverty, and heroic death before the tyrant, as well as scenes of vengeance and victory. The work is broad enough to include general human perspectives: the poem is, not so much a description of one of the numerous clashes on the Turkish border, as it is a study of man's eternal struggle against oppression and evil.

In style, Mažuranić's *Smrt Smail-age Čengića* is an example of distinctively national Croatian and Yugoslav work. It contains all the elements of Croatian culture: the old classical elements, the West-European elements, the elements of Dubrovnik and Dalmatia; but based as it is on the folk poem, all these elements are so assimilated that the Croatian tongue speaks in its most natural rhythm, and Mažuranić, as the poet, in his most personal idiom. It expresses both the social and the national aspects of the Illyrian movement in a unique fashion: the struggle of the oppressed against the privileged, the feelings of brotherhood and unity among the Yugoslavs, which Mažuranić, a Croat, demonstrated by taking an episode from the life of the Montenegrins as the theme for his greatest work.

Stanko Vraz (1810—1851) was the only writer of non-Croatian nationality who espoused the Illyrian movement in its full sense. A Slovene from Cerkovac, Styria, he went to Graz after graduating from gymnasium to study law, which, however, he abandoned in order to study languages and literature. In course of time he became conversant with all the important literature of Europe, especially Slavic literature. He sent contributions to *Kranjska čbelica*, and with the publication of *Danica* in Zagreb, he began to write in the *štokavski* dialect. He became a permanent associate of the Zagreb magazine after it published his first contributions (in 1835); and gradually he drew so close to the Illyrians that he moved permanently to Zagreb, in Croatia. There he was able to live without any major disturbances, and to concentrate on literary work. In 1846 he was appointed secretary of *Matica Ilirska,* a post which he held till his death.

Vraz was primarily a writer. He regarded his literary calling as his main pursuit in life. He joined the Illyrians because he considered that, as small nations, neither the Slovenes, nor the Croats, nor the Serbs could develop a major literature. Vraz lived for literature, he wrote, travelled, organized literary undertakings. He maintained personal and written connexions with the most prominent Yugoslav and Slavic writers of the time; and he himself was a prolific and versatile writer. During his lifetime he published three collections of original and translated poems: *Djulabije**) (1840), *Glasi iz Dubrave žerovinske* [Voices in the Žerovo Wood] (1841), *Gusle i tambure* [The gusla and tambouras] (1845).

Vraz's literary reputation is founded chiefly on his love poems in *Djulabije.* At a time when most other Croatian poets were composing patriotic poems, the young Vraz was writing about a subject uppermost in his thoughts, about love. In the simple verse of the folk poem he describes his first meetings with his beloved, his moments of happiness, their little misunderstandings, her marriage to another, his anguish, her early death. In his collection of poems his love for women gradually became sublimated into love for his homeland and for humanity in general.

Parallel with *Djulabije,* and also later, Vraz wrote poems with a more complex mode of expression. He introduced foreign poetic forms into Croatian literature: the sonnet and the ghazel. The sonnet cycle *Sanak i istina* [Dreams and the truth], the fruit of his new love, is the most perfect in form; but the fundamental features of his lyrics remained the same. Something youthfully gay and direct emanates from them, and only by degrees does the feeling of sorrow for failing to gain a secure position in life pervade them.

---

*) A word of Turkish derivation denoting a sort of delicious red apple.

In addition to his love poems, Vraz wrote romances and ballads, chiefly on national themes. As he advanced in years, he took to writing satirical poems and epigrams, lampooning his national and literary opponents, and condemning various negative manifestations in Croatian bourgeois and feudal society.

In his endeavours to link Croatian literature as closely as possible with European literature, Vraz was a zealous translator, being one of the first to translate works by Pushkin, Byron, and Dante.

With his advanced views on literature and literary life, Vraz could not remain a creator only: he regarded literature also from the aspect of its social significance — he considered the problem of the reading public and the distribution of books. He studied the background of Croatian Renaissance literature, and boldly asserted that the Croatian literature of the Illyrian movement had been created and sustained, not by the rich nobility and bourgeoisie, but by the children of the poor.

In his endeavours to raise Croatian literature to European standards, Vraz charged it with serious tasks. With a group of friends he founded the literary magazine *Kolo*. It published accounts of all Slavic literature, especially information about recently published Yugoslav books. Under the nom de plume of Jakob Rešetar, Vraz took to studying more important literary manifestations and ideas, and to taking note of everything that he thought significant in literature. He was one of the first to draw attention to the exceptional quality of Njegoš's *Gorski vijenac*, Mažuranić's *Smrt Smail-age Čengića*, and Radičević's lyrics. His criticism drew objections and attacks, but he never dropped the work he had begun.

Unlike the average Illyrian writers, who lacked conclusive views respecting art, Vraz pointed out that the purpose of Illyrian literature as a whole was to create an artistic literature on the basis of folk poetry. Accordingly he discouraged exaggerated admiration for the Dubrovnik writers, as was the vogue among the Croatian Illyrians. He contended that the Dubrovnik writers of the past centuries imitated the Italians in many respects. Hence, he also disapproved of the classical standards by which some Serbian critics, educated in classical schools, judged the works of later Serbian literature. It was for this reason among others, that he eulogized Njegoš, Mažuranić and Radičević, for it was in their works that he saw his own goal.

Primarily a lyrist, Vraz's talent never found full expression, for, as a Slovene, he could not gain complete mastery over the *štokavski dialect*. As a result, shortcomings and stiffness will be found in his poems. But if his verses are read as Vraz read them himself, it will be observed that they are truly lyrical. Coming from the Slovene countryside, optimistic and frank, Vraz was an

114

artist above all in the poems which are most eloquent of his optimistic and frank nature. They place him among the greatest Croatian poets of the nineteenth century. But his critical and ideological work does not lack significance, and Vraz was the first to indicate the course of Croatian literature — the course which it actually followed.

Petar Preradović (1818–1872) entered upon Illyrian literature with the younger Illyrians who were still at school during the early period of the movement. The son of a poor non-commissioned officer, born in the village of Grabrovnica near Bjelovar, after a period of elementary school and some junior military schools, he was admitted to the Austrian military institution at Wiener Neustadt, where he remained eight years (1830–1838). He had almost completely forgotten his mother tongue by the time he left it. But while he was there he acquired a good command of languages and literature, for there were some among his teachers who acquainted their pupils even with the attainments of Slavic literature. Having left the institution, he served as an officer in numerous Austrian garrisons. He reached the rank of general. He died away from his native land, at Fahrafeld near Vienna. His remains were finally transferred to Zagreb.

Although he was a highly efficient officer, Preradović was never able to overcome the feeling that his profession was burdensome, and on a number of occasions he decided to resign. Ardent patriot as he was, he was compelled to serve outside his native country. His first wife was an Italian from Zadar, his second was German. Being educated abroad by force of circumstances, he felt a foreigner wherever he went. Constant transfers, the death of his first wife, the death of his children, and his own illness broke him morally and ruined him financially, and he was a tired man while still young. At moments of despondency he sought an outlet in spiritualism.

Preradović began to write while he was a military cadet, and distinguished himself by producing romantic verses in German. It was while on duty in Milan — which was then under Austria — that he began to show an interest in Croatian literary trends; but only at Zadar did he begin to publish poems in his mother tongue. A literary paper, *Zora dalmatinska* [The dawn of Dalmatia], was founded at Zadar in 1844. Preradović became first a contributor to it and later its editor. His early poems immediately attracted attention because they were already mature and devoid of the usual failings of the beginner. He soon ranked among the most outstanding poets of the Illyrian movement. In 1846 he published his first collection of poems *(Prvenci* — The first-born), and in 1851 his second *(Nove pesme* — New poems). After the Revolu-

115

tion of 1848 he abandoned literature for a time; but with the restoration of constitutional conditions in Austria in 1860, he again became an associate of Croatian literary papers, and continued to write till his death.

Preradović was primarily a lyric poet. Of his lengthier compositions, he completed his epic poem *Prvi ljudi* [The first men], a story of the first man and first woman. He failed, however, to give final form to his almost completed drama *Kraljević Marko*.

Preradović was attracted to literature by Yugoslav and Slavic ideals as expressed in the Illyrian movement, which he championed in his works. Generally, it may be said that he had a profound sympathy for the whole movement and advanced its ideology in his poems.

In his early patriotic poems Preradović expressed his joy in the fact that the Yugoslavs were rising as a nation. He disclosed the feelings of a man who only through living abroad had comprehended the meaning of homeland. He glorified the function of poetry and its militant duties. He extolled the beauties of his country, its magnificence and the glory of its past. He attacked those who for personal interests disseminated disunity among the people. He extolled the beauty and expressional abilities of the Croatian language.

Preradović regarded Slavdom from the standpoint of a philosopher and prophet. The Slavs, considered merely numerically, were a vast force; but more important than numbers was their human mission, for it was to reconcile all nations and, finally, to create an era of love and happiness in the world. His ode *Slavjanstvu* [To Slavdom] tells of the vision of Slavdom in its vastness of scope and idea.

In *Kraljević Marko*, Preradović sought to produce a concise picture of Yugoslav culture and the tasks of the Yugoslav peoples. He depicted the state of neglect prevailing among the peasantry, the arrogance of the intelligentsia and semi-intelligentsia, the domestic customs, and blind acceptance of everything foreign. He was also aware of the economic problems of his period: the fateful influence of wealth in the capitalistic system. Notwithstanding all the evils he observed, his work, although incomplete, offers a picture of a future free country, happy in the work of its sons.

Preradović's art, however, did not confine itself to patriotism. He also wrote a number of love poems, touching and warm in their emotion and directness. But he was primarily a man given to reflections upon life and man's lot. He wrote a number of reflective poems in which he set forth his ideas about the most crucial problems in life (love, death, destiny, the perpetual transformations in things and manifestations). In *Prvi ljudi* he attempted to advance his views on the duties of humanity: Man will be happy only when he learns to bring about harmony between the demands of heart and mind.

Preradović was a typical European idealist of the first half of the nineteenth century; and in spite of all the hardships in his life, he was firmly confident that it was possible to create a better, finer world. For this reason his poetry is a source of optimism and confidence, even when a protest against everything happening in the universe might have been expected. Only occasionally, at moments of the deepest despair, did he raise his voice against the horror and injustice which he was incapable of comprehending.

Preradović soon eclipsed the poets of the Illyrian movement. His productiveness, the variety of his themes and his idiom shone brilliantly during the forties and later. Preradović could always select the best word to express the feelings of the majority of the Croats of his day.

Preradović was a settled nature, reticent, disciplined in expression. He was compelled to be cautious in his utterances because of his military position. Consequently he expressed himself in subdued tones, concisely, often in allegory. In his views regarding literature he was an exponent of conciseness and brevity. His writing is measured, almost cold; and only beneath the apparently cold crust is it possible to discern the noble surge of feeling.

Preradović was severely critical towards himself. Living away from his people, he was not confident in his knowledge of the language, and he even regarded his poems as worthless. Yet, notwithstanding their linguistic failings, there is real lyricism and deep nobility in them; and they touch the essential problems of life. Preradović's poetry is the ripest product of the lyrical aspect of the Illyrian movement; it held first place in Croatian lyricism till the coming of Silvije Strahimir Kranjčević in the eighties.

Dimitrije Demetar (Zagreb, 1811 — Zagreb, 1872) was the most expressive dramatist and theatre worker in the Illyrian movement, and a story-writer and stage critic besides. His greatest work is his play *Teuta* [Queen Teuta] (1844), which deals with the past of Illyria. It treats of the calamity caused by disunity and selfishness among national leaders. His best poem is *Grobničko polje* [Grobnik Plain] (1842), which he wrote in imitation of Byron's style. In various scenes he depicts the victory of the Croats over the Mongolians in the thirteenth century, with the object of rousing the fighting spirit of his Croatian contemporaries against the Hungarians.

Demetar was less a creator than he was a literary worker and organizer. Consequently he did not endure in literature: during the latter part of his life he undertook the organization of a permanent Croatian theatre in Zagreb, a task of inestimable value.

Antun Nemčić (Edde, Hungary, 1813 — Križevci, 1849) was the most prolific prose writer of the Illyrian movement. With a sense for detail, and influenced by Laurence Sterne and Heinrich Heine, he wrote *Putositnice* [Travel trifles] (1845), describing his journey through Croatia and Northern Italy. In his drama *Kvas bez hleba* [Yeast without bread], and at the opening of his novel *Udes ljudski* [The human lot], he endeavoured to describe realistically the social conditions of his day: the impoverished nobility, the struggle for employment, matrimonial infidelity, the power of money, etc.

FROM ROMANTICISM TO REALISM

1. THE POLITICAL AND SOCIAL CONDITIONS DURING THE LATTER HALF OF THE NINETEENTH CENTURY

The echoes of European romanticism left their mark on the Yugoslav literature of the first half of the nineteenth century, and extended into the second half as well. But realistic notes began to resound during the fifties of the century, and realism definitively triumphed during the last two or three decades of the century.

Revolutionary 1848 was rife with storm and stress for all the Yugoslav peoples in Austria; it was a year of great expectations and partly of great realizations. It was also a year in which the Yugoslavs fraternized in the enthusiasm of their common struggle. The leaders of the Hungarian revolution, which had been launched against the Habsburgs, tyrannized the non-Hungarian nations on the territory of Hungary. In their effort to strengthen the power of their own State, they strove to Magyarize the other nations. They thus antagonized these nations, especially the Croats, Serbs and Slovenes, to such a pitch that in their struggle for national survival they united in an anti-Hungarian camp.

In 1848 the representatives of the Yugoslavs assumed partial or complete power in their countries. In Croatia all connexions with Hungary were severed, and an autonomous government within the Habsburg Monarchy was established. In a similar fashion, the Serbs in Hungary gained autonomy in Vojvodina; the Slovenes endeavoured to imitate the government in Croatia. That year co-operation was established between Ban Jelačić in Croatia and Bishop Njegoš in Montenegro, and between the representatives of the Slovenes and of the Serbs in Vojvodina and Serbia.

The feudal system was abolished in Austria the same year, and the State administration was taken over by the representatives of the bourgeoisie. In 1848, for the first time in history, members of the common people also became members of the Croatian Sabor.

But these achievements were short-lived. With the help of Russian troops, Austria quelled the Hungarian revolution and reassumed power. In 1852, in order to consolidate power as thoroughly as possible, Austria abolished the Constitution and set up an absolutist government over the entire State. Henceforth the life of the Yugoslav peoples developed along two courses: in the Habsburg State; and in Serbia, Montenegro and the areas under Turkey.

During the period of absolutism, Austria brought heavy pressure to bear on all the non-German nations under its sway. German became the official language and the language in the schools on all the territories. In order to render government secure, a gendarmerie was organized, spies and confidential officials were employed. Croatia was flooded with bureaucrats, who were ignorant of the Croatian tongue and of Croatian traditions. The nine years of absolutist government were nine years of terror, persecution and fear. Progressive legislation was put on the statute book, it is true, but it remained a dead letter.

The people of Austria regained some freedom with the overthrow of the absolutist government in consequence of Austria's military defeats in Italy (1860), and Croatia was granted a government independent of Hungary. Meanwhile negotiations were conducted respecting the reorganization of Austria. The main issue was whether Austria should be a centralized, a federal or a dual monarchy. The Austrian and Hungarian statesmen reached an agreement after Austria's defeat in the war with Prussia (1866) known as the Austro-Hungarian Compromise (1867), under which the Habsburg Monarchy was divided into an Austrian half and a Hungarian half. Without being consulted, Croatia and the Serbs in Vojvodina were ceded to Hungary. Austria, on the other hand, got the Croats and Serbs in Dalmatia and Istria, and all the Slovene areas (Krain, Styria and Carinthia). Admittedly, the several Austrian nations enjoyed a semblance of autonomy, but the central government was in Vienna. Thus the German minority in Austria ruled the Slavic majority, while the Hungarian minority ruled the non-Hungarian majority. In Dalmatia and Istria power was in the hands of the Italian bourgeois minority. Thus were destroyed the achievements of half a century's struggle, the Slavs under Austria-Hungary being compelled to begin their struggle anew — a struggle which ended with the downfall of the empire.

Relations between Croatia and Hungary were settled in 1868 under the Hungaro-Croatian Compromise, according to which Croatia, headed by a Ban, enjoyed autonomy in some affairs (administration, schools, jurisdiction). But dissatisfaction was so general in the country that the Compromise had to be revised a few years later, and Ivan Mažuranić was placed at the head of the country in order to save what could still be saved. He was removed in 1880, however, and the Hungarians, with increasing ruthlessness, recommenced their previous designs to Magyarize the country.

What they did to the Croats in accordance with some semblance of legislation, they did unscrupulously to the other nations in the State. In Hungary they recognized only one nation, the Hungarian; the others were disfranchised nationalities. The Serbs were treated in the same way. Consequently the centre of Serbian cultural life was gradually transferred to Serbia.

During this period Serbia was also passing through various straits. Knez Aleksandar Karadjordjević was forced to leave the country in 1858, and Miloš Obrenović was reinstated. He, however, had learnt nothing in exile. He was succeeded upon his death in 1860 by his son Mihajlo. Mihajlo was an educated ruler, but he likewise refused to grant the people sufficient freedom, for he considered that Serbia must primarily prepare for war in order to deliver all the Serbs from the Turks. Nevertheless progress was obvious in the country. In 1867 Turkey surrendered the towns in Serbia which had still been garrisoned by its troops. Conditions steadily deteriorated, and in 1868 Knez Mihajlo was assassinated. Then followed a sequence of rapid changes in personalities in power, until finally the throne devolved upon Milan Obrenović, who was proclaimed king in 1882.

During these years of major political turmoil, rapid economic and social changes occurred both in Serbia and in the Austro-Hungarian Empire in connexion with the speedy development of capitalism. Labour no longer being unpaid, the feudalists in Croatia were slowly ruined, while power was taken over by the young bourgeoisie. The capitalistic system was especially ruthless in the countries with primitive methods of farming, particularly since its centres were outside the Yugoslav areas — in Vienna and Budapest — and its representatives chiefly foreigners. With their trade policy, by felling timber beyond a reasonable extent, they overtaxed the economy of Croatia, regardless of the consequences.

On account of the new economic position, the peasantry sank into debt. A period of usury ensued in which wealth was amassed quickly by some, while others were as quickly ruined. In this regard, there was no difference between Austria-Hungary and Serbia. The endeavours of the authorities in Serbia to add a European touch to the country, to run the administration with permanent Government employees, and to protect it with a regular army, required heavier funds, which impoverished the peasantry on the one hand, and brought wealth to the townsfolk on the other.

The most significant movement among the Serbian people after 1848 was the United Serbian Youth, and among the Slovenes the Young Slovene. Both movements resembled those in Western Europe (Young Italy, Young Germany).

The United Serbian Youth, which was initiated in 1847 and 1848, gained impetus during the sixties, but vanished with the victory of the counter-revolution. Having come into being with the unification of a number of youth societies into a federation, the United Serbian Youth was the first organized movement among the Serbs in the nineteenth century, the whole of Serbdom being united on a distinctive platform. It originated in the main in the ranks of the progressive bourgeoisie of Austria, spurred on by the activity of Serbs from Serbia. Its distinctive quality was that it dispensed with the traditions of Serbian bourgeois culture that had been developed in Austria in the footsteps of Central European culture. On the contrary, it encouraged the Serbian people to develop according to their own characteristics and requirements.

The Serbian youth movement especially nurtured Serbian nationalism, fundamental elements of which were the Serbian past, the Serbian peasantry and Serbdom generally.

During the eighteenth century Serbian nationalism was cultivated upon historical foundations. It was held that the Serbian people, having once had a great State, were bound to become united and great again. Serbian nationalism was distinguished by a cult of the Serbian past, hatred for the enemies of the nation, especially for the Turks, who were responsible for the downfall of the old Serbian State and still held a part of the Serbian nation in subjection.

Adopting these features of Serbdom, the Serbian youth movement intensified them in keeping with the new social conditions. Like Vuk Karadžić, who, at the opening of the century, had identified Serbdom with the peasantry, the members of the United Serbian Youth considered the peasantry as the core, the foundation of Serbdom.

The social consequences of these views were that the Serbian youth gradually dropped everything the educated Serbs had brought to Serbia from Austria during the first half of the nineteenth century in token of a superior civilization: the West-European way of life, bourgeois customs. Serbian peasant culture, as expounded by Vuk Karadžić in his works, became the model for Serbdom to follow. On the other hand, the political consequences were that the Serbian youth demanded political freedoms.

The achievements of the movement were not identical in Austria and in Serbia. In Austria-Hungary, Svetozar Miletić, the head of the movement, was imprisoned time and again by the Hungarians. After much suffering he went insane, and insane he died. In Serbia, on the other hand, the movement strove for democracy in the country, and conflicted with Knez Mihajlo's regime. After his death the movement was banned.

In Croatia, during the period of absolutism, political life had waned. With the restoration of the Constitution the Croatian politicians from the ranks of the young bourgeoisie endeavoured to revive the traditions of the Illyrian movement. They fought for an independent Croatia within Austria, and for democratic freedoms. However, the increasing efforts of the Austrian rulers to offset the political endeavours of the Slavs engendered a movement among the Croats similar to the United Serbian Youth. Its representatives (Ante Starčević, for one) gave broad publicity to Croatism, and demanded the severance of every contact with Austria and Hungary, and the formation of a Croatian State in accordance with the right of the people to a Croatian State. Believing in the perpetuity and validity of this right, the champions of the movement named their party the Party of Rights. The party became especially strong after 1868, when Croatia was incorporated into the Hungarian half of the Habsburg Monarchy.

Being without hope of bringing about an early change in the position of their country, the progressive Croatian intellectuals sought ways outside politics to sustain national consciousness and to raise resistance. "With Education towards Freedom" became their slogan. Towards the seventies it meant that however unpropitious the political conditions may be, a cultured nation cannot be annihilated: the advancement of national culture paves the way to national liberation. It was chiefly under the sponsorship of Bishop Josip Strossmayer, and with the abundant funds received from him, that the Yugoslav Academy was founded in Zagreb in 1867, the Croatian University expanded in 1874, the literary society *Matica Ilirska* reorganized under the name *Matica Hrvatska* in 1847, many elementary schools opened, and the gymnasia reorganized. The foundations of modern Croatian science, especially of national history, linguistics and literary history, were laid in the course of a few decades. The protagonists of the movement (Vatroslav Jagić, Franjo Rački, Ivan Kukuljević) continued the traditions of the Illyrian movement, but now as Yugoslavs.

Divided into four provinces, the Slovene people continued to be ruled during the second half of the nineteenth century by the German bourgeois minority. Their position at that time differed from their position during the first half of the century in that the number of Slovene lay intellectuals from the ranks of the peasantry steadily increased, and founded what was called the Young Slovene Movement. It was aimed, not so much against the rulers, as it was against the representatives of the Slovene people, the Old Slovenes, as they were known.

Janez Bleiweiss had become, during the forties, the most influential Slovene through his *Kmetijske in rokodelske novice*. In his public work an opportunist, he was for compromising with the

123

authorities and for suppressing any new and progressive idea supposedly in the interest of national unity. Besides this, his followers frequently identified their own interests with the interests of the people. They sought to play the principal part in every matter of general significance, they alone deserved all credit, no criticism dared be levelled at them. They were proud of being Slovenes, they wrote and spoke about the miserable and backward people, who required their leadership. They themselves, however, were often not clear about the characteristics of these people or their requirements. Later, Slovene culture had to fight and protect itself against them to secure its development.

The Young Slovene Movement, headed by Fran Levstik, began to oppose the Old Slovenes headed by Bleiweiss during the fifties. The movement was of social, political and literary significance. It stood for combatting pseudo-authorities, foreign influences in Slovene society, compromise in politics, conservatism in cultural matters, in favour of democracy in public life, and Slovene nationalism. Owing to the specific Slovene conditions, its significance was most telling in literature.

2. SERBIAN ROMANTICISM

A mighty transformation came to pass in Serbian literature in 1848. Vuk Karadžić, who had been almost entirely forgotten towards the end of the forties, suddenly became a central figure in literature. His views, which had been the object of attacks and jeers for several decades, now inspired the young Serbian generation (Djura Daničić). The centre of Serbian literary life was still in Austria (Novi Sad and Sremski Karlovci), and the writers were by descent mostly from Austria. The champions of the old-fashioned pseudo-classical views and the defenders of the Slavo-Serb language had retired from the literary field, leaving it entirely to the young generation, which was imbued with Vuk Karadžić's ideas. But it was unable to gather momentum during the period of absolutism in Austria and the reactionary reign of Aleksandar Karadjordjević in Serbia. After the reign of absolutism was over, however, the young generation impressed its stamp upon the whole of Serbian cultural life.

At the beginning of the sixties the Serbs, but for the mentioned exceptions, generally adopted Karadžić's literary language and orthography, while the folk poem was proclaimed the model and inspiration of all literary creativity. The literary models followed by the earlier generation were forgotten, and so was the classical style of lyrics; Branko Radičević, among the native writers, with his poetry of the heart, youth, and enthusiasm, became the paragon of the Serbian poets. The literary transformation was evolving in two directions: in subject-matter and in expression.

In subject-matter, the Serbian literature of the latter part of the nineteenth century in many ways adopted the general features of European romanticism: the predominance of sentiment and fantasy, ecstasy and enthusiasm. These elements were adapted to the conditions of the Serbian people. Serbdom, its past, its grandeur, its strivings for freedom and unification became the greatest motive power in Serbian literature. The rulers of the medieval Serbian State, Kosovo and its heroes, the Hajduks as fighters, free Montenegro, etc. became almost the only subject-matter both in lyrical and in epic poetry, in prose as well as in verse. In the more personal lyrics, the chief theme was romantic love, with all its manifestations of bliss and passion. In addition to this, there occasionally appeared other subjects customary in European romanticism: the cult of the Orient, the praise of chivalry.

All the rules adhered to by typical writers of the Slavo-Serb period were abandoned as mannerisms, and the verse-form of the folk poem became almost obligatory. Only an occasional poet essayed to sing in his own individual way; but he also adhered to the fundamental laws of Serbian metrics as had been evolved in the popular verse.

In addition to *Letopis Matice srpske*, which was the oldest literary magazine, several other literary magazines were founded in Serbian literature during the sixties, notably *Danica* (1860—1872), *Matica* (1866—1870), *Mlada Srbadija* (1870—1872).

The young literary generation cultivated every literary form, the chief among them being lyrics. In addition to a very large number of mediocre and minor writers, the period also produced some of the most outstanding representatives of Serbian literature generally.

The most prolific and most distinguished writer of his day was *Jovan Jovanović-Zmaj* (1833—1904). He was not only the foremost Serbian writer of the second half of the nineteenth century, but also one of those rare writers who worthily represent their own generation, yet with understanding approach the younger generation, and always remain fresh and abreast of the times.

Jovan Jovanović-Zmaj was born of bourgeois parents at Novi Sad. He graduated in law and medicine, and practised the latter in a number of towns (Novi Sad, Pančevo, Karlovci, Zagreb, Vienna). He was also the director of the theatre in Belgrade for a time.

Although he practised throughout his life as a doctor, Jovan Jovanović-Zmaj was primarily a writer. He wrote verses for almost all the Serbian magazines of his time. He also founded various humorous periodicals *(Zmaj, Starmali, Žiža)*. Since he frequently signed his compositions with the pseudonym "Zmaj", the name stuck to him as his permanent literary designation. During his lifetime he published several volumes of poems, the most important of which are *Djulići* [Rose-buds] (1864), *Djulići uveoci* [Withered rose-buds] (1882), *Pevanija* [Poems] (1882), *Druga pevanija* [Other poems] (1895), *Čika Jova srpskoj deci* [Čika Jova to Serbian children] (1899), *Čika Jova srpskoj omladini* [Čika Jova to Serbian youth] (1901).

He also translated poems by many major and minor poets. Most of his work was scattered in periodicals, and only many years after his death (between 1933 and 1937) was it collected in sixteen volumes.

Jovanović-Zmaj appeared in literature at the beginning of the fifties with love poems and translations. But only during the sixties did he gain full expression and win recognition, and then remained in the centre of Serbian literary life almost forty years. Both his style and the subject-matter of his poetry appealed to the Serbian public.

After Branko Radičević, Jovanović-Zmaj was the first poet to adopt completely the rhythm and language of folk poetry. The ease with which he wrote, and the clarity and limpidity of his idiom were of the very greatest intrinsic value — a value only enhanced by the theme of his poetry and by the position he held in Serbian national life.

Jovanović-Zmaj originally distinguished himself as a writer of love poems. He gave concrete substance to Serbian romantic lyrics; but lavish though they were in outpourings of love and encomiums to passion, they were frequently rhetorical and bookish. *Djulići* and *Djulići uveoci* expressed what seems to be everyday life: his love for his betrothed, whom he later married, and for his family; his sorrow over the death of his wife.

Jovanović-Zmaj definitely affected his Serbian contemporaries with his patriotic poems. He was the forerunner of a generation which harboured aspirations for liberation and for the unification of Serbdom, hatred for national oppressors, with love for the broad masses, and strivings for progress and social justice. Like most of his Serbian poetic contemporaries, he gave expression to his hatred of the Turks and of Austria. He was not, however, content with empty phrases about homeland and freedom: he had in mind the actual situation of the Serbs; and his love for his people embodied the hope that they would attain the progressive achievements of mankind. Accordingly he was not content with glorifying Serbdom: he also criticized its political and social system. During the closing decades of the nineteenth century especially, he proved to be a man of spirit and courage, who struck both at those in power in Serbia and at the corruption in the ranks of the Serbian bourgeoisie. In the course of almost four decades he heralded the most progressive tendencies in Serbian society: with the generation of Youth he fought for political freedoms; with the generation of realists he fought for social progress. In 1871 he voiced indignation at the shooting of the Communards in Paris. Through the decades he nurtured brotherhood between the Serbs and Croats.

Always a central figure in national life, Jovanović-Zmaj knew how to couch the feelings of the best Serbian spirits in the appropriate expression. The result was that even at the beginning of the twentieth century the most progressive Serbian youth hailed him as their own, while the reactionaries maligned him.

In the course of almost fifty years Jovanović-Zmaj recorded in verse, both serious and comic, every event which occurred in Serbian political and social life. He often gave the impression of being a poetic journalist, who wasted his gift on things which were often unworthy of the toil. And when it seemed that he had exhausted his fount of amatory, patriotic and satirical poetry, he took to writing poems for children.

Jovanović-Zmaj became a children's poet by transferring his fatherly love to all Serbian youth after the death of his own children. He had an extraordinary feeling for that infant world, for child interests, speaking directly the language which children understand, and establishing that contact with them of which only the rare poet of genius is capable.

In Serbian literature Jovanović's translations are also important. Among other things, he translated works by Goethe, Lermontov and Arany. His translations are frequently as valuable as an original work; he often turned an inferior model into a good poem.

In his doctrinal poem *Pesma o pesmi* [The poem about a poem] Jovanović-Zmaj exhorted poetry and the poets to encourage the disheartened, to brand the villainous, to help the suffering, and to comfort the sorrowing. Although many of his poems vary in value, if his entire work is measured, it must certainly be said that he accomplished his task. During the latter half of the nineteenth century he was one of the most prominent Serbs, helping his people in their striving for progress. He was the most national Serbian poet in the noblest sense of the word.

He was no less significant in developing Serbian verse. He was the first Serbian poet to introduce the syntax and accent of everyday speech into poetry; and in this he was the model for all later Serbian poets. He also exercised a beneficial influence on the development of Croatian metrics. Among the Croats he was familiar and popular for his amatory, satirical and children's poems.

He thus came to be the foremost poet in later Serbian literature, connecting two brotherly nations.

Djura Jakšić (1833—1878) was perhaps even more forceful than Jovanović-Zmaj in the depth of his poems and their personal features. A painter by training, a novelist and playwright by reason of his literary output, he was in temperament and expression a lyrist, and indeed one of the most impressive of Serbian poets.

Jakšić was born at Srpska Crnja, Banat. His childhood and early youth were on the whole calm. He completed four years of gymnasium and began to study art. His father, a priest, was sentenced to death by the Hungarians in 1848. Jakšić himself took part in the struggle of the Serbs against the Hungarians, and after the revolution he endeavoured several times to complete his studies in Vienna and Munich, but in vain. He emigrated to Serbia, where he took up and abandoned various vocations, among them that of teacher in elementary schools, and drawing instructor in gymnasia. Often he was jobless. Only towards the end of his life, when he was gravely ill, did he secure a transfer to Belgrade, where he died.

Jakšić entered public life with the generation of the Youth, which dreamt romantic dreams about Serbdom, freedom and national rights. To this end he took part in the rebellion in 1848, and to this end he worked for two aims in Serbia: that Serbia might unite all Serbdom, and that the Serbian people might win political rights. He fought in the war of 1876 against the Turks for the realization of the former goal; because of the latter he incurred the lasting odium of the Serbian rulers, and almost continuous persecution.

Jakšić was poor all his life. Except during the last few years before his death, he lived in extreme want. His wife and children often went hungry and lacked clothing. Aware of his own worth, his circumstances embittered and infuriated him. Because of his perpetual persecution by reactionary politicians, he went through life with the feeling of a hunted animal. He began to write as a romanticist; but gradually inclining towards the realists of the seventies, he took to describing social injustices.

Jakšić ranks among the foremost Serbian painters of the nineteenth century. One characteristic in his paintings distinguished him from every other painter: all his attention was directed to the central part of his picture, the periphery being no more than suggested. His works evince strong contrasts and an untamed temperament.

In his plays *Seoba Srbalja* [The migration of the Serbs] (1862), *Jelisaveta, knjeginja crnogorska* [Jelisaveta, the Montenegrin princess] (1868), *Stanoje Glavaš* (1878) Jakšić depicted the coming of the Serbs to the Balkan regions, the conflict between the Serbs and the western elements in Montenegro, and the Hajduk as a fighter for the freedom of the Serbs.

His first stories were founded on motifs from the Serbian Middle Ages, with their kings, knights, romantic loves, tournaments. Gradually he went on to themes closer to his own times. He recounted the sufferings of Serbian peasants under the Hungarian feudalists, the brutality of the officials in Serbia, the corruption of the petty-bourgeois intelligentsia, the pressure of the usurers and authorities on the Serbian peasantry.

Jakšić's dramas, and many of his stories, contain all the short-comings of romanticism: long-windedness, sentimentality, unreal characters, a stilted style. But they also contain a fine lyricism, a feeling for landscape, and immense dramatic strength. Their fundamental trait is the description of mighty explosions of friction between the characters. Passages of this kind render Jakšić's dramas and some of his stories valuable even when there is no doubt that as a whole they are far from perfect. By temperament a man of deep feeling, Jakšić was particularly effective in giving spontaneous expression to his inspiration. In this respect his lyrics are his most important work.

Jakšić's poetic work is not large in volume. In many of his epic and lyric poems he is often impersonal, for he wrote on the whole as the other Serbian romanticists did. But among his lyric poems there are ten or fifteen which are the most fragrant product of Serbian lyric poetry.

Luxuriant, impetuous, fiery as he was, Jakšić revealed in the best of his poems his strong feelings for Serbdom, and his keen eye for the Serbian landscape, but most of all his sufferings in life. Like no one in Serbian literature before him, Jakšić gave utterance to his loneliness, his desperate search for solace in wine as the only cure, to his hurt feelings, his boredom with life, to his longing for death.

Jakšić expressed the profound human pain which he endured with a cry, a shriek, as though subjugated and suffering humanity were racked with pain; and he did so with few words, but with the glow of red-hot iron. His best poems of this type, such as *Na Liparu* [On Lipar Hill], *Put u Gornjak* [The road to Gornjak], *Mila*, give the impression of being torn from life itself. His poems are not bookish or conventional; they are not written for the sake of verse or rhyme. Direct feeling, sudden and burning, surges from them, and fills the reader with emotion.

To be able to reveal such sentiments Jakšić had in store ample expression, both personal and deeply national. His poems seem to adhere to the rules of the folk poem — yet in such a way as to leave no doubt as to Jakšić's ability to use its expressive qualities in a new way typically his own. He is, in fact, a self-made poet: there is nothing in his verse or style adopted from foreign models.

In Jakšić, Serbian romanticism found its most sincere interpreter, its most spontaneous lyrist, and its best artist: a man who revealed his romantic sentiments in a way that was distinctively Serbian, and at the same time universal.

While Jovanović-Zmaj and Djura Jakšić were developing as men, and as poets passing from romanticism to realism, there were writers among the Serbs who remained pure romanticists. The chief among them were Jovan Ilić, Vladislav Kaćanski and Laza Kostić.

Of the prominent romanticists *Jovan Ilić* (1823—1901) was the only one born in Serbia (Belgrade). He was among the first in the country to be educated abroad (in Vienna). Later he received important positions in the State administration, and at one time he was a minister.

Ilić began to write poems in 1843, in the spirit of the Serbian lyrics of the time, in the old classical metre. With the triumph of romanticism in Serbian literature, he forsook this style and followed the new generation. In his poems he praised the Orient, sang of love and of passion *(Pjesme* — Poems — 1854, 1856; *Dahire* — The tambourine — 1891). He knew how to reproduce national expression so closely that some of his poems gained the popularity of folk poetry. Believing till his death in his romantic ideals — Serbdom, the people, freedom, democracy — he failed to adjust himself to contemporary reality; even less was he able to reconcile himself with the conditions which came about in Serbia with the strengthening of the bourgeois system.

His epic *Pastiri* [The shepherds] (1868) is regarded as a first attempt at composing an idyllic epic modelled upon popular fairy tales. The critics of realism denounced it as a false picture of Serbian peasant life.

During the romantic period, *Stevan Vladislav Kaćanski* (Srbobran, 1828 — Belgrade, 1890) was the foremost poet of Serbian militant nationalism. Born in Hungary, in 1848 he fought in the war against the Hungarians, and sang songs on the battlefield in order to encourage the fighters against the enemy. Like all the young Serbs of the period, he eulogized Slavdom. Later he became a radical. He believed in the strength of Serbdom and in that belief he died. He moved to Serbia, where he continued his patriotic work by writing verse and articles, and by running newspapers.

Except for a few love poems, Kaćanski wrote patriotic verse. In his epic poems *Noćnica* (1849) and *Grahov laz* (1862) he described the victorious Serbian battles against the Hungarians and Turks. Expressing his feelings with fervour and appeal, during the romantic period he enjoyed the distinction of being the leading Serbian poet. Several of his vigorous patriotic poems have earned him the name of Serbian bard. In his advanced years he almost entirely abandoned the writing of poetry.

Unlike the two preceding poets, *Laza Kostić* (Kovilj, 1841 — Vienna, 1910) lived a life of long literary activity, during which he remained a typical romanticist. He was born in Hungary, and after completing his law studies, he engaged in a number of different occupations at Novi Sad. He was one of the leaders of the United Serbian Youth in its heyday. Later he was elected to Parliament in Budapest. But the Hungarian authorities soon began to persecute him, and arrested him because of his politics. For this reason he moved to Serbia, and then to Montenegro. He returned to Hungary in his old age.

Kostić was the most learned of all the Serbian writers of his time. He spoke several European languages and was well-versed in European literature. He came upon the literary scene with poems written as early as 1858; he was still a young man when he made a name in literature. In his twenty-second year he published his first play *(Maksim Crnojević)*. At the same time he published romantic stories, as well as articles on literature. During his lifetime he published two volumes of poems (1873 and 1874) and two more plays *(Pera Segedinac* in 1875; *Gordana* in 1890). The greater part of his literary work, especially his aesthetic dissertations and criticism, were scattered in periodicals. He was also notable at one time for his translations of Shakespeare.

Kostić was the only prominent Serbian romanticist who was inspired to record his views on literature. But carelessly shifting from theme to theme, he failed to complete a single thought. First he was a votary of the folk poem, then he exhorted the Serbian writers to imitate their European contemporaries. Often he wrote unfavourably about the former (Radičević, Jovanović-Zmaj). Compared with the other Serbian lyrists, he was the closest to European romanticism. His mode of expression violated the traditional rules of syntax and word forms, he created new lingual combinations, caring not a whit whether his readers understood him or not. He pressed the theory of poetic licence and creative individuality to extremes. The result of all this was that his contemporaries frequently hailed him as a genius; but on the revival of realism, the critics denounced his poetry as affe ted, accusing him of being a typical romanticist possessed of all that was worst in romanticism.

Kostić had one feature in common with his lyrical contemporaries: he lauded Serbdom. But there is the least Serbdom, shallow anti-Turkish utterance and occasional poetry in his stanzas.

Although we must admit that many of his poems are the fruit of literary fashion, Kostić, more than any of the Serbian poets of his time, found an approach to eternal human problems: man and the universe, the individual and society, man and the deity. He had the courage to bare the misery of man's position in the universe, to express his hatred of tyrants and oppressors, and to deplore the lot of the superior man, oppressed as he is by scoundrels and fools. He manifested the profoundest dissatisfaction with the world order and the human race.

Kostić rarely expressed his feelings directly. He had recourse rather to irony, to unusual similes, ridiculing both himself and others. But at moments of exhilaration, he was full of fine amatory sentiments, pervaded by deeply painful undertones of disappointment with life.

Unlike the average romanticist, Kostić did not slavishly imitate the folk poem, but evolved a style of his own. In his best poems, like the ballad *Minadir*, he attained absolute simplicity and purity of expression.

Kostić's *Maksim Crnojević* is the first attempt in Serbian literature to dramatize the folk poem of the same name, and simultaneously to reach greater depths of philosophy and psychology in its motif. The historical drama *Pera Segedinac* is a picture of the struggle of the Serbian people in Hungary against the perfidious policy of Vienna, which exploited the loyalty of the Serbs; and against the corruption of the church hierarchy. Notwithstanding a certain affectation in some scenes and the complexity of the plot, *Maksim Crnojević* contains some distinctively lyrical passages. *Pera Segedinac* ensued as a strong and open protest at a time when the Austrians again began to oppress and deceive the Serbs in Hungary, after their stand in 1848.

Primarily of a lyrical tendency, Serbian romanticism admittedly, had its stories and story-writers; but it did not succeed in producing any distinctive artists in this category. Some lyrists were also story-writers (Djura Jakšić, Laza Kostić), and so were other less prominent writers, like *Milorad Popović-Šapčanin*. There were some writers during the romantic period who were chiefly story-writers, such as *Bogoboj Atanacković* (1826–1858), who also wrote a novel called *Dva idola* [The two idols].

The Serbian romantic story-writers had a feature in common in that they endeavoured to break away from their own period. They sought to dispense with sentimentality, with emotion and tension in their plots, with the Serbian Middle Ages, the knights, the Hajduks. In the novel *Dva idola*, Atanacković was relatively independent. Upon the fabric of love and patriotism he superimposed the revolution of 1848, and the part played in it by the

Serbs. In addition to this, being sensible of the social conditions, he depicted the sufferings of the Serbian peasant under the Hungarian feudalists.

The only Serbian narrator of that period who created his literary profile with his own effforts was *Stjepan Mitrov Ljubiša* (1824—1878). He was born at Budva, Dalmatia. He was completely self-taught, and learnt to read and write when he was fourteen years of age. But his was such a bright intelligence that at nineteen he was already a notary in his birth-place. In his mature years he was the most prominent Serbian public figure in Dalmatia, a national representative in Vienna, and the speaker in the Provincial Sabor of Dalmatia. In his time, elections for the Sabor were held in accordance with a law which gave a negligible Italian bourgeois minority predominance over the overwhelming Croatian and Serbian peasant majority, because of which fierce controversies were conducted for national freedom.

Ljubiša began to write in 1845. He translated works by Italian writers into Serbian, wrote occasional poetry, etc. Only during his middle years, having gained the necessary experience, did he begin to write stories. His only collection of stories, *Pripovijesti crnogorske i primorske* [Stories of Montenegro and the coast], was published in 1875, when he was already fifty-one years of age. He started to publish his second work in 1877, *Pričanja Vuka Dojčevića* [The tales of Vuk Dojčević], his intention having been to write a hundred stories around a single character. He had written only thirty-seven at the time of his death in Vienna.

Being a man from the people, Ljubiša clung to romanticism in literature. He was indifferent to the Serbian writers of his time, and maintained that if they vanished, the folk poem would still remain. He considered that his stories were not original in any way, that they were impressions of the past of his region and of Montenegro, which he had culled from the people.

In *Pripovijesti crnogorske i primorske*, as well as in *Pričanja Vuka Dojčevića*, Ljubiša described his native region, the Montenegrin coastland, as well as Montenegro itself, and the border regions, notably Albania. He portrayed people and recounted events from the sixteenth, seventeenth and eighteenth centuries, when the Turks and Venice fought over these regions. A period which teemed with changes, murder, unbridled passions, baseness and gallantry, it offered him an opportunity to produce plots tense with unexpected turns, with human passions and conflicts brought to a climax. His longest story, *Skočidjevojka* [The maiden's leap; otherwise the name of a promontory], is the story of a girl whose father wants to give her in marriage to the youth whom she loves. Her stepmother, however, wants to marry her to a Venetian. There follow conflicts and diplomatic controversies, and the girl finally sees no other outlet from her predicament but to leap into the sea. *Prokleti kam* [The accursed stone] tells of the endeavours of Venice to destroy an Orthodox monastery. A Serb who is attracted by the promise of a reward, poisons the monks. His reward is poison for himself secretly administered by his employers.

The plots of Ljubiša's stories are not original, for he took them from folk tales. He recast parts of them, making use of stories by foreign writers (Manzoni). Almost all of them abound in strange provincialisms frequently difficult to understand. Actually, both the plot and the motif were merely the tools employed by Ljubiša to depict people as he saw them, two features being outstanding in this respect: Ljubiša's views of the individual, and his views of the nation.

Ljubiša's numerous characters are the result of his experience of people. Except for a few respectable characters, the majority are intriguers, egoists, scoundrels. The honest are victims through whom the corrupt and the criminals gain money and power. In addition to this, Ljubiša compares his own primitive but honest people with the representatives of the refined, but morally exhausted civilization of the Dalmatian towns and of Venice.

These features brought Ljubiša's stories abreast with the times. For the most part they reflected the experiences and views which guided him in his struggle against the Italian bourgeois minority in Dalmatia.

Ljubiša's stories are vivid character-studies of people; he presents his matter economically and in high relief. In view of the redundancy from which typical romantic stories suffer, Ljubiša's are as though hewn out of stone: hard, massive, plastic. Deeply true in their human and literary qualities, they are completely national in subject-matter and form, highly aesthetic in expression.

3. CROATIAN ROMANTICISM; FROM ROMANTICISM TO REALISM

Through political and social causes, writers changed rapidly in Croatian literature after 1848. A number of men ceased to write in 1848, and devoted themselves, in the new conditions, to politics instead. Several of the major writers (Vraz, Nemčić) died about this time. During the period of absolutism, most of the Croatian intellectuals withdrew from public life out of fear of being persecuted. The absolutist government punished every liberal public manifestation, literary activity included. In 1849 the literary paper *Danica* stopped publication. A new literary magazine named *Neven* was founded in 1852; but it suffered chronically from a shortage of contributors and subscribers. In 1858 it was moved by its founders from Zagreb to Rijeka, where it stopped publication a year later.

There were no notable writers in Croatian literature during the period of absolutism. Its representatives realized the necessity of primarily saving the achievements of the Illyrian movement: Croatian national existence, the literary language and orthography; and, notwithstanding all their difficulties, they succeeded in this endeavour.

The Croatian literature of the fifties tended to reach Vraz's goal of the preceding period: to be national in spirit and style. In consequence of this conception, as among the Serbs, poetry was almost completely pervaded by the verse of the folk poem in mode and expression, and by folklore in theme. The literary form which prevailed consisted of the story founded on themes from the past, the historical play, and lyric poetry.

In regard to the quality of its subject-matter and style, the Croatian literature of that period was more akin to romanticism than it was in the Illyrian period. Its writers described events from the Middle Ages, with their knights, feudalists, Hajduks, avengers, lingering especially upon the struggle with the Turks. They wrote of love with its trials, abductions, poison; of murder as a means of resolving differences. Only occasionally did they attempt to show real life, with all its problems and frictions.

Mirko Bogović (Varaždin, 1816 − Zagreb, 1893) became the central literary figure. He achieved distinction with his lyrics during the forties. He was the first editor of *Neven* during the period of absolutism, and the first writer whom the authorities jailed for his writing. His plays *(Frankopan, Stjepan, Matija Gubec)* and stories engendered hatred for the Habsburgs, because of their deceitful policy towards the Croats, and exhorted the Croats to unite. While the feudalists were still politically strong, he glorified in his play *Matija Gubec* the unfortunate leader of the peasant rebellion of 1573 who was cruelly put to death by the feudalists.

Other writers who shared Bogović's distinction during that decade were Luka Botić, Janko Jurković and Paskoje A. Kazali, three intellectuals from the ranks of the people.

Luka Botić (Split, 1830 − Djakovo, 1863), the son of a poor charwoman, recounted in verse *(Pobratimstvo* − Brothership; *Bijedna Mara* − Wretched Mara; *Petar Bačić)* and in prose *(Dilber Hasan)* the tragic love stories of members of different religions: the Orthodox, Catholic and Moslem; and the conflicts which always occurred during the centuries of blind religious hatred. Although he drew on the past for his material, his works nevertheless contained in the main that which inspired him in life: his craving for

135

beauty and liberty, his endeavour to free himself from poverty and injustice, from social and religious bounds. He wrote all his works in the style of the folk poetry.

Janko Jurković (1827–1889) from Požega, was a story-writer, a writer of comedies and a critic. He was one of the first Croatian writers who had the courage to describe people and the manifestations of his times as they were. In numerous stories and plays he depicted the petty bourgeoisie, the intellectuals and the would-be intellectuals, the village priests, the teachers and the retired officers, with their rural loneliness and their daily cares. In his criticisms and aesthetic dissertations he attacked the stream of literary dilettanti, and warned them of the profound significance of literature. His better-known plays are: *Kumovanje* [The christening], *Čarobna biljeznica* [The magic note-book], *Novi red* [The next line]; and his stories: *Pavao Čuturić*, *Seoski mecenati* [The village maecenases].

Paskoje A. Kazali (1815–1894) was born in Dubrovnik. He was a priest, and the only Croatian writer of his time to rise against the theory that literature must imitate folk poetry. He was conversant with the works of writers from Western Europe, notably with those of Byron. In his poems *(Zlatka; Trista Vica udovica —* Three hundred widowed Vitsas; *Glas iz pustinje* — The voice in the wilderness; *Grobnik)* he broached eternal problems: the conflict between love and duty, the meaning of pain, the meaning of life. Without a firm mastery of the language, and owing to his uneven mode of expression, he was unable to rise above mediocrity.

After *Neven* ceased publication, a literary paper called *Naše gore list* was founded in Zagreb in 1861. It attracted all the better writers, and revived the traditions of the previous decade. But it was again necessary to create a new circle of writers, for after the restoration of the Constitution, numerous Croatian bourgeois intellectuals had devoted themselves to politics. In addition to it, a second magazine called *Slavenac* was founded in the provincial town of Požega. They were both succeeded by a magazine founded in Zagreb called *Dragoljub*. But in 1865 two members of the younger literary and scientific generation, August Šenoa and Vatroslav Jagić, warned that the Serbian and Croatian literatures were far from reality. Šenoa especially emphasized that however rich the life of the Croats and Serbs was, their literatures were pale.

Criticizing current literature, both Šenoa and Jagić advised that it should have more in common with reality, and that it should show more artistic creation. This was the task of the literary generation which appeared at the beginning of the sixties. But only in 1869 did it come forward as an organized body, having founded a literary magazine in Zagreb named *Vijenac*, which was the principal Croatian literary paper till 1903.

The chief representatives of the new generation were August Šenoa and Franjo Marković. Josip Eugen Tomić also distinguished himself as a prolific writer.

August Šenoa (1838—1881) was the foremost Croatian literary figure of his period, and at the same time one of the most distinguished Croatian writers in general. He became known as a prolific, varied and modern writer. Like Vraz during the Illyrian period, Šenoa was aware of the fundamental problems in Croatian literature, and made earnest endeavours to solve them.

Born in Zagreb of petty-bourgeois parents, Šenoa studied law in Zagreb, Prague and Vienna. He was later a journalist in Zagreb, and then a senior employee in the Town Council. For a time he was also art director of the theatre.

Šenoa made a start in literature at the beginning of the sixties with poems. He continued to write epic and lyric poems till the end of his life. The political conditions in Austria, as well as the need to support himself compelled him to pursue journalism for nearly ten years. In addition to writing newspaper articles, he also wrote feuilletons, and thus became the first distinctive Croatian writer in this genre. His interest in the theatre resulted in his becoming a dramatic critic and in his writing a comedy called *Ljubica* (1866). He also wrote literary criticisms. From 1874 up to his death he was the editor of *Vijenac*. His other literary work included the translation of plays and short stories, usually from French and German.

His most important work, however, was fiction. At the beginning of the sixties he transformed some of his feuilletons into short stories; and in 1871 published his historical novel *Zlatarevo zlato* [The goldsmith's gold], after which he devoted himself primarily to story writing. He wrote numerous stories on themes of his own times *(Prijan Lovro* — Friend Lovro; *Mladi gospodin* — The young gentleman; *Kanarinčeva ljubovca* — The canary's love) as well as several full-length historical novels *(Seljačka buna* — The peasant rebellion — 1877; *Diogenes*, 1878) and novels of contemporary life *(Prosjak Luka* — Luka the beggar — 1879; *Branka*, 1881). He failed to complete his most extensive work, the historical novel *Kletva* [The curse], because he died while writing it.

Šenoa regarded his literary calling in connexion with the general national and social views of his day, for in his eyes writing was an instrument of national and social activity. As the position of Croatia in the Dual Monarchy deteriorated during the seventies, he began to look upon literature as a weapon of resistance, of national enlightenment and economic advancement. He expounded his ideas in his articles, as well as in his works.

Maintaining that the most important function of literature was its social function, Šenoa exhorted the writers to write for the broad masses of the people — the townsfolk and peasantry. In his ideas he was a stanch supporter of realism throughout his lifetime. He reminded young story-writers of the abundant material lying to hand in contemporary life. He discouraged them from giving conventional and lifeless portraits, advising them to study people continually. In his opinion, the models to be followed by Croatian literature were the Russians Gogol and Turgenev, and the French realists.

Šenoa's poems dealt chiefly with the current and educational trends of his time, as well as with social problems. The strength of his poems lay in the fact that they were the best expression of what the average progressive Croat of his period felt. He extolled freedom, the constitution, education, industriousness, courage, social justice. Only occasionally did he reveal his own feelings of pain or joy.

A dramatic critic for twenty years, Šenoa touched on every problem of the Zagreb theatre. He demanded that it should climb to higher realms of art, that its members should be more realistic in their interpretations. He was in favour of replacing the repertoire of German works with one of Slavic and Romance works. He especially recommended the French realists.

In his feuilletons, collected under the common name of *Zagrebulje*, Šenoa described scenes from Zagreb society in the course of some twenty years, and advanced observations on numerous cultural problems.

In his literary criticism Šenoa endeavoured to mediate in an easy and humorous manner between the reading public and the writers. He brought out the artistic, national and social characteristics of original or translated works. Although he wrote his criticisms without a clearly defined critical method, he would point out the chief merits of a work in a few sentences. He had a particular influence on the young generation.

In his stories Šenoa was primarily concerned with the bourgeois, petty-bourgeois and peasant folk, and with their development during the transition from the feudal system to full bourgeois domination. He portrayed the extinct Croatian small nobility at home, with their altercations and petty disputes; the bourgeoisie and petty bourgeoisie as they prospered or went to their ruin. He described the disintegration of the peasant cooperatives, the struggle of the peasants to climb the social ladder, the disappearance of the last of the old feudal families. In his more extensive works he discussed current educational and social problems: the position of the village schoolmistress in humiliating and contaminating surroundings *(Branka);* the conflict between town and village *(Prosjak Luka).* He presented a rich variety of types from every social section, particularly from among the oppressed who till then had been given no place in literature.

Šenoa, however, devoted himself chiefly to the historical novel. Having himself been raised to a certain degree on works of this kind, and living at a time when Croatia took a special interest in history, he sought to revive the atmosphere of different historic periods, endeavouring in particular to give an artistic presentation of those periods of Croatian history which involved some fundamental problems of national life. By drawing a comparison between events from the past and events of his day, he sought to exercise a guiding influence on his contemporaries. In his most popular novels he resurrected figures and events from the fourteenth to the eighteenth century. He recounted the struggle of the peasants and bourgeoisie against the feudalists and rulers, the struggle of the representatives of Croatia to prevent the Germans and Hungarians from violating the national and political rights of the Croats.

In his novels Šenoa also presented class struggles from the past. His sympathies are always with the oppressed. His *Seljačka buna* is a monument to Matija Gubec, the leader of the greatest peasant rebellion in Croatia.

Šenoa's historical novels, which are based on a thorough study of historical material, are pervaded by the progressive views of his time. Written at a period when the Croatian peasantry and bourgeoisie were prospering, and when fierce battles were again being fought for Croatian national and political existence, Šenoa's works also constituted a militant weapon. Better than anyone before or after him, Šenoa knew how to present both the glorious and the tragic sides of Croatian history: both the reverses and the successes, both the vices and the virtues of his people. And he did all this as though he were writing about his own period. In this respect he is the most Croatian of writers, and an advocate of unity and brotherhood among the Yugoslav and the other Slavic peoples.

Šenoa appealed to the reading public primarily because of his narrative genius, for with his opening sentence he attracted the reader's attention and held it till the end. He was skilled in casting living and varied types of characters, in leading them into different situations, in letting them speak, think, act. He knew how to alternate serious scenes with comic situations, pathos with sentimentality, the bloody events of war with pictures of domestic happiness. He revelled in depicting festivals and the broad movements of the masses. In order to add to the interest of his historical novels, he often had recourse to the requisites of the romanticists: love at first sight, irreconcilable quarrels, spies, intriguers and murderers.

But he also gave a faithful picture of the petty bourgeoisie: the tradesmen of Zagreb, the wrangling women on the market place, intimate family life.

All Šenoa's work had a strong influence on the young Croatian generation in their national and social development. His criticisms, editorial work, and theoretical articles definitively rid Croatian literature of dilettantism. He was the first to direct it towards realism. The strength of his personality cast its warmth upon the young writers of his time, but they resented his supposed literary dictatorship. They failed, however, to pull him down from the position he occupied: he was overthrown only by his premature death, at the age of forty-three.

The rapidity with which Šenoa wrote, and his tendentiousness often caused him to neglect aesthetic values in his works, and in many cases he gives the impression of being a representative writer rather than an artist. However, the artistic qualities of many of his pages are indisputable.

Franjo Marković (1845—1914), who was younger than Šenoa, earned a name in literature even before the latter did. Although they had identical views on political and literary matters, their methods and forms of work differed. Their paths were also different.

Marković was born in the Croatian interior, at Križevci. He was the son of a small nobleman. He graduated from elementary and secondary school, and gained a doctorate of philosophy in Vienna. He was twenty-nine when he became a professor at the University of Zagreb. He was also soon admitted to the Yugoslav Academy of Science.

Marković wrote poetry while in gymnasium. He composed his epic poem *Dom i svijet* [The home and the world] at the age of twenty. The subject was the period of absolutism. But he did not dare have it published at the time. His first more extensive printed work, *Kohan i Vlasta* (1866), was an epic on the life of the Slavs of the Elbe and Baltic areas. In addition to these two works, he wrote a number of romances and ballads during his early creative period. In 1872 he published two plays in *Vijenac* on Croatian history: *Karlo Dracki* and *Benko Bot*. He published most of his verses and his first epic in 1883 in a volume entitled *Iz mladih dana* [From youthful days]. Later, devoting himself to criticism and to the theory of literature, he almost gave up writing poetry. In numerous treatises, he expounded his views on the foremost older and latter-day Croatian writers (Gundulić, Mažuranić, Preradović, Šenoa, etc.). He set forth a synthesis of his views on art in his extensive work *Razvoj i sustav općenite estetike* [The development and system of general aesthetics] (1902).

Marković was an opponent of realism in principle because in his opinion it revealed naked, unpurified reality. He was a pure romanticist and idealist, and he contended that a poet must portray life, not as it is, but as it ought to be; that an artist must aspire, not after the passing favours of his period, but after the eternal ideals of beauty: there are eternal laws of beauty by which every writer must abide.

Believing in the eternal ideals of love, Marković only once, in *Dom i svijet*, presented life in Croatia as it really was: the heavy burden that the absolutist rule imposed on the Croatian people. For all his other works he sought his themes in history: in *Kohan i Vlasta* he related the endeavours of the Germans to gain power over the Slavs on the Baltic by deceit; in *Karlo Drački* he portrayed this fourteenth-century minor Hungaro-Croatian ruler as the protagonist of the struggle for the freedom of the human being; in *Benko Bot*, upon a background of historic events, he described a conflict between love and duty. He composed his dramas in accordance with the Aristotelian views on tragedy. Only in his epics did he imitate the Polish romanticist, Mickiewicz. Because of this, his works, except *Dom i svijet*, leave a cold impression.

Actually, Marković's plays are all in their own way the product of his times, with their political, cultural and material conditions. They are a voice of protest against the subjection in which the Slavs were held, a cry for freedom. Each of them was directly inspired by the current events (absolutism, the Austro-Hungarian Compromise). *Karlo Drački*, with its demands for freedom, reflected the spiritual circumstances in Croatia at the beginning of the seventies, when the young bourgeois intellectuals endeavoured to gain every freedom at a single stroke, as it were.

Marković's works derived from the same source as Šenoa's, and their tendency was similar. But Šenoa spoke openly to his contemporaries, while Marković seems to have always had the distant future before his eyes. There is yet another difference between them: Šenoa endeavoured to carry out the tasks of his day; Marković, like Preradović, had before his eyes those distant times when all peoples would live in brotherhood and freedom. The fundamental motifs in his works were, not only Croatian national ideals, but general human perspectives of forgiveness, brotherhood and love as the ultimate goal of the Slavs on earth.

In his critical dissertations and in *Estetika* Marković set forth the principles on which he composed his own works. Contending that beauty lies in form, he analyzed different works in accordance with the rules of formal aesthetics. He trained generations of young scholars and critics to his own views. His method was already rather obsolete while he used it. But it is due to him that Croatian criticism, having rid itself of superficial impressionism, set out to seek the general laws of artistic and literary development. Besides all this, Marković had an accurate feeling for art. The majority of his views have survived.

During the times of August Šenoa and Franjo Marković, the Croatian writer who enjoyed the widest popularity was *Josip Eugen Tomić* (Požega, 1843 — Zagreb, 1906). He wrote lyric poems, humorous pieces, plays, historical novels. He is known best for the works in which he described events in Croatian history *(Zmaj od Bosne* — The dragon of Bosnia — 1879; *Emin-agina ljuba* — Emin Aga's love — 1888; *Udovica* — The widow — 1891; *Za kralja, za dom* — For king and country — 1894-5, etc.). With a sense for reality and social criticism, he also depicted the ruin of the Croatian nobles and aristocratic families *(Melita;* 1899).

4. SLOVENE ROMANTICISM;
THE TREND TOWARDS REALISM

Modern Slovene literature proceeded in its development on the whole side by side with European literature and with that of the other Yugoslav peoples. But during the nineteenth century, the literary strivings of the Slovenes were concerned, not so much with literary trends, as they were with an outlook upon the world and upon questions vital to the Slovene people. This was already evident during Prešern's time, and still more so from the fifties onwards, during the time of Fran Levstik, who was the principal ideologist of later Slovene literature and, indeed, its founder. Parallel with him there appeared several writers of prominence among the Slovenes who determined its trend. The most important were Josip Stritar, Josip Jurčič, Simon Jenko and Janez Trdina.

Fran Levstik (1831—1887) was born in the village of Spodnje Retje near Velike Lašče. As a gymnasium pupil he distinguished himself by his profound knowledge of language and literature. Although an excellent pupil, he was unable to matriculate, because his·catechist endeavoured to fail as many candidates as possible in order to compel them to take up theology. Levstik also began to study for the priesthood at Olomouc. In 1854 he published a collection of poems which roused the enthusiasm of the young, and elicited the resistance of the older, conservative Slovenes. His former gymnasium catechist having charged him with immorality before his theological principals, he was compelled to abandon his studies. His entire later life was a perpetual fight for existence, a struggle against poverty, during which his opponents endeavoured to deprive him of the very essentials of life. He was in turn tutor, journalist, editor, publisher, lexicographer; he was also frequently without work. He lived in Ljubljana, Trieste and in Vienna. Only before his death, physically and spiritually broken, did he obtain permanent employment in the Ljubljana Library. He died in Ljubljana.

Levstik's first publication was the book of poems for which he was vilified. During his later poetic progress he continued to write and publish poems, but usually under a nom de plume. The most important of his lyric cycles were *Tonine pesmi* [Poems to Tona] and *Franjine pesmi* [Poems to Franja], composed in memory of his two loves, which had terminated, as Prešern's great love had, because of his poverty. Levstik evinced his strength of expression, his wit and sincerity in his poems; but he did not write with Prešern's succinctness. His poems for children are excellent.

Levstik earned the greatest merit in Slovene literature with his criticisms. Cultural life in the Slovenia of his day was saturated with the German spirit, with the spirit of the German bourgeoisie; and the Slovene literary language teemed with barbarisms. Following the example of Vuk Karadžić, Levstik launched a struggle to cleanse the Slovene tongue of foreign impurities and to render Slovene literature a mirror of Slovene life.

Having been brought up in his family to have a fine command of the Slovene language, Levstik soon noticed that even the best educated Slovenes wrote poorly. In his dissertation *Napake slovenskega pisanja* [Errors in Slovene writing] (1858), he drew urgent attention to the poor level of literacy of the Slovenes of his day, and laid down principles for the purification of the Slovene literary language.

Writing on art, Levstik assailed the writers who published imitations of German literature under guise of Slovene works, alluding chiefly to Ivan Vesel Koseski. He cited Prešern as the model to whom, in his opinion, Slovene literature should return. Levstik was the first Slovene to appreciate Prešern, and advised a return to the course which he had given Slovene literature. It was he who first prepared a new edition of the latter's poems.

Speaking of subject-matter and character-study in literature, Levstik urged Slovene writers to utilize Slovene folklore. He himself collected and published folk tales and indicated motifs which could be used.

Levstik was also an excellent prose writer: he was one of the founders of Slovene prose. He wrote a clear style, concisely, and with a sense for simile and humour. A special place in Slovene literature has been accorded to some of his writings, such as *Putovanje iz Litije do Čateža* [A journey from Litija to Čatež] (1858), and *Martin Krpan z Vrha* [Martin Krpan from Vrh] (1858).

143

Putovanje iz Litije do Čateža is a description of a journey on foot between these two neighbouring towns, in which Levstik gave a simple and realistic portrayal of the Slovene peasants whom he met on the way. He presented them as they were: at their wine, in conversation, as they stated their views on life and men; and he drew his characters skilfully, in a few strokes.

Martin Krpan is a story by Levstik, founded on a folk tale, about a Slovene peasant of enormous physical strength, who alone was able to save the emperor in Vienna from the giant Brdavs, his enemy. He was offered the place of court jester as a reward. In the end he was allowed to carry salt openly from one place to another — an article which he had always smuggled till then.

Martin Krpan is commendable in language, composition, characterization and plot. It recounts the fate of the Slovene nation in Austria, which gave what it could, yet was rewarded by being held up as a laughing-stock.

Martin Krpan resembles Ljubiša's *Kanjoš Macedonović* in motif and tendency. Kanjoš is a little man but shrewd; like Martin Krpan, he saves his enemy, the Venetian, from the giant.

Levstik was not a creator in the full sense. Apart from the poems and the writings referred to, he left no works which merit classification among the lasting achievements of Slovene literature. It is true, he attempted to write plays, stories, and even a novel; but he failed to complete his undertakings. All his work is fragmentary, for he tried his hand at everything that needed to be done among the Slovenes of his day: from composing lyric poetry and satire to writing newspaper articles and compiling a dictionary. His work is of general national significance rather than of literary significance. Levstik was the first Slovene writer to grasp the Slovene national problem as a whole, and it was he who initiated the Young Slovene Movement.

The problem was how the Slovenes were to rise, without a real literary language, without a befitting social and political position, to the status of a full-blown nation with clearly defined political, cultural and social aims. Levstik's whole work amounted to a struggle of principle, for the development of the Slovene people on the basis of the independent peasant element, and against the residue of the half-German bourgeois individualities.

Levstik was not only a man of letters, but also the spokesman of the progressive young Slovenes. He launched the struggle against false patriotism, against politics as a trade, backwardness, and cliques. He was opposed by the leading figures of that time, such as Bleiweiss, and by the majority of the clergy. But he had the backing of the progressive, the distinctively Slovene, the vigorous and the militant.

It was during Levstik's struggles that the first purely Slovene literary papers were founded *(Slovenski glasnik* — The Slovene herald — at Klagenfurt in 1858; *Zvon* — The bell — in Vienna in 1870). *Slovenski glasnik* was published by Professor Anton Janežič, *Zvon* by Levstik's friend and partisan, Josip Stritar, apart from Levstik the most influential Slovene writer of the nineteenth century.

Like all the Slovene writers of the latter part of the nineteenth century, *Josip Stritar* (1836—1923) was the son of peasant parents from the village of Podsmreka near Velike Lašče. He came under Levstik's influence in gymnasium. But whereas Levstik failed to matriculate, Stritar went on to receive his degree at the Faculty of Philosophy in Vienna, and was thereafter able to develop freely. He was an excellent pupil, and his was the typical youth of a gifted son of Slovene parents. He tutored the children of the well-to-do, earned some money, acquired good manners, and saw part of the world, especially Western Europe. He also read assiduously. He passed the examinations required to become a teacher, and settled down in Vienna to follow the career of a secondary-school master. But he continued to maintain contact with his country, to which he returned after the defeat of Austria-Hungary. He died at Rogaška Slatina.

Stritar stands for three things in Slovene literature: critic, creator and pedagogue.

Stritar wrote verse while he was still in gymnasium. But afterwards he abandoned writing for many years, and devoted himself to reading. He wrote an aesthetic analysis of Prešern's poems, as an introduction to the edition which Levstik published in 1866. The analysis was the first literary piece of this type in Slovene. Stritar wrote it with feeling and artistic ease. It was an epoch-making event in Slovene literature, for he stabilized Prešern's standing forever and destroyed Koseski's definitively. In this work he was concerned, not so much about the person, as he was about the principle. His aim was to free Slovene literature of the fetters of local dilettantism, to raise it towards the level of European literature.

In his entire public work Stritar, as a critic, supported Levstik, and they shared both friends and enemies. In order to be free in his work, Stritar founded a literary paper in Vienna *(Zvon)*, around which he rallied the best Slovene literary men. In Vienna the younger Slovene writers went to him as a supreme arbiter. He enjoyed unsurpassed esteem on account of his vast literary erudition and his ability to set down his thoughts with wit and ease. In his *Zvon* he dealt with various literary manifestations, both domestic and foreign.

In principle Stritar was definitely a romanticist, an idealist. Literature, in his opinion, should present an ideal world, not the crudities of every-day life.

Stritar sometimes wrote as a creative artist. He published numerous poems under the name of Boris Miran, thus giving evidence of his skill at versification and in the use of different European poetic forms. His lyrics are sentimental, pessimistic, pervaded by a feeling that it is useless to live: the world is bad and life is an evil; and the poet is more poignantly aware of this than anyone else. It is, therefore, his duty to express it. And Stritar did so in poems of high artistic accomplishment. He also wrote satirical verse aimed at his Slovene adversaries, the Old Slovenes *(Dunajske elegije —* Viennese elegies).

Stritar wrote stories and novels *(Zorin, Rosana, Gospodin Mirodolski)* in which it is possible to discern elements from Goethe's *Werther* and *Wilhelm Meister;* but in them the writer was chiefly concerned with portraying himself. Like his lyrics, his novels with their European background and the problems they dealt with also made an exceedingly strong impression on his Slovene contemporaries.

In the cultural life of the Slovenes Levstik and Stritar supplemented each other's deficiencies, their goal being one: to advance the Slovene nation and its literature. But Levstik laid more stress on local, Slovene, rural, realistic elements; Stritar on European elements. Stritar was, nevertheless, a Slovene and a Slav to the bottom of his soul. Like Herder and the Illyrians, he believed that the Slavs were destined to save the world from wars and hatred among nations.

At the peak of his work, Stritar exercised a deep influence upon Slovene literature, and his lyrics and prose enjoyed nationwide popularity. But it was already clear during the eighties that his strength lay in his deftness and ability of formal expression rather than in creative power. Having become aware that as a creator he was no longer what he had been, Stritar began to write for children. He was past seventy when he abandoned this field of literature. Stritar's significance in Slovene literature is of such magnitude, however, that its development would have been inconceivable without him and Levstik. Moreover, he represented the European factor and skilfulness in Slovene literature, while Levstik was primordial, Slavic, rustic.

Levstik's disciples were Simon Jenko, a lyrist, and Janez Trdina, a prose writer.

Simon Jenko (1835—1869) came from the country (Podreče near Kranj). He studied in Vienna, where he earned his living as a tutor in the homes of the rich. Having received his law degree, he became a clerk in a law office.

At nineteen Jenko was second only to Prešern in lyrical talent among the Slovenes. He sang about his sorrowing country, insignificant and unrecognized, evoking the past grandeur of Slavnom and its sad present. His expression of the national feelings of the Slovenes and Slavs was spontaneous. His poem *Naprej, zastava slave* [Onward, flag of glory] became the Slovene national anthem. He also wrote love poems and nature poems with youthful sincerity. His lyrics, imbued with the spirit of the Slovene folk poem, breathe youthfulness, freshness, genuine contact with the soil — nature in its eternal youth; and the painful recognition that everything but man changes in life.

An edition of Jenko's poems (1864) was attacked by the conservatives as immoral with such violence that it broke his heart. His early death (at Kranj) is believed to have been the result of this reverse.

Janez Trdina (1830—1905) was also the son of peasant parents. He was born in the village of Mengeš near Kamnik. Having graduated at the Faculty of Philosophy in Vienna, he became a gymnasium teacher in Croatia. Persecuted for political reasons, he retired at an early age, and settled in the country. He died at Novo Mesto. He considered that it was the chief task of a Slovene writer in his time to put folk tales down in writing, and to describe folk customs, which he did with diligence. He appears to be, not so much an original writer, as a scholar of folklore. But whatever he wrote is pervaded by so real a personal note that it is obvious he was able to give a personal touch to whatever matter he handled. Besides this, he was a master of the Slovene tongue: in fact, Ivan Cankar, the later Slovene prose writer, looked to him as a model.

His autobiographical pieces are important. They are a vivid description of events in Croatia and Krain, written with sincerity, and based on history *(Bahovi husarji in Ilirji* — Bach's hussar's in Illyria; *Hrvaški spomini* — Croatian monuments; *Autobiografija* — An autobiography).

The most outstanding Slovene story-writer of the nineteenth century, and the founder of Slovene fiction was *Josip Jurčič* (1844—1881). His parents were poor country people from Muljava in Dolenjsko. His whole youth was a struggle, and he began to earn a living by writing while he was still a gymnasium pupil. Finally he reached the university in Vienna, but owing to poverty he was unable to take his degree. Later he made a living by journalism. He died of consumption in Ljubljana.

Like Trdina, Jurčič was aware of the importance of Levstik's rule that the Slovene writer must study Slovene rural life. He noted Levstik's advice that Slovene folk tales, Slovene history and Slovene social life were sources of interesting literary material, and strove to study and make use of it. He was a pupil in the fourth grade of gymnasium when he succeeded in writing a tale he had heard from his grandfather, and in getting it published. In the seventh grade he was already regarded as the best Slovene narrator on the basis of a group of published stories *(Jurij Kozak, Domen)*. By the time he left gymnasium he was widely known as a fiction writer. He also soon wrote the first Slovene novel, *Deseti brat* [The tenth brother] (1866). Up to his early death he had written numerous stories and several novels: *Cvet in sad* [The flower and the garden] (1867); *Doktor Zober* (1876), *Med dvema stoloma* [Between two stools] (1876), and some plays *(Tugomer, Veronika Deseniška)*.

During his development, Jurčič came under various influences. He was especially impressed by Sir Walter Scott, whose influence is particularly marked in *Deseti brat*. He occasionally attached more importance to his story than he did to moulding his characters. But this deficiency did not eclipse his good qualities: he was the first writer to present the Slovene life of his day in Slovene stories and novels as he experienced and understood it.

In his historical novels and stories Jurčič described the Ljubljana of the fifteenth century *(Hči mestnega sodnika — The daughter of the local judge)*, the Turkish sorties into Styria *(Jurij Kozak)*, the period of Cyril and Methodius *(Slovenski svetec in učitelj — The Slovene saint and teacher)*. In novels and stories about contemporary times he depicted the peasantry, the intellectuals of peasant descent, the nobility and clergy. No matter what period or social milieu he described, he diffused the same Slavic and democratic spirit. He described the sufferings of the Slovene peasants and townsfolk at the hands of foreigners, the hardships to which ordinary people are exposed by the mighty. His works abound in incredible, romantic scenes, abductions, conflicts between kinsmen. Jurčič recounted with such vividness, and added such lively details to his stories, that he held the attention of his readers from start to finish. All his more important works demonstrated his ability to present the Slovenes in everyday life, in good and ill. He is in fact the originator both of the story of Slovene town life and of the story of Slovene village life.

The best successor to Stritar in poetry was *Simon Gregorčič* (1844—1906). He was also born in the country, in the village of Vrsno near Ljibušnje. Like his juniors, he wanted to attend university after graduating from gymnasium. But poverty forced him to choose the priesthood, although he had never had any special liking for this vocation. Besides, he was in love. Sensitive, persecuted by the ecclesiastical authorities and by his brethren, his life became one of bitterness. He died at Gorizia.

Gregorčič established himself as a man of letters during the seventies. His first collection of poems *(Poezija;* 1882) was his best and most characteristic. His poems were the product of experience and of the hardships he had endured. Born in the mountainous part of Slovenia, near the Italian border, he was so devoted to it that he was unable to live elsewhere. Most of his poems are of love and longing for the heights. Forced to remain in the profession for which he had no inclination, he felt like a prisoner, and sang about birds in cages. He described the pain he suffered and his weariness with life, and expressed his sympathy for sufferers and for the downtrodden worker. He extolled his country and his small, oppressed nation, which was always threatened by predatory neighbours *(Soči).* He sang about love, altruism, peace, understanding among men, Christian tolerance; and in some of his poems, with circumspection, he poured out his own sentiments of love. Gregorčič's best poems are distinguished by warmth and freshness. Less philosophical than Prešern's, and less furbished than Stritar's, they resemble the Slovene folk poem, though they aspire towards perfection in form. Many of them, however, are marred by the atmosphere of the pulpit, a reminder of the poet's calling. But this did not prevent the Slovene public from recognizing Gregorčič as their poet, and his first volume soon disappeared from the bookshops.

This volume of poems drew down the condemnation of clerical circles, who regarded literature from the standpoint of their own teaching. The fanatical theologian, Anton Mahnič, the forerunner and pioneer of militant clericalism in the making, attacked Gregorčič's poems for their pessimistic note, for the elements of love they contained, and for their lack of piety. Mahnič had the support of the majority of the clergy, and Gregorčič suddenly felt scourged and ostracized, he knew not why.

Gregorčič continued to write, and published his books. However, his original success was not repeated. As though he had changed, or wished to appease his opponents, it was only rarely that a lyrical spark emanated from his verses. Nevertheless he was the most popular Slovene poet before Oton Župančič appeared, and was dubbed "The Nightingale of Gorizia".

REALISM

While traces of realism are evident in the subject-matter, technique, trend and style of some Yugoslav writers (Jovan St. Popović, among the Serbs; Antun Nemčić, among the Croats) towards the end of the first half of the nineteenth century, it was during the three last decades of the nineteenth century that the movement prevailed as a whole in Yugoslav literature. Owing to the social and economic conditions, the development of realism in Yugoslav literature was varied.

Considerable political changes took place in Yugoslav literature during the last quarter of the nineteenth century. In 1878, in accordance with the decision of the Congress of Berlin, Austria-Hungary occupied Bosnia and Herzegovina on the pretext of establishing order and setting up European methods of administration under Turkish sovereignty in it, and began to construct roads, railways and public buildings in the country. All control was in the hands of foreigners, notably Germans and Hungarians; the native population was kept at odds by religious differences as a means of widening the cleavage already dividing it, so as to facilitate their rule.

1. SERBIAN REALISM

In many respects the outcome in Serbian romanticism was extremely favourable. The romanticists had expanded the subject-matter in Serbian literature, improved its mode of expression, intensified its feelings of Serbdom, and attracted increasing numbers of reading public. But their dreams of a greater Serbian State, of liberation, and the unification of all the Serbs, brought them into conflict with reality: in Hungary pressure on the non-Hungarian nations was redoubled; in Serbia the economic and social conditions came to be deeply involved.

The efforts of the authorities in Serbia to organize the country according to West-European ways demanded heavier funds, which the backward agriculture was unable to supply. The mounting taxes and the growing need for money caused the peasant cooperatives to break up, the usurers to foreclose the mortgages which they held. The importing of industrial goods into Serbia engendered greater requirements in the Serbian countryside. Besides this, the government employees poorly paid as they were, yet desirous of the pleasures which the townsfolk could afford, became more susceptible to corruption. The towns alone benefited from the economic and social unrest. Till then inhabited chiefly by Turks, Greeks and Zinzars, the towns assumed a more Serbian hue with the greater influx of the Serbian country population. In the United Serbian Youth circles the more progressive elements drew attention to the outstanding economic problems. Nationalistic slogans lost their appeal. The protagonists of the new views were Serbian students who had been studying abroad at the expense of the State in order to become its highly qualified servants. The foremost among them was *Svetozar Marković*, a student of engineerind in St. Petersburg and Zurich who was born at Jagodina or Zaječar in 1846. Familiar with materialistic philosophy and with the social sciences, he sought to apply his knowledge in Serbia.

Svetozar Marković's work was extensive and varied: he was a theorist, an ideologist, an organizer. Marković introduced socialism in Serbia, initiated the organization of producers' and consumers' cooperatives, founded newspapers, organized political movements. And he persistently drew attention to the economic and educational backwardness of Serbia. It was in his most important work, *Srbija na Istoku* [Serbia in the east] (1872), that he observed the position of Serbia as an island in the capitalistic sea. He contended that in its economic development Serbia would be able to overleap the capitalistic phase and, evading its unpleasant consequences by sustaining the old cooperatives, step directly into socialism.

Svetozar Marković exercised a tremendous influence on Serbian life, particularly on its youth. At the beginning of the seventies, Serbia had produced a type of youth who was versed in materialistic philosophy and socialism. Instead of dreaming romantic dreams of a greater Serbia and Dušan's Empire, the progressive Serbian youth shifted emphasis in their work to the present and future. Faith in science gained ground; idealism and mysticism were discarded. A struggle was fomented in writing and orally against capitalism, the bourgeoisie, and bureaucracy, and for full democracy and equality. The movement roused the authorities to resistance; one of the victims of the struggle was also its champion Marković, who died of consumption in Trieste in 1875 at the age of twenty-nine.

Conditions in Serbia did not evolve entirely as Svetozar Marković had predicted in *Srbija na Istoku*. It was impossible to arrest the development of capitalism. The cooperatives rapidly fell to pieces, the towns grew, the general race for wealth intensified in fury. And the peasants sank deeper into poverty. Oppression by the bureaucrats, economic unrest and general insecurity forced men to take to the woods, from where, as Hajduks, they committed robbery and other crimes, often with the connivance of the authorities. King Milan, who had set up an autocratic government, was forced to leave the country. His son Aleksandar was no better as a ruler: he was assassinated by a group of officers in 1903.

The movement which had been founded by Svetozar Marković did not fade with his death; instead, it assumed a different aspect. In keeping with the social conditions in Serbia, it abandoned its socialist foundations little by little, and evolved into a peasant movement, the purpose of which was to combat bureaucracy, to fight for democracy and for the principles of parliamentary government. Now calling itself the Radical party, it enlisted most of the peasants and some townsfolk. The party fought King Milan and the house of Obrenović in general. The leaders of the party were persecuted, arrested and murdered; attempts at rebellion were suppressed in blood. The party adopted its own foreign policy: whereas Milan Obrenović was an Austrophile, the Radicals sought support in Russia and in the democratic countries of Western Europe, notably in France. This had an effect also on cultural problems.

Towards the end of the sixties, Serbian romantic literature came under the criticism of the youth movement. Two of Svetozar Marković's articles influenced literature especially: *Pevanje i mišljenje* [Singing and thinking] (1868) and *Realnost u poeziji* [Reality in poetry] (1870). Imitating the Russians Chernyshevski, Dobrolyubov and Pissarev, he criticized Serbian romantic poetry for its shallowness, pretentiousness and falsity, for its sentimental declarations of love, its attacks against the Turks, and its rhetorical patriotism. He exhorted the writers to describe life as it was and to be useful to society. He recognized merit only in a few Serbian writers, such as Jovanović-Zmaj and Djura Daničić. He brought influence to bear upon some of the older writers, but more so upon the younger ones. It was the coming of Svetozar Marković that initiated the period of realism in Serbian literature which lasted till the end of the nineteenth century.

During the closing decades of the nineteenth century, an important change also took place in Serbian literary life: Belgrade became the literary centre of liberated Serbia, while those centres in Austria-Hungary lost their importance. Literary newspapers *(Letopis Matice srpske, Brankovo kolo)* continued to be published in the Austro-Hungarian centres, but they gradually assumed provincial significance.

A number of new magazines were founded in Belgrade during the seventies, such as *Mlada Srbadija* [The young Serbs], *Rad* [Labour]. The magazine *Otadžbina* [Fatherland] (1875—1892) was especially important in literature, for it survived the longest, and had more literary significance than any of the others.

Unlike the preceding periods, when the writers came mostly from regions in Austria-Hungary, the period of realism was distinguished by the fact that the outstanding writers were either from Serbia or had moved permanently to Serbia.

Realism among the Serbs was originally identified with literary tendentiousness. During the years in which the writers held that it was necessary to solve the main problems in Serbian national life, art was also judged according to its usefulness. Their paragons were the Russian materialistic critics. The more radical Serbian theorists even preached the principle that aesthetics was an unnecessary element. There were controversies in Serbian literature about realism and naturalism, in favour of Zola and against him, with observations on pornography and other subjects. These controversies led to the translation of foreign works, notably Russian and French (Gogol, Turgenev, Hugo, Zola, Daudet).

The controversies subsided during the eighties, and gradually assumed the character of discussion of principles regarding artistic methods in realism. The radical theorists retired, leaving the field to the artists.

Whereas Serbian romanticism had fostered lyrics as its chief literary category, Serbian realism produced the story and the novel. It dealt with the conditions of the entire Serbian nation, particularly with the countryside. The peasantry gradually came to be the chief source of literary inspiration inasmuch as it constituted the overwhelming majority of Serbian society. It might even be said that the story of rural life was the fundamental achievement of Serbian realism. In view of the growth of the towns in Serbia, the Serbian petty-bourgeois story and novel of this period are also significant.

The first Serbian realist — in temperament rather than in programme — was *Jakov Ignjatović* (1824—1888). Born in the year of Branko Radičević's birth, he was also Radičević's literary contemporary. He was already recognized and gained eminence during the fifties, and he was appointed editor of *Letopis Matice srpske*. He was then writing historical novels and stories *(Djuradj Branković; Krv za rod* — Blood for the nation; *Manzor i Džemila)*, which contained all the elements of romanticism. Only during the sixties and during the period of realism at its peak, did he develop his distinctively realistic talent. He wrote a number of novels: *Milan Narandžić* (1860—1863), *Čudan svet* [Strange world] (1869),

Trpen spasen [Endurance is deliverance] (1874–75), *Vasa rešpekt* (1875), *Večiti mladoženja* [The eternal bridegroom] (1878), *Patnica* [The sufferer] (1888). He also wrote numerous stories of bourgeois and petty-bourgeois life.

Ignjatović came of a well-to-do bourgeois family from Hungary (Szentendre, near Budapest). During his youth he witnessed the frenzy for wealth which had seized the bourgeois folk of that country; he also watched the ruin of many. His was a stubborn nature, which, for one thing, kept him from passing through the higher schools. He took up the Hungarian cause in the rebellion of 1848, being an opponent of the Serbian majority. He was forced to flee with the collapse of the Hungarian revolution. In Paris he became acquainted with French literature, notably with Balzac's works. On his return to his country, he took up writing and politics. But his path through life continued to be a tortuous one. As a prominent writer, he was elected to the Assembly in Budapest by the Serbs in Hungary, but again he championed the Hungarian cause. He died at Novi Sad with the disrepute of renegade, and his literary work was forgotten. Only with the revival of realism, during the twentieth century, was the literary position he deserved restored to him.

Before Svetozar Marković began to set forth his views on realism in literature, Ignjatović had already been portraying the world as he knew it in his childhood and youth and as he saw it in his manhood. In his novels and stories, starting with *Milan Narandžić* he describes Serbian bourgeois and petty-bourgeois society in Hungary as it had taken form during the period of prosperity and social change. He produced countless characters: merchants, lawyers, officers, students, soldiers, maidservants, cooks, barbers, shop-assistants, journeymen. They constituted the section of society which had been busy during the early period of capitalism either in amassing wealth or otherwise advancing thanks to the new order. Ignjatović told of parents who had made fortunes by hardship and self-denial, and of their offspring who, living in plenty, could not make their wealth last. He described the niggardliness and heartlessness of the rich, the cheating and exploitation carried on by those whose duty it was to uphold the law. In his works the reader encounters mercenary marriages, law suits over trifles, endless quarrelling between neighbours.

As a story-writer, Ignjatović recounted the fullness of the life of his day. He realized that in the bourgeois system success was the reward of the ruthless and daring, and that everything else followed as a matter of course. The lesson to be learnt from his works leaves no room for question as to the importance of education, nobility of spirit, altruism. He depicted with extreme care characters who fought their way through the world with audacity, irrespective of schooling or breeding.

Ignjatović appealed to his reading public with the fidelity of detail in which his works abound, and with the fluency of his narrative. But he was often feeble in composition and psychology, and in moulding his characters; and for this reason his novels, especially his long ones, often seem long-winded. But when he took the necessary care, he was able to produce works of artistic completeness, with the characters sculptured to perfection, and psychologically complete. Such, for instance, is his novel *Večiti mladoženja*, which is important as an illustration both of the times and of their people. It is the story of a young man whose father had given him an education and left him money. His milieu is polite bourgeois society, and he is welcome everywhere. He is always on the point of getting married, and on a number of occasions the business is almost brought to a head. But he lacks the fortitude to surmount the last remaining minor obstacles. And so old age finds him still a bachelor.

The first distinctive story-writer from Serbia who joined Svetozar Marković's movement was *Milovan Glišić* (1847—1908). He came from the country, from the village of Gradac near Valjevo. He began to go to gymnasium when he was seventeen, and in order to attend school he had to work. Later he studied engineering and philosophy, but he did not obtain a degree in either. He earned his living as journalist, proof-reader, translator, librarian, and in other capacities. In his endeavours to improve his general education he mastered the more important European languages. He cultivated his taste for literature by studying the works of Russian writers, a number of which he translated into Serbian. He died at Dubrovnik.

Glišić occupied himself with literature during the seventies and eighties. During that time he wrote numerous stories, and two plays *(Dva cvancika* — The two Zwanzigs; *Podvala* — The hoax). A good-hearted man and a jester, a votary of Gogol, he gave a humorous picture of the characteristics of the Serbia of his day: the curruptibility, rapacity and stupidity of the bureaucrats, the violence of the authorities, types of village moneylenders, the inability of the average intellectual to adapt himself to conditions among the peasants.

Although he regarded his subjects from a humorous side, Glišić painted the harsh reality of the Serbia of his times: the Serbian village as the target of capitalism, oppressed as it was by bureaucrats and moneylenders. A peasant by nature till the end, Glišić presented the village during its transition from the patriarchal system to the domination of money economy. He pictured its sufferings, beliefs, superstitions and its resistance against the powers that corroded it.

He was most a poet when he portrayed the peasants in their own environment. His *Prva brazda* [The first furrow] is a Serbian idyll. It tells of a woman whose husband was killed in the war, leaving her with a family of small children. Although she has suitors, she refuses to remarry, for she is reluctant to break up the home her husband left. She toils and endures till she has put her children on their feet. Her greatest moment of happiness comes when her eldest son reaches the age when he is able to plough his first furrow.

Four years younger than Glišić, *Laza Lazarević* (Šabac, 1851 — Belgrade, 1890) was also in the youth movement of the seventies. He took a medical degree in Berlin, and was one of the first Serbian writers of his day who studied West-European science at its source. Lazarević, who was born in a Serbian provincial town which was little more than a village in its way of life, respected the Serbian patriarchal system grounded in firm traditions and in the authority of the elders. But he also kept an observant eye on the road which was being trodden by the young Serbian intellectuals and Serbian petty bourgeoisie, in view of the new economic system, the sudden social changes, fashions, wars, and the striving for a higher standard of living.

He wrote nine stories *(Švabica* — The maiden from Swabia; *Prvi put s ocem na jutrenje* — For the first time at Mass with father; *Školska ikona* — The school icon; *Sve će to narod pozlatiti* — The people will make good for everything; *Verter; Na bunaru* — At the well, etc.). They primarily describe life in Serbia, the patriarchal order of which had been disturbed: the attempts which were made to dissolve the cooperatives, the appearance of individualism, the idyll of rural life, the collision between the old outlook on the world and the new. He portrayed the petty bourgeoisie during its rise, with its yearning for frivolous pleasures. He particularly described the Serbian intellectuals whom contact with the West and with science had rendered weak-willed and turned into soft sentimentalists.

Lazarević composed his stories carefully: he was fastidious about every word, and drew his characters in a few strokes, but these were strong and original. Keeping in mind the effect of his plot, he would develop his story in such a way as to bring his reader to a high pitch of anticipation, and then end it suddenly and unexpectedly. Everything about his work is calculated almost to perfection, all his stories are almost masterpieces. Because of this, some critics regarded him as an efficient craftsman rather than as an artist. Regardless of such judgments, however, his stories have survived through all the periods of Serbian literature by virtue of their own vigour, right down to our own time.

The most fruitful, and for a time the most popular Serbian writer of stories of the village was *Janko Veselinović* (1862–1905). The son of a village priest, from Crnobarski Salaš, in the Mačva region, he went back to his village to be a schoolmaster after finishing four years of gymnasium and teacher's training college. As a schoolmaster he became closely attached to the peasantry, living their way of life, and understanding all their habits and failings. And he slowly acquired the habit of taking down tales he heard from peasant women, and events which he observed. Having published a number of country sketches in a provincial newspaper, which attracted notice, he soon contributed to literary magazines and began to publish books, the first of which was *Slike iz seoskoga života* [Scenes from country life] (1886, 1888). In the course of two decades he continued to produce matter similar to that in his original stories, giving various titles to his collections: *Poljsko cveće* [Field flowers], *Rajske duše* [Heavenly souls], *Zeleni vajati* [Green huts], etc. He was a writer of repute when he moved to Belgrade. There for a time he wrote plays, and was the editor of the literary magazine *Zvezda*. He yielded himself completely to bohemian life, became ill and died at his father's home at Glogovac.

In his early collections of stories Veselinović gave a picture of the Serbian village before it was seized by the depression caused by the domination of money economy, and while it still preserved its internal peace. His stories are full of joy, love and song. They contain conflicts caused by love, offended pride, disregard of family ties, and by similar reasons. But almost always they have a happy ending. Attempts to undermine the foundations of the cooperative life are almost always defeated by patriarchal ideas. Veselinović sought to give a synthetic picture of the country as he knew it in his novel *Seljanka* [The countrywoman] (1893), in which he follows the life of a typical Serbian peasant woman from childhood to old age.

In his later stories Veselinović presented aspects of country life engendered by the new economic system: usury, the exploitation of the poor by the rich men of the village, the pressure of the bureaucrats. In his unfinished novels *(Junak naših dana* — The hero of our days; *Borci* — Fighters) he sought to describe the new political manifestations in Serbia: the careerism and demagogy of the young educated Serbs, the struggle of the politicians to win democratic freedoms. But these works seem to be strained. He was in his element only in describing the country idyll. One-sided as he was, he was nevertheless a poet in this type of story. Veselinović also wrote a historical novel, *Hajduk Stanko* (1896), which treats of the times of the First Serbian Insurrection. He presented the historic figure of the Hajduk, who fearlessly fought the Turks and fell in battle. But only those parts of the novel in which he describes the idyllic Serbian village are really successful.

The last major Serbian writer born in Hungary (Senta) was *Stevan Sremac* (1855—1906). Like all the Serbs from Hungary, he was more imbued, owing to their political position, with feelings of Serbdom than concerned with social problems. Brought up on romantic ideas, he studied history at the Belgrade High School, and then went to be a gymnasium teacher at Niš, a town in Serbia which had just been taken from the Turks, in order to carry on nationalistic work among the local population. He moved to Belgrade ten years later. He died at Soko Banja.

As a historian, Sremac was inspired by the glory of Serbia's past. He was opposed to the attempts to repudiate legend for the sake of scientific truth. He was a severe opponent of Svetozar Marković, and later of the Radical party. In private life, likewise, he preferred what was old-fashioned, and hated everything new. He liked to visit the small cafés frequented by ordinary people, with their free-and-easy atmosphere.

Sremac began to write late in life. His first stories from the Serbian past appeared in the magazine *Bosanska vila* in 1888. In a solemn and lofty style he sought to describe the main events in Serbian history in the form of a legend. His first important work, however, is his novel on life in Niš, called *Ivkova slava* [Ivko's feast], which was published in his fortieth year. During the next ten years he was extremely prolific, writing numerous stories and several novels, mostly humorous: *Limunacija na selu* [Torchlight in the country] (1896), *Pop Ćira i pop Spira* [Father Ćira and Father Spira] (1898), *Vukadin* (1903), *Zona Zamfirova* (publ. 1907). He soon gained wide popularity with the Serbian and Croatian reading public. A humourist in temperament and an untiring observer of detail, for ten years Sremac kept the whole of Serbia laughing.

Sremac was a conservative in his theoretical views and outlook on life. He was remote both from socialism and from the idea of literature used as a medium of creating better social relations. But he was a realist by instinct. His was a keen eye for the minutest details of significance, and he endeavoured to put them down in writing instead of giving himself up to dreaming. Being of a sociable nature, he endeavoured to get to know people in speech, movement, habits and in their pet expressions, unconsciously gathering material for his works.

Sremac's characters moved in the same kind of circles as those of their creator: Niš during the eighties, the Serbian province and Belgrade during the same period; and Banat in Hungary towards the close of the nineteenth century. Unlike most fiction writers in

Serbia who primarily described the country, Sremac wrote about the bourgeoisie and petty bourgeoisie of Serbia during the last decades of the nineteenth century, at the time when they were emerging from the patriarchal and Oriental ways of life, and adopting West-European views and ways.

The characters in Sremac's novels and stories are tradesmen, small merchants, clerks, priests, provincial actors, innkeepers, waiters. The events in his stories occur most often in small cafés, in the offices of junior clerks, in village schools, in the kitchens of petty-bourgeois families. They chiefly revolve around the question as to how the junior clerk or officer is to gain promotion, how a marriage is to be arranged, if some individual will succeed in a commercial adventure, how a small shopkeeper will manage to swindle an unsuspecting customer. He described with relish feasts, intrigues, drinking-bouts. He particularly loved to portray ordinary people with their narrow horizons and petty pleasures.

There is scarcely any plot in the usual sense of the word in Stevan Sremac's novels and stories. *Ivkova slava* is a description of a drinking-bout. *Pop Ćira i pop Spira* is a duel between two clerical families over one prospective bridegroom. *Vukadin* illustrated the endeavours of a junior clerk to gain promotion. *Zona Zamfirova* is the story of a small shopkeeper who, by clever strategem, wins the hand of a rich man's daughter.

The strength of Sremac's narrative lies in the extraordinary multitude of detail, which he presents with fidelity and animation. The later chapters of his novels often do not advance the action beyond the point reached in the earlier ones. But their abundance of the truth of life compensates for their lack of plot.

Because of his political views, Sremac's opponents regarded him as a reactionary, particularly after he had devoted a whole novel — *Limunacija na selu* — to satirizing a follower of Svetozar Marković. His habit of describing intrigues, quarrels, drinking-bouts, banquets, cafés, caused the critics to observe that he interpreted Serbia merely in terms of food, sprees, intrigues, gossiping.

Actually, Sremac was a lyrist at heart. At the bottom of his stories lies love for the human being, a search for the beautiful, a hope that there exists something better, finer, more perfect. Though many of his works evoke roars of laughter, on the whole they leave an impression of sadness. In Serbian literature Sremac was the greatest and most genuine humourist, who observed people and their paltriness with the eye of a commiserator, looking on with anguish and yet with a smile at their exertions to emerge from poverty, oppression, neglect.

Sremac's works are a picture of Serbia towards the end of the nineteenth century, with its bickering political parties, its rotten bureaucracy, the strivings of its petty bourgeois folk to rise above their circumstances by any means. With humour, yet faithfully, Sremac pictured his country, which seemed to have hurriedly discarded the old and familiar, without realizing what it really wanted, being consequently carried away by shallowness and phraseology.

As a whole this picture is not negative. Besides the multitude of intriguers, careerists, drunkards, mean souls, Sremac observed and depicted characters of rare integrity and human greatness (Ibiš Aga, Čiča-Jordan). He possesses something in common with all the great humourists: his works reflect human misery, yet also the belief that it can be avoided. The road of mankind, indeed, runs through filth and baseness, but the triumph of good and beauty is visible at the end. In his stories and novels victory does not go to the representatives of wealth, ambition, cruelty, but to the champions of nobility and perfection.

A new, personal, note was introduced in Serbian realism by *Simo Matavulj* (1852—1908). Born at Šibenik, Dalmatia, nurtured on Romance literature, he was the most at home with Italian verism and French realism. He learned Italian in the teachers' training college at Šibenik, and French by reading books in an out-lying Dalmatian village, in which he was a schoolmaster. He was later transferred successively to Southern Dalmatia (Hercegnovi), Montenegro and Belgrade, where he taught in secondary schools or worked on newspapers. He travelled widely, also visiting Paris. Absolute truth and objectivity were his literary principles. He wrote his memoirs and views on art in *Bilješke jednog pisca* [The notes of a writer].

Matavulj began to write in his youth, composing verse and tales. But it was not until 1880 that he published his first important story, which was a realistic description of a beggar. His main books of stories are *Iz Crne Gore i Primorja* [Montenegro and the Littoral] (1888, 1889), *Iz primorskog života* [Life in the Littoral] (1890), *Sa Jadrana* [From the Adriatic] (1891), *Iz beogradskog života* [Life in Belgrade] (1891), *Iz raznijeh krajeva* [Various places] (1893), *Beogradske priče* [Belgrade stories] (1902). In addition to these stories, he published two novels *(Uskok*, 1892; *Bakonja fra Brne*, 1892).

Matavulj's works may be divided into three groups according to the regions he described: the Dalmatian, the Montenegrin, and the Belgrade group.

Matavulj's most distinctive stories are those from Dalmatia. They portray faithfully types of the Dalmatian petty bourgeois folk: clerks, small shopkeepers, priests, ruined feudalists, with their idiosyncrasies, customs, conflicts. Characteristics of Matavulj's narrative are conciseness, precise expression, faithful portrayal of physiognomy and character. Matavulj forcefully exposed the atmosphere of the small Dalmatian localities, their monotony and opressiveness. Deliberately unemotional, he gave the impression of being an unbiased recorder of events rather than a poet. It is from his relation with Dalmatia that his best work, one of the finest in Serbian literature — *Bakonja fra Brne* — springs.

Bakonja fra Brne describes life in a Catholic monastery. The theme is the spiritual and physical development of a youth, who evolves from an untamed village urchin into a friar who is possessed of human weaknesses and virtues, like any other human being.

The novel contains an extraordinary multitude of traits peculiar to man and his nature. In his effort to present his friars primarily as human beings, he stripped them of the halo of piousness and holiness, bringing them, with their human attributes, close to the reader. The great wealth of detail, the variety of characters, the abundance of types render this novel a treasury of human documents, and imbue it throughout with an understanding for man and his weaknesses.

In his stories of Montenegro and in his novel *Uskok*, Matavulj introduces the Montenegrin at the close of his heroic period, when he still lived for the memories of the glory he had won in battle against the Turks, when a man's worth was assessed according to the number of Turks he had beheaded; and also at a time when mean souls, petty plots and intrigue were beginning to dominate. On coming to Montenegro, Matavulj seemed to yield to its spirit and to live in it. His stories of Montenegro are without the coldness of his Dalmatian motifs: he is carried away by enthusiasm and ecstasy over the heroism of the past.

In his stories of Belgrade, Matavulj sought to describe city life: the horrors of the human ant-hill, into which humanity drifts from all sides, in which a man advances only at the expense of his neighbour.

The period of Serbian realism ended with *Svetolik Ranković* (1863—1899). He was brought up on the Russian novel. He had no connexion with the theory of Serbian realism; for all that, he was closely in touch with life, and gave a vivid picture of Serbia during the last of the Obrenovićs.

The son of a village priest from Moštanica in Šumadija, Ranković also chose theology, which he studied in Belgrade and Kiev. He earned a living as a teacher of religion in gymnasia. He grew to manhood just at the time when the Serbian village, impoverished by the impact of money economy and by usury, was writhing in the throes of severe depression. He had the tragic experience of seeing his father murdered by Hajduks. He died in Belgrade of consumption.

Ranković wrote a number of stories and three novels: *Gorski car* [The czar of the mountains] (1897), *Seoska učiteljica* [The country schoolmistress] (1898), *Porušeni ideali* [Shattered ideals] (1900). His stories, which he appropriately named *Slike iz života* [Pictures from life], give details of the social and moral manifestations of his time. In his novels, on the other hand, he dealt with all the negative aspects of the Serbia of his day.

Gorski car is a novel about the Hajduks, and the fundamental task of the book was to disprove the romantic legend of the Hajduks as the embodiment of freedom, and to show them up for a social evil. The hero is a man who could have been a useful member of society. But owing to his unfortunate surroundings, he becomes a lazy, careless youth, and finally falls under the influence of the head of a band of Hajduks, who seeks to exploit his physical strength and discontentment. He begins with petty theft, and ends by committing murder and sinking deep into crime, while the beneficiary is the organizer, who lives comfortably in a town. Any attempt by the Hajduk to free himself spells ruin for him.

In his novel Ranković presents the moral downfall of the Hajduks, the surroundings in which they move, and the psychology of their captains and accomplices. He also gives the psychology of the Hajduk worshipper for whom the Hajduk is a hero till disappointment opens his eyes.

Seoska učiteljica is a novel of the Serbian village and the small Serbian official. It is the story of a young schoolmistress who dreams of a wonderful, comfortable future. She is further and further oppressed by the harsh life of the country, by the backwardness of the peasants and the arbitrariness of the bureaucrats, till she commits suicide: a Madame Bovary of the village. Ranković related the case of his country schoolmistress, not as an isolated instance, but as a part of the picture of a society in which her development was logical and inevitable. In addition to his heroine, Ranković presented types of junior government employees who are driven from place to place by the authorities; he described the corrupt bureaucrats, who exploit the helplessness of the weak; he pictured the Serbian countryside, suspicious, and incapable of understanding the need for intellectuals. He dealt with his subject broadly and deeply, the destiny of his main characters being the inevitable result of living conditions.

Porušeni ideali to some extent resembles the case of Dositej Obradović: the flight of an inexperienced boy to a monastery, his piousness, his disillusionment, illness and death. This novel, which he wrote in haste, almost on his death-bed, lacks Dositej's optimism.

163

Motifs similar to Ranković's were employed by other Serbian and Croatian writers. Of all of them Ranković was the most complete realist: he never strove to represent individuals as fearless fighters against the depraved community, but as organic components of the community and as its issue; and for this reason they are impressive in their plausibility.

Serbian realism in its militant phase engendered analogous poems. It produced poets who expressed the current political and social programmes of their day. During this period Jovanović-Zmaj was still publishing his forceful satirical and political poems. But there was only one other genuine lyrist during that whole period: Vojislav Ilić.

Vojislav Ilić (1862—1894) was born in Belgrade. He was the son of the poet Jovan Ilić, and the son-in-law of Djura Jakšić. Ilić at first drew on his immediate surroundings for his literary training. He expanded it later by reading the Russian poets, notably Zhukovsky and Pushkin, and the works of West-European writers translated into Russian. Instead of finishing his schooling, he took various government posts in Belgrade and elsewhere. He was very poor most of his life, and he was continually persecuted by the authorities because of his progressive views. Although he died of consumption at the age of thirty-two, he had written so many lyric and epic poems by then, that he had already won for himself an unprecedented literary name, and exercised a strong influence on Serbian and Croatian poetry. He published three editions of his poems during his lifetime (1887, 1889, 1892).

Like his Serbian predecessors and contemporaries, Vojislav Ilić wrote patriotic poems, glorifying the Serbian past and freedom. Like the progressive part of his generation he denounced conditions in Serbia under the Obrenovićs. In his satirical and epic poems and odes he dwelt upon the corruptness of the authorities, the poverty of the peasants, the vacuity of the most prominent representatives of culture in Serbia during that period, and upon similar subjects. But his appearance was significant, not so much for the subject-matter or ideas which he dealt with, as for the distinctively individual character of his poems, and for their expression. In this respect Ilić is a notable reformer in Serbian poetry, being second only to Branko Radičević.

The difference between Vojislav Ilić and his typical predecessors and contemporaries is that they worked on hackneyed patriotic themes, without any true bent for creating. They anathemized the Turks and cursed the enemies of the nation with false emotion and overworked phrases. On the contrary, Vojislav Ilić declared that a poet should write only when he is truly inspired, irrespective of the literary vogue. He demanded that man himself in all his aspects, and not merely the patriot, should find expression in poetry. At the same time he exhorted the real poet to present a picture of his period, and not, like the typical romanticist, only to seek escape in the past.

Vojislav Ilić vastly expanded the field of Serbian poetry to include the whole of man, with all his yearnings, weaknesses and frustrations. He discarded the style adopted by the romanticists, and found his own mode of expression. Thus he reverted somewhat to the earlier tradition of Serbian poetry, to that of his father's period, which he adopted in his own way.

Delicate, sensitive and ailing, living in times of political stress and merciless struggle for career and wealth, Vojislav Ilić revealed his own sorrow at the existing conditions: the sorrow of a man in contact with the transience of things, with a yearning for something impalpable and remote. His poetry is pervaded by sentiments evoked by nature in delicate souls during their dying moments. It is permeated by sighs for the irretrievable. It is imbued with the feeling and consciousness that life is miserable and worthless, and man weak and helpless in perpetual change and transience. His verse breathes hopeless affliction, depression and even pessimism.

In his poems Vojislav Ilić presented nature, sketches from ancient Greek and Roman life, from the Serbian Middle Ages, from Spain, and from the Orient. The essence of his poems lies, not in the descriptions of nature and people, but in the lyrical impression made on him by nature and people. Whatever his theme, his poems are impressive, not so much for their distinct picture, as for the strength of their mood, for an indefinable, vibrantly living, musical emanation which rises from them.

In reviving the traditions of earlier Serbian verse, Ilić did not revert to the scheme of the old classical rhythms in their formal sense. He used them only as a means of varying the monotony in Serbian poetry which had been instilled into it by the mode of expression of the inheritors of the tradition of the folk poem, Jovanović-Zmaj and Jakšić. The old classical moulds were filled by Ilić with Serbian speech, with a feeling for the strength of Serbian accentuation and for the laws governing the Serbian tongue. He discarded so-called poetic licence, elision, offences against tense and syntax, the creation of new terms as an expedient. With the skill of a fine artist he elicited every shade of expression, all the music of its accents, from the Serbian tongue. His style is extremely mellow and smooth; his rhythms are like the wafting of a gentle breeze, the trembling of a leaf: what was fine and almost intangible, yet forceful and personal, Vojislav Ilić felt and succeeded in putting into words. His poems are both intelligible and simple; yet, with their wealth of expressive media, exuberant and varied. They seem to flow joyfully, like a placid brook sparkling with light and colour.

165

Although the world of his feelings and senses was neither particularly broad nor particularly deep, Vojislav Ilić was the most individual Serbian lyrist. This did not prevent him from being also a herald of the progressive trends of his day, a poet of action and battle.

2. CROATIAN REALISM

In Croatian literature August Šenoa was already the theoretical representative of realism. But realism became a definite trend only after his death, occupying a dominant position till about the end of the century. If we exclude Šenoa from this period, it coincides with the times of immense political and economic happenings in Croatia.

During the eighties, the political position of the Croatian people inside Austria-Hungary was becoming worse. Supported by Vienna, the Hungarian authorities sought to implement the dualistic principle without compromise, and to consolidate their power in Croatia. After a few tentative ventures, they nominated Count Khuen Hederváry as Ban of Croatia, a man who was Hungarian by birth and sentiment. The twenty years of his rule (1883–1903) amounted to twenty years of economic, political and cultural oppression, the purpose of which was to crush the resistance of the Croats and to turn Croatia into an ordinary Hungarian province in which the people would be Magyarized in the course of time. Violence during elections, ruined lives, political persecution, censorship and espionage were the instruments of his reign of terror. Khuen Hederváry succeeded in wrecking the biggest Croatian political party, the inheritor of the Illyrian traditions, and in attracting a section of its members to support him. He deliberately fomented discord between the Croats and Serbs in order to enlist the Serbs to his cause. Under these conditions, the most radical and militant Croats joined the Party of Rights, which refused to recognize that Croatia was under any legal obligation to Hungary or Austria. But its romantic idealism often benefited the authorities rather than hampered them.

The social process in Croatia, which had begun in 1848, had more or less reached its conclusion. New economic and social problems began to make their appearance. The small nobility of Croatia were on the whole economically ruined. Only the high aristocracy succeeded in winning the struggle for survival. Formally without political privileges though they were, the feudalists continued to be a major political force, for they held the most influential and lucrative offices in the State administration and Army. This being the case, they were ready to come to terms

166

with the Hungarian authorities. The Croatian bourgeoisie steadily became prosperous in the capitalistic system, but the greatest benefits from the economy went to foreigners. The new banks, factories and major business concerns were in the hands of foreign capitalists; they were managed by foreign boards and run by foreign personnel. The majority of the Croatian bourgeoisie, the petty bourgeoisie, continued to live a narrow way of life, given to romantic dreams and to verbalistic revolutionism. In some regions, the overwhelming majority of the Croatian people, the impoverished peasantry, turned proletarian, or went abroad, especially to America, to seek work. As emigration increased towards the end of the century, Hungarians and Germans, supported by the authorities, settled on Croatian land. The educated Croats, in a country poorly developed economically, were compelled to seek government jobs, and so were held in subjection by the authorities. The more remunerative professions — medicine and engineering — were practised by outsiders or by the children of the well-to-do. The better-paid posts in the government administration, in finance and in the railways, were held by Hungarians, mostly individuals who could not speak Croatian.

The eighties and nineties in Croatia were a period of steady economic and national decline of the Croatian people, of increasing pressure of alien power and alien money, of growing despondency among the elite of Croatia, helpless to prevent the domineering foreigner from over-running the land.

On account of growing economic adversity and impoverishment from the seventies onwards, the socialist movement rapidly gained ground in Croatia.

During the seventies Šenoa demanded that the Croatian writers should present Croatian life realistically, and suggested to them a multitude of economic, political and cultural problems suitable for literary treatment. His request was generally accepted during the last years of his life. The younger generation regarded themselves as realists, and during the eighties their realism assumed various aspects. Some of them were naturalists after Zola, verists after Verga, and realists of the Russian type.

Attempts were made by Evgenij Kumičić to transplant French naturalism into Croatia, while Italian verism was introduced by the Dalmatian writers. But neither of these was generally adopted. Naturalism and verism were opposed by most writers, who were more inclined to the realism of the Russian type. They contended that naturalism and verism amounted to pornography, aesthetic deformity; that these two schools jeopardized morality. Heated and extended controversies supported by polemics and pamphlets and by other forms of attack followed. The principal Croatian magazine *Vijenac*, vaccilating between naturalism and realism, remained, nevertheless, conservative in the main, by realism. New magazines *(Hrvatska vila, Balkan)* were founded in consequence, naturalistic in tone, in some of their numbers at least.

The struggle over naturalism, verism and realism filled Croatian literature till almost the end of the century, when new trends began to make their appearance.

An array of prolific story-writers such as had never been seen before in Croatian literature, appeared during the realistic period, who presented Croatian life from various aspects. The main literary form at that time was the novel, the task of which was to deal broadly with the entire Croatian scene; with the ruin of the feudalists, the rise of the bourgeoisie, the fate of the intellectuals in bourgeois surroundings, the political situation in Croatia, the pressure of the authorities on the Croatian people, the problem of the Croatian peasantry and the economic conditions of the country. The novel had its parallel in numerous stories, dealing in the main with the same themes.

Unlike Serbian realism with its rustic story, the Croatian novel and story dealt during the period of realism on the whole with the Croatian bourgeoisie and petty bourgeoisie, and also with types who belonged neither to the peasantry nor to the bourgeoisie. Croatian literature of that time also endeavoured to include all other classes of society, from the aristocracy down to the working class.

The fundamental characteristic of Croatian realistic literature was critical philosophy. The writers tried, not only to describe, but also to analyze and appraise various manifestations. The literature of this period was no small help to the resistance of the Croatian people against the authorities, for it raised their consciousness, buoyed their spirits and revealed the causes of Croatian misery. During one period or another, all the more outstanding Croatian writers of the time belonged to the Party of Rights, the most radical party in Croatia, some of them also being supporters of socialism. Almost every Croatian literary work of that period was written with a definite tendency, which was the offshoot of Croatian reality.

Because of these features Croatian literature was hampered in its development by the authorities, who confiscated Croatian magazines and books, and prosecuted the writers. Not a single distinctively realistic Croatian writer could obtain any good government post or practise one of the professions, and many of them even suffered imprisonment.

Towards the end of the century, as the decline of the country became glaringly obvious, and the position of the Croatian people grew more distressing, Croatian literature lost its militant nature. Even during the period of realism it had uttered notes of despondency and resignation.

Croatian literary criticism developed in the novel and story during the period of realism, parallel with critical philosophy. Its chief objective was to judge the extent to which Croatian literature conformed with the principles of realism, and the extent to which it was art. Its most outstanding and most distinctive representatives were *Janko Ibler* (Desiderius) and *Jakša Čedomil* (the nom de plume of Jakov Čuka). Ibler purposely defended the new trends; Čedomil introduced methods of West-European literary criticism in Croatian literature.

Realistic tendencies also began to manifest themselves in drama and poetry, but no work of lasting value appeared in the dramatic field during that period. Verse produced but one distinguished poet, Silvije Strahimir Kranjčević.

Evgenij Kumičić (1850—1904) was the first Croatian writer to introduce a new trend, Zola's naturalism, in literature, and his programme had the impact of a storm. Born at Berseč, in Istria, he graduated in history at the Faculty of Letters in Vienna, and continued his studies in Paris, where he became familiar with French literature. After a brief period of teaching in the gymnasium in Zagreb, he resigned and turned to politics, becoming one of the more prominent members of the Party of Rights, which he represented in the Sabor, and also practised as a journalist. He made a living at journalism and literature. He died in Zagreb.

Kumičić took to literature relatively late in life, at the close of the seventies; but being prolific as well as radical, he eclipsed all the Croatian story-writers. He published a number of novels on contemporary subjects: *Olga i Lina* (1881), *Jelkin bosiljak* [Jelka's basil] (1881), *Začudjeni svatovi* [The astounde wedding guests] (1883), *Gospodja Sabina* [Madame Sabina] (1883), *Sirota* [The orphan] (1885), *Pod puškom* [Under arms] (1886), *Teodora* (1889), etc. His historical novels are *Urota Zrinsko-Frankopanska* [The Zrinski-Frankopan conspiracy] (1892—3), and *Kraljica Lepa* [Queen Lepa] (1902). He also wrote a number of stories and plays.

In the main two factors moulded Kumičić's literary profile: his nationalistic sentiments, and his conception of literature.

Kumičić was born in Istria, where an Italian bourgeois minority dominated the Croatian peasant majority with the assistance of the authorities. He lived at the time of Croatia's bitter struggle against Khuen Hederváry, the exponent of Hungary. And all this was inspired by the Viennese politicians. He regarded Rome, Imperial Vienna and Hungarian Budapest as the worst enemies of the Croatian people. Besides this, he regarded the reverses of the Croatian people as the fault of the Croatian bourgeoisie, which was willing to compromise, and was opportunistic and pleasure-loving, and therefore servile towards the authorities. He contended that it was the duty of literature to expose every aspect of life, the worst included, if it was to have a moral effect.

Kumičić exercised his every literary effort towards exposing the enemies of the Croatian nation, towards warning the Croats of the source of all their evils and towards drawing their attention to their own deficiencies. He was inspired in his works by the regions in which he had lived: Istria, the Croatian Littoral and Zagreb, and also by Croatian history.

Kumičić portrayed all sections of Croatian society and many walks of life: the bourgeoisie and petty bourgeoisie; government employees, politicians, merchants, captains, seamen, fishermen, peasants, priests, moneylenders, procuresses, writers, aristocrats. He pointed to the dissolute force of money, the corruptness of the politicians, the extravagance in the homes of the civil servants, the careerism and the lack of character of the bureaucrats. Side by side with the Croats he depicted the representatives of the Istrians, the Hungarian and Austrian authorities. Whatever his subject, he always placed the Croat side by side with the foreigner, usually in contrast to the cunning, in order to emphasize the former's integrity and poverty. Whereas he wrote with bitterness about the enemies of the Croatian nation, he described his Istrian villagers and the islanders of Cres and Krk with almost childish enthusiasm.

The plots of Kumičić's novels were exciting and romantic. Being a skillful narrator, and imbuing his works with current political tendencies, he won remarkable renown among his followers and among the discontented Croats generally. Since his novels and stories frequently dealt with crime, immorality and depravity, his opponents accused him of naturalism in a disparaging sense, and underrated his works.

Kumičić's historical novels were written for the same reason as his works on contemporary life. He sought to describe three important periods in which the Croatian people came into conflict with the same forces as persecuted them during his time: with the policy of Vienna, Budapest and Rome in relation to Croatia; but he succeeded only in showing the relations between the Croats on the one side, and Vienna and Rome on the other.

In *Urota Zrinsko-Frankopanska* he presented events of the seventeenth century, when the representatives of the Croatian and Hungarian aristocratic families united against Vienna. The conspiracy was discovered and two of the most prominent Croatian noblemen, Petar Zrinski and Fran Krsto Frankopan, both men of letters, were imprisoned and executed. *Kraljica Lepa* describes the last years of the medieval Croatian State, when the Pope had the national ruler of Croatia taken prisoner in order to install an obedient vassal in his stead, and later a Hungarian.

As the political situation in Croatia altered, it was easier to perceive the shortcomings in Kumičić's works: their partiality, the excessive emphasis on plot, his political bias, his romantic elaborations, the exaggerated expression of personal feelings in his works. Their merits were nonetheless manifest: the writer's courage in openly criticizing Croatian society, his ardent patriotism, the warm idyll of the Istrian countryside, seascape and coast, and his indubitable gift for narrative.

Ante Kovačić (1854–1889), who was actually Kumičić's predecessor, made his entrance into literature with lyric and epic poems, and in 1875 he joined the literary journal *Vijenac*. At first he pursued the path followed by the older Croatian writers, notably Šenoa; but from 1880 onwards he turned against them for political rather than literary reasons. Towards the end of Šenoa's life, Kovačić became his most bitter opponent, for he demanded more realism and more Croatian nationalism in literature.

Kovačić was the son of a poor peasant, born at Marija Gorica, in Hrvatsko Zagorje. Being an especially gifted child, he was sent to school. He lived chiefly from grants and by tutoring. Having completed his law studies, he worked in law offices in Zagreb and at Karlovac. He was granted a licence to set up as a lawyer at Glina just before he died. He died in the hospital at Vrapče near Zagreb.

Forced to struggle all his life for his livelihood, Kovačić was unable to develop systematically as a writer. His command of foreign languages was superficial, and his chief models were the domestic writers. He was familiar with some foreign writers (Turgenev, Voltaire, Hugo); but both in literature and in politics his pattern was Ante Starčević, with his radicalism, intransigence and inflexible style.

Kovačić's main works are his novels *Baruničina ljubav* [The baroness's love] (1877), *Fiškal* [The solicitor] (1882), *U registraturi* [At the registrar's] (1888); a number of stories: *Ljubljanska katastrofa* [The Ljubljana disaster], *Ladanjska sekta* [The country sect], and poems and feuilletons.

Kovačić's earliest writings showed no unusual promise, and consisted mostly of lengthy ballads on events from Croatian history. His early stories are markedly romantic, and his first more extensive works *(Baruničina ljubav, Fiškal)* are also romantic in subject-matter, dealing with strangely complex human destinies. But at that time Kovačić had already learnt how to knit up what he saw into literary and fantastic plots. Being descended from the poorest Croatian social section, he became a delineator and critic of social relations. He described the Croatian bourgeoisie, nobility and peasantry as he saw them. In the declining feudalists he saw, not well-bred people who were proud in their defeat at the hands of modern times but egoists, fools, intriguers, with neither wealth nor honour, who lived by cheating and deception. Of everything that they had formerly possessed, only their contempt for the common folk now remained. In the Croatian bourgeoisie and petty bourgeoisie Kovačić saw merely selfishness, narrow-mindedness, petty scheming, intellectual poverty, and the endeavours of individuals to present themselves as something better than they really were.

From his earliest stories down to his last novel, *U registraturi*, Kovačić steadily evolved towards realism. His best features — his unswervingly faithful view and picture of social reality — found their deepest expression in his last work.

The novel *U registraturi* is the biography of a poor country boy called Ivica Kičmanović. As he is a gifted boy, his teachers send him to town to study, to become a gentleman. His supposed patron, a debauchee, gives him board and lodging, but abandons him to the servants, from whom he learns nothing but evil. The home of his patron is the scene of his affair with his patron's mistress. Then follow numerous entanglements, poisoning and murder. By the time Ivica becomes a clerk in a registry office, and after his many difficulties and trials, he is a broken man. Then one day the documents in the case against his former mistress, who was the cause of his misfortunes, come into his hands. As he reads them, he relives the unhappiness of his whole life, sets fire to the registry office and burns to death in it.

The novel is full of fantastic scenes. But as a whole it is a picture of Croatian life during Kovačić's day, especially of the social and cultural conditions. Kovačić was skillful in drawing true-to-life portraits of the representatives of all sections of society: peasants, priests, teachers, aristocrats, merchants, literary men, clerks, servants, the rich men of the village, procuresses. The fundamental theme of his work is the advance of a child from the country and from the class of its fathers to the society of the educated class. Whereas the slogan in Šenoa's period was "With Education towards Freedom", Kovačić's aim was to describe the path which led to education. In his novel he clearly demonstrated that the passage from a rustic milieu to the higher, educated classes ran through sufferings and humiliation, and ended with the breakdown of the individual and with the distress caused to the whole environment from which such a person springs.

In his main work Kovačić dealt with that period of Croatian life in which the peasantry grew poorer owing to money economy. There were individuals, it is true, who amassed wealth in the country by usury and avarice. But the process of the pauperization of the peasants was obvious.

Kovačić's novel is distinguished by ruthless frankness. Instead of the usual rural idyll, such as the average Croatian bourgeois writers presented, Kovačić presented almost uncanny scenes of rural life as the consequence of the economic forces which were at work in every milieu: the friction between the rich and the poor, conflict, spiritual backwardness, envy, the struggle for higher social standing. In the bitterness of his observations Kovačić created extremely vivid and almost unique types, and the pages in which they appear remain a lasting memory. Such are those which contain the description of the childhood of his hero, the scene in the servants' hall, the portrait of the depraved peasant lackay, to mention but a few. In addition to the pages which are striking for their bitterness and emotion, there are deeply tender passages, full of youthful gaiety and innocence.

Apart from those of his experiences in the country, Kovačić's novel contain ample descriptions of his experiences in the town. He depicted the hypocrisy and falsity of the town philanthropists, who were in fact tyrants, voluptuaries, and exploiters of the poor. He revealed the misery of the government employees and the vanity of the superficial literati.

A peculiarity in Kovačić's works is that he mixed the blatantly romantic with the realistic, that he connected the products of his own fantasy with scenes from reality. His characters grow to extraordinary proportions, often becoming phantomlike and grotesque.

Kovačić had a forceful creative talent, but as a writer he was insufficiently developed. He was more eruptive than capable of giving his ideas quiet expression. His style is luxuriant, volcanic. He is now a caricaturist and then an elegist; now he curses and then he weeps. His art, however, is impressive in its internal harmony, irrespective of the patchiness of his detail and heterogeneity of his technique. His talent was the fruit of that social chaos which set in with the inglorious downfall of feudalism in Croatia, while the new people, rising from the broad masses, were not yet strong enough to resist the new forces of scheming and money. It emerged from the distressing circumstances which the Croat experienced in the turmoil which had needlessly taken as its toll so many men of talent. All his country characters, who temporarily make their way up in society, sooner or later come to grief through poison, drunkenness, fire, madness.

Some of Kovačić's passages rank among the best in Croatian prose for their truthful observation, daring expression, condensed and precise style; and on this account he often served as a model for the younger generations.

Ksaver Šandor Djalski (1854—1935), the most prolific writer of Croatian realism, also comes from Hrvatsko Zagorje, from Gredica Castle, near Zabok.

Djalski's real name was *Ljubomir Babić*. He studied law in Zagreb and Vienna, and became a government employee. But he was soon dismissed for political reasons, and he then turned to politics. He was elected to Parliament, and distinguished himself in the struggle of the Croatian people against the regimes of oppression sustained in Croatia by the Hungarian authorities.

In his aesthetic development Djalski passed through several phases. By family upbringing he was a follower of the Illyrian ideas expounded in the Yugoslavism of Bishop Strossmayer. For a time he was also a member of the most radical Croatian political party, the Party of Rights. He subsequently passed through a phase of socialism. He was one of the first Croatian writers whose works, as a token of brotherhood and unity, were published in Belgrade during the Austro-Hungarian period.

Djalski spoke several languages, was widely travelled, read Turgenev, Balzac, etc. He studied philosophic and economic works, and the social sciences, and for a time he also occupied himself with occult studies. All these things left their impress upon his literary work.

Djalski began to write at an early age, but only after he was thirty (in 1884) did he succeed in penetrating into literature with his story *Illustrissimus Bathorych*. He soon earned the name of the foremost realistic story-writer in Croatia. His major collections of stories are *Pod starim krovovima* [Beneath old roofs] (1886), *Tri pripovijesti bez naslova* [Three stories without title] (1887), *Bijedne priče* [Tales of misery] (1888), *Iz varmedjinskih dana* [From varmegye days] (1891), *Diljem doma* [The country from end to end] (1899). His novels are *U noći* [During the night] (1886), *Djurdjica Agićeva* (1889), *Osvit* [Dawn] (1892), *Za materinsku riječ* [For a motherly word] (1906).

Djalski began his literary career as a poet of that social class of which he was a member by birth: the declining aristocracy. Later he widened the compass of his literary interest, but in essence he did not change.

As distinct from other Croatian story-writers of the realistic school, who represented the period of feudalism as a period of oppression and exploitation, Djalski portrayed the feudalists with affection, as people with human virtues and weaknesses. His first novel was a kind of protest against the habitual presentation of the feudal lords as being oppressors of the peasantry. He pictured the feudalist, who suffers because of his fine breeding and because he cannot bear the coarseness of the peasant masses.

174

In describing his native region, Djalski depicted the nobility as unable to accustom themselves to the conditions which came into being after 1848. He described their intimate and their social life, their parties, their financial cares. He depicted their conflict with the new times, as well as their reflections upon bygone days. He described their romantic loves, as well as the misery to which they fell prey owing to their obstinacy, ignorance, and the ruthlessness of their creditors during the years in which they found themselves without unpaid labour. He described both the aristocrats who resigned themselves to their ruin and those who endeavoured to adjust themselves to the economic relations. Djalski speaks lyrically about the aristocratic Croatian families, the Croatian landscape, the beauty of tradition and the past. All his affections were given to those who were sinking into ruin, although he himself realized that their ruin was inevitable.

In his further work Djalski endeavoured to deal critically with the entire life of the Croatia of his day. He described the political problem when compromise and opportunism were couched in radical phraseology *(U noći)*. He presented the destiny and downfall of the cultural workers in bourgeois and petty bourgeois surroundings *(Radmilović, Djurdjica Agićeva)*, the moral and political pressure exercised upon the Croat by the authorities *(Tri pripovijesti bez naslova)*. His more extensive works also comprise two historical novels *(Osvit, Za materinsku riječ)*, in which he described the period of the Illyrian movement, with its inspirations and successes, as a contrast to his own time, with its bourgeois egoism, political apathy and servility.

Djalski's novels and stories revealing philosophic questions and problems of life in the next world may be said to form a separate group *(Janko Borislavić, Mors)*.

In volume and scope, Djalski is the most comprehensive Croatian writer of the nineteenth century. His novels and stories form an extensive document of political, social, economic and cultural life in Croatia from the beginning up to the end of the nineteenth century. Whereas other Croatian writers presented a single region or a single section of society, Djalski founded the political, social and psychological novel and story. Notwithstanding his birth, he tried to be socially progressive: he wrote stories even about the most wretched members of society *(Bijedne priče)*. He was the first Croatian writer whom the critics declared to be European in spirit, for he endeavoured to introduce problems into Croatian literature which transcended the bounds of that country. During his time he exercised a militant and progressive effect on Croatian readers, and he opened new horizons for writers. Indeed, the entire younger generation of the end of the nineteenth century regarded him as their master. During the literary controversies which raged at that time he always took their side, in opposition to the conservative writers.

The artistic value of Djalski's works is not always equal to their ideological, critical and national significance. Djalski wrote at a great pace, and often the propaganda or intellectualistic elements in his works outweigh the creative. What strikes the reader is that his plots are artificial and his delineation one-sided. There is the most artistic vigour and truth of life in those stories in which, with the sensibility of an artist, he depicted the patriarchal life of the Croatian nobility. His stories show him to be, not so much a preacher and critic, as the poet of a vanished period in which he, nevertheless, found beauty. His earliest stories *(Pod starim krovovima, Iz varmedjinskih dana)* are his best.

Janko Leskovar (Valentinovo, 1861—1949) was born in the same part of Croatia as Kovačić and Djalski. He was the last of the Croatian realistic story-writers. He worked as a schoolmaster in many parts of the country, but after retiring he went back to his native region, to his family estate.

Like Djalski, Leskovar began his literary career in mature manhood. Having published a number of stories and two novels *(Propali dvori* — Ruined mansions — 1896; *Sjene ljubavi* — Shadows of love — 1898), he gave up writing.

Leskovar portrayed the Croatian junior government employees and schoolmasters, who were persecuted by the authorities and harassed by poverty. On the other hand, like Djalski, he also wrote about the Croatian nobility in its economic decline. But he was concerned, not so much with economic problems, as he was with presenting his characters in relation to the perpetual problems of man and eternity, sin and punishment, man and woman. He was less concerned with the turbulent events of the day than he was with the psychology of his characters. In analyzing apparently insignificant psychical manifestations, he sought to investigate those problems which bear on man's happiness or unhappiness. His heroes are deeply sensitive, and suffer because of their sins. They live their lives, not so much in action, as in self-analysis. Hence their inertness; hence also the concern with ethics and the pessimistic note in Leskovar's works, for sins are never forgiven.

In view of his subject-matter, the realists regarded Leskovar as one of themselves, while the modernists of the late nineteenth century regarded him as their predecessor and as belonging to their own ranks, for he had attained the goal to which they themselves aspired: psychological analysis, man in relation to eternal problems.

Josip Kozarac (Vinkovci, 1858 — Koprivnica, 1906), an outstanding realist, came from Slavonia, the most prosperous part of Croatia. Having studied forestry in Vienna, he was employed as a specialist in many parts of Slavonia till his death.

Kozarac's first essays in literature were verses and romantic stories. Then he turned to writing comedies, in which, in the style of Molière, he depicted types from Slavonia, or composed superficial plots based on love and money. These pieces contained neither art nor real life. While studying forestry, he also devoted himself earnestly to reading works on economics and sociology. Having lived for years in the Slavonian countryside as a practical worker, with few books to hand, he described the world as he saw it.

Kozarac published his first realist story in 1887, and with it he established himself as a mature artist. After his initial triumph, he published story after story *(Tena; Proletarci* — The proletaries; *Slavonska šuma* — The Slavonian woods; *Tri dana kod Sina* — Three days at my son's; *Rodu u pohode* — A visit to my relatives; *Krčelići neće lepote* — The Krčelići want no beauty; *Mira Kodolićeva; Oprava* — The dress; *Tri ljubavi* — Three loves). He also wrote two novels: *Mrtvi kapitali* [Dead capitals] (1889), *Medju svijetlom i tminom* [Between light and darkness] (1891).

Calm, measured, almost without lyricism, Kozarac presented his region in both his shorter and longer works as he had grown to know it during one of its most important periods.

Capitalism had penetrated rapidly into Slavonia. The region, rich in ancient forests, was flooded by aliens to exploit its wealth and the cheap labour of the Slavonians as speedily as possible. Having plenty of money, they were able to purchase whatever they sought: both forests and wives. The crashing of the old tree-trunks and the disintegration of the cooperatives were accompanied by the disappearance of the old morality. New requirements and new desires sprang up, including the desire for easy living; the influx of the population into the towns mounted, impoverishment increased rapidly.

Kozarac reviewed with an observant eye this economic and moral process. He depicted the Slavonian, sound in body and mind, but often lazy, who allowed his estate to waste away. He described the Slavonian woman, beautiful and sensual, whom either weakness or extravagance forced from the road of honour. He portrayed the Slavonian intellectual of peasant origin, who vaccilated between adherence to the bureaucratic pseudo-gentry and the need to advance Slavonia economically. He observed the gap between peasant parents and their children, who were educated at higher schools without becoming any happier. He observed the rabble who, without a thought for the future, gathered around the sumptuous tables of the foreigners and flared up for a moment in false brilliancy. In his novels *Mrtvi kapitali* and *Medju svijetlom i tminom* he endeavoured to give a clear picture of Slavonia and the result of his studies, advising a return to the soil and economic advancement, instead of flight from it.

In most of his stories Kozarac showed himself to be an economist and sociologist rather than an artist; nevertheless his artistic abilities are indisputable. Without seeking for literary effect, without falling into literary sentimentality, without inventing tense plots, Kozarac presented his observations and shaped his characters conscientiously and succinctly. At heart he was less a rationalist than a tender man who felt the poetry of the woods, the beauty of youth and love, the superiority of feeling over cold reason. At the same time, he was tragically aware of the laws to which man must submit even in his most intimate sentiments of love. From an analyst of society and a painter of nature he gradually became a psychologist, a painter of human souls *(Oprava)*.

Of all the Croatian realists, Kozarac was the least productive, with the least number of distinctively literary features, yet the most realistic and the most concise. Several of his stories *(Tena, Tri dana kod sina, Slavonska šuma)*, with their excellent psychological picture of economic and moral decline, with their perfect descriptions of social conditions during the transition from one economic system to another, and with their clear, forceful pictures of nature, rank among the best Croatian stories of their kind.

Apart from Djalski, the most prolific Croatian realistic narrator was *Vjenceslav Novak* (1859—1905). Of petty bourgeois origin, born at Senj, in the Croatian Littoral, Novak was first a schoolmaster, then a music teacher in the Conservatorium in Zagreb, where he also died. He published his first book in 1881, which is a romantic account of battles between the Bosnian Turks and Christians, which he had never seen, and fought in a region with which he was not familiar. But soon dropping this method of work, he endeavoured in his later stories and novels to describe realistically the world in which he lived. In the course of more than twenty years he filled the Croatian magazines with short stories and published book after book. His most important are *Pavao Šegota* (1888), *Podgorske pripovijetke* [Tales from Podgora] (1889), *Pod Nehajem* [Beneath Nehaj] (1892), *Podgorka* [The Podgora woman] (1894), *Nikola Baretić* (1896), *Dvije pripovijesti* [Two tales] (1897), *Poslednji Stipančići* [The last of the Stipančići] (1899), *Dva svijeta* [Two worlds] (1901), *Zapreke* [Obstacles] (1905). The novel *Tito Dorčić* was published after his death (1906).

Like the other Croatian writers, Novak also wrote stories and novels about his birth-place (Senj) and its surroundings. He presented the Senj of the nineteenth century, with the gradual decline of its patrician families, with the changes in commercial routes, with the domestic life of its small merchants, housewives, clergymen, pupils. Parallel with this, he described Podgorje, an extremely poor region south of Senj, in which begging was a profession, with its

178

own perculiar notions of morality, with the struggle it waged against poverty and adversity.

With his horizon broadened by visits to Prague and Zagreb, Novak gradually expanded the scope of his stories, entering more deeply into the problems they dealt with as he did so. He showed how young Croats in big cities suffered through inexperience, poverty and illness. He observed his fellow countrymen from the Littoral in various intellectual professions, and their reaction to the political and cultural conditions in Croatia. He presented the Croatian artist in his struggle with petty bourgeois surroundings *(Dva svijeta)*, the hardships and duties of the village priest *(Zapreke)*, the fate of the children of peasants and craftsmen at school and among the townspeople *(Tito Dorčić)*.

Being of petty bourgeois origin himself, during his most mature period of writing Novak mostly portrayed the bourgeoisie and petty bourgeoisie. Small clerks, merchants, priests, gendarmes, teachers, pupils, servants, chamber-maids, with their views and desires, hardships and tragedies, such as every social group has, alternate in his works. He observed everyday life with almost photographic fidelity, and he presented his scenes without polish, in the endeavour to reach down to the depths of the human element in them.

Novak was not only the best portrayer of the Croatian petty bourgeoisie — he was also its poet and its critic. He spoke with unconcealed affection of the petty bourgeois way of life, of petty bourgeois morals of saving and gaining. But he was also ruthless in condemning its faults: petty bourgeois narrow-mindedness, suspicion of higher cultural attainments, pretensions to fashion, desire for extravagance. Some of his novels and stories are a most vehement condemnation of the petty bourgeoisie, which with its narrow outlook and self-interest destroyed every stimulus and everything that was not profit-bearing.

From a portrayer of the bourgeoisie Novak gradually became a poet of the poor. In his stories and sketches he presented the town poor, the manual and intellectual workers, the inhabitants of the slums and cellars of Zagreb, the fate of the beggar school-boy, etc. In these stories he did not instruct and upbraid so much as reveal the human wretchedness he knew. He found words of forgiveness for the offences of the poor, and branded the social order which had made such misery possible. Novak was, in fact, the first Croatian story-writer to give scenes from the life of the workers, the unhappy creatures who frequented stuffy wine-shops and slept in garrets.

Vjenceslav Novak's entire art, which began as purely national romanticism, and continued by picturing and criticizing the bourgeoisie, developed into a means of exposing the life of the most neglected members of society. It became a voice of protest against the capitalistic system, in which a negligible minority ruthlessly oppressed the overwhelming majority.

Novak was an extremely keen observer. He used the method of some European writers in noting down incidents which could later be used as a framework for his stories and novels. He holds first place in Croatian realistic literature for his wealth of material, and by reason of the multitude of problems with which he dealt. But owing to the rapidity with which he wrote and to his illness, his works often seem to be hardly more than sketches. He was an indisputable artist when he described human misery, the psychology of the suffering and downtrodden. Several of his stories of this type *(Iz velegradskog podzemlja* — From the city underground; *U glib* — In the mud; *Janica)* are significant, not just as pictures, but as works of art which occupy a place in the anthologies of Croatian stories.

The most outstanding writer in Croatian lyrics directly after Šenoa's death was *August Harambašić* (Donji Miholjac, 1861 — Stenjevac, 1911). In his poems *(Slobodarke* — Songs of freedom — 1883) he sang of the freedom-loving spirit of the Croats, of their revolutionary struggles against their oppressors in Vienna and Budapest. His fiery utterances reflected the bitterness which had been aroused in the best men in Croatia by the decline of the Croatian people. Following in the footsteps of the Serbian poets Jovanović-Zmaj and Jakšić, and imitating the folk poem, he made Croatian verse lighter, more supple, more orderly; but as he became interested in politics, his lyrics fell to the level of journalism, and he soon ceased to write.

During the years of Harambašić's retirement from serious literature, *Silvije Strahimir Kranjčević* (1865—1908) was steadily rising. He was also born at Senj. His father was a junior clerk. Failing in his matriculation, Kranjčević took up the study of theology, for which he had no inclination. He abandoned his studies and went to Zagreb, where he attended a course for school teachers, and as a schoolmaster he was sent to Bosnia. He was frequently transferred from one small town to another. He reached the peak of his career in Sarajevo as the headmaster of the commercial school. He died after a protracted and painful illness at the height of his literary work.

Kranjčević published his first collection of poems, *Bugarkinje* [Bugarštice], in 1885. Although it is permeated by pathos like Šenoa's, it contains some new notes of an especially social character. Later Kranjčević became a contributor to the foremost Croatian literary journals. During his lifetime he published two more collections of poems: *Izabrane pjesme* [Selected poems] (1898), *Trzaji* [Spasms] (1902). He did not live to see the publication of his last book, *Pjesme* [Poems]. He also wrote some prose, which was collected after his death in a book entitled *Pjesnička proza* [Poetic prose]. He edited the Sarajevo literary paper *Nada* for many years.

Through Kranjčević's veins coursed the blood of his ancestors who had fought for centuries against the Turks and Venice, and had never let their rebellious spirit be broken. Like his generation, he also dreamt of national freedom, hating his Vienna and Budapest oppressors, and got to know Croatian socialism in the making. He spent the years of his young manhood in Croatia, under the reign of Khuen Hederváry, and the rest of his life in Bòsnia, which the Austrians had sought to reduce to a subservient province irrespective of the feelings of the Serbian and Croatian population. Although he cultivated his literary taste upon the works of August Šenoa, he endeavoured all his life to enhance his literary culture by reading the works of world writers.

During the period of his full creative powers, Kranjčević's poetry derived from the realization that the world was harsh and unjust. Kranjčević was primarily a poet of national, social and cultural freedom. He fought against all those who suppressed these freedoms. He was a bitter opponent of the national oppressors of Croatia, and equally an opponent of the hollow rhetorical patriotism customary in Croatian politics. He drew attention to the economic background of Croatian life, to the poverty and wretchedness of the Croats. He sang of the misery of the landless, of the ruthlessness of the strong. He thundered against sycophants and careerists. He rose against the official Church, which subjugated and exploited the weak in the name of Christianity.

No matter what he sang about, Kranjčević was always a poet of justice, freedom, of the broadest human views. He expressed his emotions with rapture and warmth, with tears and imprecations, in prayer. From his whole art there emanates that profound human pain which comes from the realization of the anguish the human being must suffer. He was, therefore, not merely a poet, but the preacher of a better, finer order in the world.

From criticizing human relations Kranjčević went on to criticize general universal relations, his anguish becoming thus cosmic in its proportions. From a poetic critic and prophet he became an artist who represented the sufferings of the whole of mankind. He drew attention to the disharmony between emotion and reality, between human aspirations and the prospect of their fulfilment. In the name of suffering humanity he equally criticized the universal order in which an inexplicable force inexorably crushed the fruits of men's labours. From an artist whose works pointed to the deformities in human society Kranjčević became a thinker who exposed the deformities in nature itself with bitterness and indignation.

Although often overwhelmed with bitter anguish, and driven to sarcasm, Kranjčević's was not a poetry of absolute hopelessness. It always contained hope of something better, something brighter. Kranjčević believed in the value of work and of the worker; and because of this the progressive people in Croatia always regarded him as their poet.

Kranjčević was an artist with a strong inner life. He expressed himself better than anyone else in nineteenth-century Croatian literature. He perfected Croatian poetic expression to a greater extent than anyone else, availing himself of the achievements of August Šenoa and August Harambašić, and of Djura Jakšić and Vojislav Ilić in Serbian literature. No one before him was capable of exploiting the powers of the Croatian language to the extent he did. Tender feelings of calm in his works alternate with strong cries of protest. He was capable of conjuring up the coldness of lonely winter evenings, the cheerful moods of spring, the idyll of happiness on the stony shores of his birth-place. He was capable no less of widely embracing the whole of the universe. Although traces of the influence referred to are evident in his poetry, he created a style of his own, completely personal.

Owing to the conditions in which he lived, and to internal unrest, it is possible to detect traces of incoherence in Kranjčević's poetry. His poems rarely contain complete internal harmony, they are hardly ever tuned to a single key. They are characteristic of inferences, allusions. They often contain irony and sarcasm, the sting of which was best felt by the poet himself. Many of Kranjčević's poems are horrifying, gloomy, rambling monologues, with obscure passages proceeding from moments in which the pictures of the imagination are indistinct and its workings unfold at the edge of consciousness.

Kranjčević was extolled during his lifetime by the progressive Croats, and disparaged by the reactionaries, the backward, the mystics who, after his death, exposed the aesthetic shortcomings in his poems. Although the greater part of Kranjčević's verse is the product of forced effort, he is, nevertheless, the author of ten or fifteen poems which rank among the best in Croatian literature. In the perfect balance of subject-matter and expression they are the profoundest revelation of the relations of the individual towards the nation, society, the universe, and of his personal emotions of suffering, solitude, distress. These qualities put Kranjčević among the most brilliant Croatian minds, who — even at the cost of tribulation and sacrifice — directed the Croatian nation to the roads of struggle, justice and freedom.

182

3. SLOVENE REALISM

Among the Slovenes, realism evolved side by side with the realism of the Serbs and Croats. Both their theoretical foundations and their literary paragons were the same: the Russian and French realists. But in Slovene literature, cultural policy was more important than trend: the point was whether the Old Slovenes or the Young Slovenes should lead the people.

The Slovene people were still divided in various provinces: Krain, Styria, Carinthia and Istria, with their provincial autonomies, while the central government was in Vienna. In these provinces the German and Italian minorities succeeded in holding almost all power, while the Slovene peasants remained disfranchized. Besides this, the secondary-school system being German, Slovene was only one more subject. The Slovenes who wanted to attend higher schools, were compelled to go to the German centres of culture, to Vienna or Graz. As usual, many Slovene intellectuals lived in these towns as employees, the result being that apart from Ljubljana, these towns were also, in a manner, centres of Slovene culture up to the disintegration of Austria-Hungary.

The economic and social development of Austria-Hungary, with the strengthening of capitalism, spread also to the Slovene regions. Of all the Yugoslav areas, Krain with its iron-mills and coal-mines was industrially the most advanced. The mills and mines were of much older foundation, but only during the eighties of the nineteenth century did they acquire full importance. Krain, in addition, had a chemical and a glass industry. Neither the capital nor the management was of Slovene origin. The Slovenes supplied the labour, which was poorly paid, and the men were forced to work in difficult conditions.

The capitalistic system, with growing industrial production, penetrated even to minor localities, in which it destroyed the old-fashioned handicraft workshops. Increasing numbers of small artisans, farmers and workers were unable to earn their living in their own country, and had to leave for Croatia, Bosnia, America, where they were employed at the hardest jobs, as timber workers, miners, servants.

The number of lay intellectuals of Slovene origin steadily multiplied during the eighties. For opportunistic reasons some of them joined the typical German-Slovene bourgeoisie of the Slovene towns or the clerical elements, who were still strong. But the majority espoused the cause of the Young Slovenes. During the last twenty years of the nineteenth century they comprised a sizable group, which fought for positions in society and for predominance in politics. They consolidated especially in literature, in which they had always been the strongest. They fought, not so much for a literary trend, as they did for a world outlook. Liberal by conviction, they strove to weaken the hold of the Church on the peasantry, to spread free thought and democracy.

As a result, there were many discrepancies in the cultural life of the Slovenes. There were among the Slovenes some who spoke and wrote of progress and patriotism; but their main goal was to approach the German liberal bourgeoisie in way of life. The men of the Church, on the contrary, ideologically conservative as they were, were cleverer in maintaining contact with the peasantry and in tightening their grip on it. There were public men who spoke frankly about science and free thinking, and regarded themselves as the protagonists of progress. But they left contact with reality to others. On the contrary, the Slovene conservatives, particularly the militant ecclesiastical figures of the eighties, took the offensive against the Young Slovenes. It was from their militant Catholic platform that they regarded all the cultural and political manifestations of the Slovene people. They sharply criticized everything that resembled liberalism and religious tolerance. The most persistent in this struggle was Anton Mahnič, a theologian. The clashes between the liberals and conservatives were extremely bitter. They dictated the tone to the entire political and spiritual life of the Slovenes.

In Krain and Styria society continued to be led by representatives of the nobility who still possessed property, and by the highest class of the bourgeoisie. Indeed, they possessed castles and land in Slovenia, to which they repaired only in the summer time, and even then they kept aloof from the Slovene language, customs and way of life: in the main, they felt German. The rest of the year they lived in Vienna.

The petty bourgeoisie and the intellectuals of Slovene origin, often the children of peasants, — whose first generation was still unable to accustom itself to bourgeois and aristocratic society — vaccilated between the nobility and peasantry. The offshoot were a special type who were Slovenes by descent, but Germans by political conviction.

The struggle of the Young Slovenes was of particular political and cultural significance, because the Old Slovenes compromised with the authorities and the German political parties to further the ecclesiastical interests. Liberalism, positivism, faith in science, anti-clericalism, and such principles became both political and cultural slogans. The conditions grew even more involved as controversies broke out among the Young Slovenes themselves.

In spite of all this, progress was clearly visible in the cultural field among the Slovene people during the closing decades of the nineteenth century. Increasing numbers of children from the towns and villages went to high school, though often at the cost of severe privation. The result was that more and more people among the townsfolk took to reading, which went to increase the demand for printed books and magazines. Continuing Stritar's and Levstik's efforts, the liberal Slovenes founded the magazine *Ljubljanski zvon* in Ljubljana in 1881. Under the editorship of Fran Levec it reached a considerable literary level. The conservative writers, meanwhile, launched their own journal, *Dom in svet*, in 1888. In literary matters there were seldom any disputes between them; indeed, some writers even contributed to both magazines.

The period of realism produced two writers of considerable stature in Slovene literature: Janko Kersnik and Anton Aškerc. Their leading contemporary was Ivan Tavčar, the writer of short stories.

Unlike the majority of the Slovene writers, who were of peasant origin, *Janko Kersnik* (1852—1897) was the son of a wealthy landowner from Brdo near Lunovica, and a notary. Like most Slovene intellectuals, he also had studied law in Vienna and Graz, where he enlarged his knowledge of letters. He died in Ljubljana.

In a way Kersnik carried on the tradition of Josip Jurčič as a narrator; moreover he completed one of Jurčič's unfinished novels. He continued Jurčič's story-writing with a realistic trend. He was the most faithful contributor to *Ljubljanski zvon* for many years. In it, as well as separately, he published several novels: *Na žerinjah* [At Žerinje] (1876), *Cyclamen* (1883), *Agitator* [The agitator] (1885), *Jara gospoda* [The upstarts] (1893), and a number of stories *(Kmetiške slike* — Country scenes; *Lutrski ljudje* — The Lutherans).

Kersnik described the process which was taking place in Slovene society before his very eyes: among the nobility, bourgeoisie and peasantry. His characters are aristocrats of foreign descent who possess land in Krain, but live most of their life in Austria, speak German, and only occasionally stoop to approach the Slovenes personally. In some of his works he describes political life among the Slovenes, with the opportunistic Old Slovenes, whose deputies in Parliament are aliens, who proclaim themselves Slovenes out of self-interest, although they are Germans in attitude and mentality. His most frequent characters are intellectuals of peasant descent who occupy various official posts, their dilemma consequently being whether they should ingratiate themselves with the section in power or be loyal to their origin. The settings of his story and novel are the small Slovene towns and the castles of the nobility, where the representatives of conflicting classes in ferment meet for varied periods of time, clashes, friction, complications being the outcome.

A considerable place in Kersnik's narrative is occupied by stories of the country. Kersnik gathered his experience of the peasantry in his official capacity. He describes peasant disputes which lead to law suits, the ruin of peasant estates owing to legal quibbles, the suffering of innocent peasants owing to the stubbornness and formalism of the juridical authorities, peasant niggardliness, obstinacy, and hatred between relatives.

The plots of his novels and stories often place Kersnik closer to romanticism than to realism. He recounts unhappy love affairs between members of different classes, which usually end tragically, the hero and heroine being the victims of petty misunderstandings or of the callousness of their families. Occasionally the cause of separation between the young couple is a secret which is discovered too late, when nothing can be done to clear up the misunderstanding. In general Kersnik worked out his plot laboriously; and he often borrowed his denouement from foreign examples.

Kersnik was a keen observer, an able analyst, with the courage to present life as he saw it. His picture of the early generations of the Slovene bourgeoisie is by no means encouraging. He revealed the ideological tergiversation, the petty scheming, the intriguing and the opportunism of the average Slovene intellectual who had just emerged from the ranks of the peasantry. Except when he strove to interest his readers in the intricacy of his plot, he was a keen critic and observer, especially when he depicted civil servants, peasants, and the nouveaux riches (*Jara gospoda*). He introduced witty dialogue into the Slovene story, and amusing descriptions of meetings and excursions of Slovene intellectuals. It was he who first introduced the intellectual woman into Slovene literature. Although Kersnik was not as gifted a narrator as Jurčič, as a discerning thinker and conscientious writer he produced a number of highly successful, truthful and touching pictures of the Slovenes towards the end of the nineteenth century (*Jara gospoda* and *Kmetiške slike*).

Anton Aškerc (1856–1912) experienced a literary fate similar to that of Gregorčič. He came of a poor peasant family from Globoko near Rimske Toplice, and joined the priesthood. He distinguished himself by publishing verse in *Ljubljanski zvon* under the nom de plume of Gorazd. It was at this moment that Anton Mahnič first attacked him. Following the publication of his *Balade in romance* [Ballads and romances] (1890) the attacks intensified in bitterness. Like Gregorčič before him, he did not expect them; but once they came, he took up the challenge, gradually drawing away from the men of the Church and Catholicism, and approaching the Young Slovenes, the liberals, defending religious tolerance, free thought, liberalism, and fighting against dogmatic Catholicism. In this struggle he dropped his clerical profession and became a keeper of the archives in Ljubljana. For many years he was the most distinguished representative of anti-clerical trends among the Slovenes. He was for a long period editor of *Ljubljanski zvon*, and one of the most influential Slovene writers. He was also widely travelled. He died in Ljubljana.

Aškerc's first essays in literature were lyric poems. He was not a gentle and sentimental nature like Gregorčič, but a fighting spirit. As he was wont to say, his muse was not a pale-faced lady but a belligerent Amazon. Unlike Stritar, he refused to sing about universal pain; rather he extolled industry and resistance. In this way he became the most eloquent interpreter of Slovene bourgeois liberalism towards the end of the nineteenth century. At the same time he was deeply patriotic and charitable. His poetry is pervaded by protest against the degrading position of the Slovenes and the Slavs generally. It is imbued with longing for freedom, justice, equality. Affected by the social conditions of his time, and by the worsening situation of the workers and peasants, Aškerc demanded social justice and the exposure of the injustices caused by the rich and mighty.

Aškerc's supple expression, the ease with which he wrote, the progressive ideas which he championed, and his realism soon won him popularity among the liberal Slovenes. In their eyes he was the greatest of Slovene poets, a philosopher, the leader and teacher of his people. The conservatives, however, redoubled their attacks against him.

Aškerc was a prolific writer. Following his first book, he published collection after collection of lyric and epic poems and travel sketches *(Lirske in epske poezije* — Lyric and epic poetry — 1896; *Nove poezije* — New poetry — 1900; *Četvrti zbornik poezije* — The fourth collection of poetry — 1904; *Zlatorog* — The golden horn — 1904; *Primož Trubar,* 1905; *Mučeniki* — The martyrs — 1906; *Junaki* — Heroes — 1907, etc.).

Aškerc was an epic poet rather than a lyrist. Consequently he gradually devoted himself to ballads and romances. He published extensive epics describing the religious struggles and persecution of the Slovenes during the Reformation *(Primož Trubar, Mučeniki)*. For his ballads and romances he took material from Slovene history, from the period of the Yugoslav peasant rebellions, from the wars with the Turks, from the history of the Croats and Slavs generally. He had an especial foundness for Oriental motifs and characters.

As he recounted Slovene history and the past of the Slavs, Aškerc presented such characters as he was able to connect to some extent with the current problems of his day. He called for unity among the Slavs; he revealed their magnificence and their decline; he extolled their successes in battle against the Turks. Portraying his own times, on the other hand, he set forth the conflicts between the mighty and the rich, the callousness of the wealthy, the suffering of innocent village girls because of their innocence or the duplicity of city men.

Aškerc's poems with Oriental motifs, particularly his parables, contain a topical trend. He often cloaked the Slovenes of his day in oriental disguise. These poems were designed to arouse the reader's interest in immediate things through tales of foreign lands. In this way Aškerc was able to touch upon relations between the Slovene people and the ruling circles in Vienna, towards the Church, the wealthy. He wrote of the innocent rejoicings of the people at any change of government, although even worse oppression was to follow. He depicted Oriental rulers, who under the guise of wanting to remove the wretchedness of the people intensified their oppression. He dwelt upon the inability of the average Slovene to help himself instead of waiting for help from others. Many of Aškerc's poems contain the ideology of the Slovene liberals of the late nineteenth century, with their faith in the power of thought, with their hatred of superstition and of the reactionary tendencies of the churchmen.

As he advanced in years, Aškerc became more productive; but, while it must be admitted that he demonstrated extreme skill, he evinced little creative strength. About 1900 the younger generation who had grown in his shadow regarded him as out-of-date, and demanded art and not rhetorics in literature. Aškerc's fate was in a way like Stritar's: first came fame, then came oblivion. Nevertheless Aškerc's importance lies in the fact that he perfected the Slovene poetical mode of expression, and that, at least during the earlier period of his work, he wrote a large number of ballads in which he foretold the destiny of the Slovenes, the destiny of the Slavs, and of mankind in general.

Besides Kersnik, there appeared among the Slovenes during the eighties a number of writers who described in their own different ways various aspects of Slovene life (Fran Detela, Janez Mencinger).

The most fruitful among them was *Ivan Tavčar* (1851—1923), the son of poor peasants, and in later life a distinguished lawyer and political figure. In cultural and social significance he was the most distinctive leader of the Young Slovene movement during the phase in which it was the party of the Slovene liberal bourgeoisie. In addition to his varied professional and political work, Tavčar occupied himself with literature.

Tavčar published his first compositions (the stories *Donna Clara; Povest v kleti* — The story in the cellar; *Antonio Gledjević*) during his school-days, and continued to write stories after becoming a lawyer (*Med gorami* — Among the hills; *Vita vitae meae; Ivan Slavelj; Ivan Solnce; Grajski prior* — The palace chaplain; *V Zali* — In Zala). In addition to his stories, short and long, he ventured into the field of novel writing *(Mrtva srca* — Dead hearts). His longest work is his historical novel *Izza kongresa* [After the congress] (1906—7), describing men and events in connexion with the congress held in Ljubljana in 1821. His last works are the long story *Cvetje v jeseni* [Flowers in the autumn] (1917) and the historical novel *Visoška kronika* [The chronicles of Visoko] (1919).

Tavčar was not as profound a literary erudite as Stritar; besides this, he was able to devote only a part of his time to writing. This fact, as well as his political and social activities, reflected upon his literary work.

In most of his stories Tavčar strove to be merely a narrator. He composed tense stories of love hampered by almost insurmountable obstacles, and endeavoured to produce original denouements. Although from the country, he generally wrote of the aristocracy — that section of society which ruled the Slovenes, but was not closely related to them. His longest novel, *Izza kongresa*, does not describe men and times so much as it does love affairs in a small town which has suddenly been inundated by many distinguished personages (Prince Metternich and others). For these reasons he has been described as a romanticist.

In a considerable number of his stories and novels *(Vita vitae meae, Visoška kronika)* Tavčar depicted the Slovene past, especially the period when the nation was divided into two hostile camps in the struggle for Protestantism and against it. Alluding to the conditions of his time, with an eye to militant clericalism, he described brother fighting brother, the one ruthlessly destroying the life and property of the other. Although his sympathies were clearly on the side of the Protestants, he endeavoured to be unbiased. He held his clerical opponents, especially Mahnič, up to ridicule in his Utopian novel, *"4000"*.

Notwithstanding his social rise, Tavčar remained deeply attached to the Slovene countryside. He portrayed the Slovene peasants of his native region in a series of sketches in *Med gorami*. He went even further in this direction in *Cvetje v jeseni*, placing the Slovene peasants above all the other Slovene social strata. The last, and the best of Tavčar's works, *Visoška kronika*, is a synthesis of all his literary endeavours, and the peak of his artistic abilities. The work is distinguished by calm and fluent narration, by the working out of the characters and figures in high relief, by the clear light in which it presents Slovene history. The novel describes the religious struggles during the period of the Reformation, the social conditions among the Slovenes in view of relations towards the nobility and clergy. It brings out the positive side of the Slovene peasant, as well as the negative, but with the realization that it is just this peasant, steadfast, patient and hard-working, that is the soul of the Slovene people.

189

CHAPTER EIGHT

THE TWENTIETH CENTURY

FACING EUROPE

The movements which appeared in literature and art in Western Europe at the end of the nineteenth century in the form of neoromanticism, neoidealism, symbolism, decadence, modernism, etc. influenced Yugoslav literature by devious channels, either parallel with developments in Western Europe or later.

The position of the Yugoslav peoples, particularly that of the Yugoslavs in Austria-Hungary, compelled their political representatives to revise their relation towards the Dual Monarchy. The Slavic nations and the Yugoslavs were beginning to realize that if they wished to resist Vienna and Budapest, they must close their ranks. In Croatia a policy of Serbo-Croatian unity was continually pursued, while in the Austrian part of the Dual Monarchy, the representatives of the Croats, Slovenes and Serbs advanced their views with increasing unanimity. Owing to the worsening conditions, the idea of unification soon took the place of unity. All these manifestations left their mark on literature, on cooperation between Serbian, Croatian and Slovene writers in magazines and on their meetings; and tended to lessen the differences which distinguished the three languages, and to familiarize the three nations with one another's literature.

i. SERBIA AT THE BEGINNING OF THE TWENTIETH CENTURY; WESTERN TRENDS IN SERBIAN LITERATURE

The social and economic developments predicted by Svetozar Marković towards the end of the sixties of the nineteenth century had taken place by the end of it. Capitalism in its rapid advance had overrun the old social system. Whereas Serbia was still a patriarchal agricultural country during the middle of the nineteenth century, without factories or transport facilities, towards the end of the century it already had railways, a number of factories and a lively trade, and a distinctively Serbian bourgeoisie had firmly established itself. The development of capitalism in Serbia was rapid and visible: banks were founded, mansions sprouted up beside the miserable hovels that still stood even in the larger towns. Thus, the picture which presented itself to the passer-by was a symbol of the whole of Serbia: on one side was the bourgeoisie with its West-European way of life, on the other was the wretched Serbian village.

The process was accelerated during the twentieth century. The gap between the bourgeoisie and the working masses widened. The Serbian socialist movement strengthened, and even the Serbian peasants sought support from the political parties, which promised to remedy their economic condition.

Following the death of the last of the Obrenovićs in 1903, the throne devolved upon the house of Karadjordjević in the person of King Peter. The chief supporter of the monarchy was now the Radical party, which had been persecuted till then. Ruling almost continually, either alone or in coalition with others, the Radicals came to be a distinctively bourgeois party, representing a class which was thriving in the capitalistic conditions. The other parties also evolved in a similar direction.

Serbia made conspicuous headway in its economic and technical development during the first ten years of the twentieth century. The dismal, pessimistic mood of the Serbs of the late nineteenth century, expressed to some extent in the poetry of Vojislav Ilić, slowly made room for a brighter attitude. Cultural activity gained considerable momentum towards the turn of the century. The High School of Belgrade was raised to university rank in 1905; and as in the past, many young Serbs went abroad to receive an education, mostly in France and England, and no longer in Russia and Germany. They introduced West-European views and ways of life in their country; they were an intellectual cadre with the highest qualifications, and they formed the connecting link between Serbia and the West.

Economic, technical and cultural progress placed Serbia in a position to surmount many dangers, and prepared it for the events that were to come. In 1908 it survived the crisis which Austria-Hungary provoked by annexing Bosnia and Herzegovina after occupying that region for thirty years. In 1912 Serbia, with its Balkan allies Bulgaria, Greece and Montenegro, attacked Turkey and in a victorious war liberated the subjugated Serbs and Macedonians, and regained the territory once belonging to medieval Serbia.

Serbia's prestige grew steadily after 1908, and the more progressive and militant Yugoslavs in Austria-Hungary now began to regard it as the core of their future common State.

The Serbs of Bosnia and Herzegovina, who became the legal subjects of Austria-Hungary after 1908, endeavoured to adapt themselves to the new conditions. The country was still organized on feudalistic lines, Moslem beys being the landowners. The Serbian bourgeoisie was prospering, and endeavoured to find common ground for cooperation with the authorities. Serbian literary magazines were also founded in Bosnia and Herzegovina (*Zora* — Dawn — at Mostar; *Bosanska vila* — The Bosnian fairy — at Sarajevo). Only a small Serbian party, headed by Petar Kočić, regarded Austria as explicitly hostile, and adjusted its tactics accordingly.

As in economy and politics, the main goal in the Serbian literature of the early twentieth century was to attain the level of the cultural life of Western Europe. Whereas the models for the Serbian writers during the period of realism were the Russians, towards the end of the nineteenth and early in the twentieth century the young educated Serbs looked towards France.

Serbian cultural life was transformed by the young intellectuals trained in Western Europe. This transformation began during the nineties with the foundation of the magazine *Srpski pregled* [The Serbian review] (1895). It was consummated during the twentieth century with the foundation of the magazine *Srpski književni glasnik* [The Serbian literary herald] (1901) by Bogdan Popović. *Srpski pregled* sought to alter the very trends towards which Serbian literature had been proceeding. Its chief spokesman, Bogdan Popović, proclaimed that every literature should follow some model; if the model is lacking at home, it must be sought abroad.

The models followed by most of the Serbian writers of the late nineteenth and early twentieth century were no longer the folk poem, Jovan Jovanović-Zmaj and Vojislav Ilić, but the French writers, particularly the Parnassians and the symbolists. Western influence on Serbian literature was intensified especially during the period when *Srpski književni glasnik* was edited by Jovan Skerlić, a socialist and rationalist. An excellent and productive writer, with a feeling for literary values, he was the leading figure in Serbian literature for almost ten years; and during his time he suppressed the vestiges of romanticism, built the reputation of some and ruined the reputation of others.

The transformation in Serbian literature was sudden and definitive. Whereas all literary tyros copied Vojislav Ilić's style during the nineties, at the beginning of the twentieth century almost everyone who hoped to make a name in literature renounced his former beginnings, and took to emulating French writers in subject-matter and mode of expression.

Literature in Serbia was brought into proximity with the literature of Western Europe without any serious upheaval, which was not the case in Croatia or Slovenia. The reason was that the representatives of western trends in Serbia, the young Serbian bourgeoisie, held every position of importance in the editorial offices, schools and literary institutions. Bogdan Popović, for example, had been a professor of comparative literature for ten years; his brother Pavle was a professor of Yugoslav literature, while Jovan Skerlić was a professor of Serbian literature. Thus they were in the best of positions to make their influence felt: Bogdan Popović's university lectures were the last word in science; Jovan Skerlić's brief notes in *Srpski književni glasnik* were the acme of judgment.

Writers who were opposed to western influence, who favoured romanticism and national poetry, gathered in remote coffee houses, where they protested helplessly against the omnipotence of the bourgeois literature as delivered from the Chair. Their literary magazines were short-lived; their weakness lay in that their opponents were superior to them even as theorists.

Lyricism and story-writing, and especially literary criticism were prominent in Serbian literature at the turn of the century.

Since Vuk Karadžić there have always been literary critics among the Serbs. None of them, however, held criticism to be their chief literary pursuit. As an independent literary category, however, criticism developed in Serbian literature only with the coming of Ljubomir Nedić, and even more so with the writings of Bogdan Popović and Jovan Skerlić.

The initiator of *Srpski pregled, Ljubomir Nedić* (1859—1902). a student of philosophy at German universities, by mercilessly analyzing the works of some Serbian writers in his literary reviews *Iz novije srpske lirike* [From later Serbian lyrics] (1893) and *Noviji srpski pisci* [Later Serbian writers] (1901) drew attention to the want of logic, to the artificiality and to the vagueness in the works of some Serbian writers, including the most outstanding (for example Zmaj, Kostić, Lazarević). He wrote clearly, logically, rounding off his thoughts, and with conviction, although there is no doubt that his conclusions were often unjust, for he was a conservative, and was not endowed with an innate feeling for art.

Bogdan Popović (1863—1944), from Belgrade, wrote relatively little. He dealt more with foreign than with Yugoslav writers. His principal works are *Ogledi* [Essays] (1927), *Bomarše* [Beaumarchais] (1925), *Članci i predavanja* [Articles and lectures] (1932). He spoke on literature, painting, music, drama, general aesthetic matters. His criticism was concentrated on the analyzing of style and composition: he asked "how" rather than "what". Nevertheless in his work *Bomarše*, he presented the revolutionary social significance of the French writer. He was punctilious and weighed every word he wrote. He exercised a forceful effect both on writers and on the public, both personally and through his disciples. But his influence began to weaken after the first world war.

Jovan Skerlić (1877—1914), also from Belgrade, was distinguished by his extraordinary fertility. During his short lifetime he dealt with every important period in later Serbian literature in a number of exhaustive works, and with all the major Serbian writers in a collection of brief essays entitled *Pisci i knjige* [Writers and books]. The synthesis of his work is *Istorija nove srpske književnosti* [A history of later Serbian literature] (1914). A disciple of Bogdan Popović and Georges Renard, and a follower of Guyau, Skerlić regarded literature in connexion with social and political manifestations. He set a high value on the progressive writers in Serbian literature, such as Dositej Obradović, Svetozar Marković, Jovan Jovanović-Zmaj and Milan Rakić. He detested romantic extravagance, verbosity and literary pessimism, accentuating soundness, optimism and frankness in literature.

During the first ten years of the twentieth century, Serbian writers strove for high artistic value, for perfection of form. In lyricism this was demonstrated in a devotion to style; in story-writing and drama it was demonstrated in attention to detail. A feature which all the more notable Serbian writers of that period had in common was extreme subjectivity in subject treatment. The initial result was a devotion to the principles of beauty and good taste, individualism, escapism and seclusion from society. But owing to the crisis provoked by the annexation of Bosnia and Herzegovina, and to the war of 1912, Serbian literature gradually awoke to its duties towards the people. After 1912, and on the eve of the first world war, it was a militant, optimistic literature, which fired the enthusiasm of the nation to resist the enemy, and touched the depths of fortitude in suffering, which it demonstrated in the war.

After the death of Vojislav Ilić, for a time the most outstanding Serbian lyrist was *Milorad Mitrović* (1866—1907). In flowing verse, without many personal references, he used motifs from medieval Western Europe, described his own experiences, his rebellion against the government of oppression, his horror of the social conditions. His ballads were especially commended; but his name was soon overshadowed by those of two Herzegovinians, Jovan Dučić and Aleksa Šantić.

Dučić and Šantić had formed a literary circle at Mostar in Herzegovina towards the end of the nineteenth century, and

195

founded a magazine called *Zora* [Dawn]. They were both influenced by Vojislav Ilić at that time, but Dučić rather less so.

Jovan Dučić (1874–1943) was born at Trebinje, Herzegovina. He graduated from the teacher's college at Mostar, where he also taught for a time. As he had distinguished himself in literary work, the Serbian Government granted him a scholarship to study abroad. He stayed in Geneva and Paris for a number of years, making himself thoroughly familiar with French literature. Finding himself at the source of new models, he discarded everything he had written till then. As a Serbian diplomatic official, and later as a representative of Yugoslavia, he resided in the most important centres of culture of Europe, which gave him deep erudition and made him a man of the world. He died in America during the second world war.

Dučić contributed to Serbian literary magazines with verse and prose. His collected works (1928–1932) comprise four volumes of poems, a volume of aphorisms *(Blago cara Radovana* — The treasure of Czar Radovan) and a volume of travels *(Gradovi i himere* — Cities and chimeras). There are still a considerable number of articles on literature and writers which as yet have not been put together in collected form.

In Serbian literature Jovan Dučić is the foremost champion of western trends. His poems are distinguished both by substance and by form. He is the first individualist and aristocrat of Serbian lyrics, a poet who declared that he wrote, not for the crowd, but about himself, about his adversities. Every poem, every piece of prose that he wrote was composed with extreme care. From him springs the paradox that a poet is an in-door toiler engaged upon the laborious job of rhyme and rhythm.

In many of his poems Dučić depicts sunsets, afternoon heaviness, rustling leaves. In many others he sings of love in its many variations: ecstasy, passion, anxiety, sorrow, dissatisfaction. In others, again, he gives pictures of the Serbian Middle Ages and of Dubrovnik. In his profoundest poems he deals with the eternal problems of life, the relation of man to the problems of love and death. A special place in his work is occupied by his prose poems, which are composed with the utmost precision; as well as by his travels in many countries (Spain, Switzerland, Greece), which he wrote less for the information they offered than to explain the psychology of a region.

Whatever his subject, Dučić was always a lyrist. Nor in his travels did he describe foreign countries and towns so much as he did the condition of his own soul in connexion with them. His essays are also of value inasmuch as he perceived traits similar to his own in the writer of whom he wrote. And the fundamental trait in Dučić's lyrics is sensuousness — a quality with which he sensed the world more poignantly than his intellect was capable of transmitting his impressions. His eyes seem to be open to every colour, tint, shade of light and shadow. All his senses seem to be working simultaneously, tuned to a high pitch to touch everything the human being is capable of apprehending.

Every motif in Dučić's poetry seems to be connected with his main awareness of life, which reflects on his amatory, patriotic and philosophical poetry. His amatory poetry is not poetry addressed to women as a whole, but to their attractions: in one it was her bearing that appealed to him, in another it was the tone of her voice, in a third it was the special lustre in her eye. As a result, his lyrics are imbued with enthusiasm for everything beautiful in the world; and with impatience at the thought that all the luxuriance of life can never be entirely embraced. For this very reason his lyrics contain intense pain.

To express his feelings Dučić developed a specific verse. According to some, his verses have the colour and brilliancy of metal. They are melodious, their vowels and consonants graduated. All his literary works are distinguished by an opulence of colour, a rich variety of dazzling detail.

Before the outbreak of the first world war, and to some extent between the two wars, Dučić's poetry with its quality and expression was regarded as the peak of poetic creativity. In him the Serbian bourgeoisie, always with an eye to western models, had found a poet to its liking, a poet of glitter and elegance. He was their Prince of Poets. There is no doubt that he raised Serbian poetic expression to a high degree of excellence and sang perfect poems in his way. But his doctrinal Westernism, his trend towards individualism and aristocracy deprived his poetry of much of its appeal during the periods when poets were confronted with concrete duties towards their nation and society.

The life-road and literary development of Dučić's fellow countryman *Aleksa Šantić* (1868—1924) were different. Up to the foundation of *Srpski književni glasnik* he industriously wrote poems after old-fashioned models. Although he was wounded by the adverse criticism of Bogdan Popović in *Glasnik*, he did not lose heart; rather, he endeavoured to adapt himself to the new views. And indeed, he succeeded: the critics soon began to count him among the worthier poets. But, unlike Dučić's his stay in Western Europe did not produce the desired results. Unable to accustom himself to the western way of life, he returned home.

Šantić was the son of a merchant, and an extremely active social worker who lived almost his whole life in his native town. But he was impeded by an insufficient knowledge of foreign languages and foreign literature. In his poems Šantić expressed the feelings and views of the Bosno-Herzegovinian, his cares, troubles, hopes. Unlike the champion of western trends and the individualist Dučić, Šantić dealt more deeply with the conditions of his people, with their political and social problems *(Pjesme* — Poems — 1911).

In his best verses, Šantić portrayed the life of the peasant in his attachment to his soil; he branded the exploiters of his toil; he glorified the nobility of tilling the soil. In a series of patriotic poems he extolled the Serbian people and their freedom. During the time when signs of Austria-Hungary's disintegration were already showing, Šantić was the most popular Serbian revolutionary poet. But his patriotism did not degenerate into verbalism: it was alive to the existing social problems, to the actual relations between the Yugoslav peoples. Šantić hailed the inception of Yugoslavia as a dream fulfilled.

Šantić's poems often seem artificial. There is no doubt that he frequently found the fitting word to express what everyone else felt: his was not an inherent source. The truest lyrics flow from his love poetry, with its wistfulness, passion and awareness of the passing of youth. In these poems he is sincere and personal.

Yet another diplomat won prominence in Serbian lyricism. He was *Milan Rakić* (Belgrade, 1876 — Zagreb, 1938). He came of Belgrade bourgeois parents, and in his early youth received the best education possible. He took a law degree in Paris. He alone of all the Serbian poets of his period did not continue the traditions of earlier Serbian lyrics: from the beginning of his literary endeavours he stood out as a French graduate. Although he was educated in Western Europe and championed western ideas, during the early years of his diplomatic career he served in the Turkish province of Macedonia in order to lend nationalist support to the Serbian population. Only with the victory of Serbia in the war of 1912 and with the foundation of Yugoslavia, when this work was no longer necessary, was he transferred to Western Europe as the representative of Yugoslavia in Rome, Paris and in other European capitals.

Into Serbian lyrics, which till then had been pervaded by romantic nationalism, extravagant expression, Rakić introduced intellectualism, philosophy *(Pesme* — Poems — 1904; *Nove pesme* — New poems — 1912). His poetry is not the product of momentary inclinations, but the profound emotion of an intellectual who believes he has penetrated into the essence of human relations and into the core of things. Its fundamental feature is pessimism, not the pessimism of one complaining of injustice personally endured, but of one who has reached the conclusion that life is painful and miserable.

The fundamental feeling in Rakić's poetry is one of decay and misery. Misery is not fortuitous: it is law; consciousness and knowledge do not elevate: they are merely the source of even greater suffering; death is the only panacea, and horrible is the very thought that there may be life after it.

Rakić also wrote love poems. They too contain a pessimistic note, for the poet is aware of the transience of love, that even in love people are false to each other. The only advantage it has to offer is illusion.

Rakić wrote very little: about thirty poems in all. He wrote only when he was in the mood. His manner is measured, precise, with a touch of heaviness and gloom in it. Unlike Dučić, who dazzled with his variety and colour, Rakić is more to the point, more concise and full. With pride he emphasizes how very far he has improved Serbian poetic expression as a member of his generation.

At first glance it may be observed that, imitating Baudelaire, Rakić introduced fashionable decadent notes into Serbian literature, into the literature of the young peasant nation. Although in form it stood at towering heights, his poetry merely reflected western trends, which were extraneous to Serbian surroundings. In point of fact, Rakić gave utterance to that whole course of development which most of the Serbs had experienced, as the country, undergoing rapid economic transformation accompanied by suffering, sacrifice, wandering and fatigue, discarded the old way of life. In this respect Rakić was both direct and sincere.

Although a decadent, Rakić was no weakling. In contact with the difficulties of his own nation, he found a way out of pessimism. In his Kosovo cycle, written on the even of the Balkan War, he drew attention to the national duty and to the necessity for sacrifice in verse which was moderate enough but nonetheless unmistakable in tone. He thus drowned his personal anguish in national sentiment, becoming a prime mover in action. His poetic visions soon materialized in the victorious wars.

In his most personal poems Rakić continued to be a skeptic, a philosopher, a pessimist, but with a pessimism which was elevating, not depressing. This is what renders Rakić's poetry both national and positive.

The extremes of pessimism and individualism were represented in Serbian lyrics by *Sima Pandurović* (1883) and *Vladislav Petković-Dis* (1880—1917).

His volumes of verse, *Posmrtne počasti* [Obsequies] (1908) and *Dani i noći* [Days and nights] (1912) introduced Pandurović as a poet who sang of the graveyard, of death, of the clouded mind. In heavy, gloomy verses he uttered his grief for his dead love, his helplessness, and the disgust he felt towards life. In his earliest volumes he proved to be a confident master of versification, and he demonstrated a faculty for finding new modes of expression and a keen ear for melody. Between the two wars he was an editor, a critic and a translator.

Vladislav Petković-Dis showed himself to be a poet of extreme despair in his first book of poems entitled *Utopljene duše* [Drowned souls] (1911). Although his opponents accused him of emulating western writers, his poems contain all the bitterness of the intellectual proletariat of Belgrade, the misery of the rabble, the headiness of drink, the ghastliness of solitude, of the grave, of insanity and of death. His poems are, however, melodious, and he proved capable of describing the condition between the conscious and the subconscious. His collection *Mi čekamo cara* [We await the emperor] (1913), following upon Serbia's victory in the Balkan Wars, signified deliverance from pessimism.

Completely opposed both to Rakić's type of pessimism and to western models was the poetry of *Milutin Bojić* (1892—1917), written on the eve of the first world war. Bojić was brought up on the views of Jovan Skerlić, and he accepted what the previous generation (Dučić and Rakić) had achieved in form; but in his extremely melodious poems *(Pesme — Poems — 1914)* he expresses joy of life, strength, gaiety, almost sensuousness, and absolute faith in his people.

A patriotic poet who criticized conditions among the Serbs in Hungary particularly in his *Rodoljubive pesme* [Patriotic poems] (1912), *Na pragu* [On the threshold] (1914), was *Veljko Petrović* (1884). Petrović was also a prolific story-writer, describing chiefly the Serbian bourgeoisie and the petty bourgeoisie of Hungary. The work he had begun before the first world war he continued between the wars and after the second world war.

Isidora Sekulić (1877) demonstrated many West-European elements in her earliest works *(Saputnici — Fellow travellers — 1911; Pisma iz Norveške — Letters from Norway — 1913)*. Erudition, an ability to observe psychological differences, and numerous associations render her stories, travels and essays highly original in Serbian literature, although her style is frequently bizarre. She published a vast number of stories, essays and studies between the two world wars, and after the second war. They are even more eloquent of the qualities inherent in her earliest works.

Among the Serbian story-writers born in Serbia, prominence was won first by *Radoje Domanović* (1873—1908), who belonged to a generation which was as active in politics and in social work as it was in literature. Domanović was born in the country, in the village of Ovsište; he took a degree in letters in Belgrade, and then became a secondary-school teacher. Persecuted under the Obrenovićs for political reasons, he was frequently dismissed from his post. He retired with the coming to power of the new dynasty in Serbia.

Domanović began his literary career with stories of the country and with tender and charming children's stories. In Serbian literature he earned a name with his allegorical stories *(Stradija* — The land of Stradija — 1902) in which he describes an imaginary country called Stradija. In that country the loyalty and value of its subjects are estimated according to the amount of oppression they can bear, and according to the number of decorations adorning the breasts of their oppressors. The masses in Stradija blindly follow the leaders, unable to see that they too are blind. In his story *Kraljević Marko po drugi put medju Srbima* [Kraljević Marko again amond the Serbs] Domanović alluded to conditions in Serbia during a period full of noisy talk of heroism, in which the people appeal to Marko Kraljević, the hero from folk poetry, to save them. But when he does come to their rescue, they give him the post of police constable.

Domanović's satire is bitter. He ruthlessly brands the mentality of the authorities, the executives, and the Serbian people. Domanović described the tragedy of his people, who had lost all sense of pride and the will for resistance under the tyranny of the blackguards in power. The strength of Domanović's pen lies in the unswerving logic with which his allegorical story unfolds, each phase in its development being true to the conditions he allegorizes.

Petar Kočić (1877—1916), from Bosnia, was similar in temperament to Domanović. He played a dual role in the Serbian national life of his native region, for he was both a politician and a writer. He was born in the country (in the village of Stričić, near Banja Luka); he studied for a degree at the Faculty of Letters in Vienna, and sought to be an educationist. But he could not endure conditions either under the Austrian authorities or as a subject of Serbia: he became a journalist and politician, and was finally elected to Parliament. Among the Serbian politicians in Bosnia, most of whom were always ready to compromise, he was an irreconcilable enemy of Austria, and the champion of the poor peasants, who were still in a state of serfdom. For this reason he clashed with the authorities and with the Serbian bourgeois politicians, the result being that he spent most of his life in prison.

Kočić's literary work is small in volume: three books of stories under the common title of *S planine i ispod planine* [From the mountain and from under the mountain] (1902, 1904, 1905), his stories *Jauci sa Zmijanja* [Screams from Zmijanje] (1910) and a long story called *Sudanija* [Judgment] (1912).

201

In his stories Kočić gave a truthful picture of his native region. He portrayed the men and women, the mighty and insatiable, with their unquenchable passions. He depicted individuals in their conflict with nature and with the authorities. On the other hand, he wrote about the wretchedness following in the wake of the occupation of Bosnia by Austria-Hungary, which was supposed to bring happiness with it, but brought, instead, an army of officials who were ignorant both of the language and of the customs, and unhappiness to the people of Bosnia.

Kočić had a temperamental and lyrical nature. It is with profound tenderness that he speaks of the peasants of his region, describing their customs, loves and failings. But he speaks with bitter irony of the newcomers from Austria, who, supposedly the bearers of culture and civilization, endeavoured to stamp out the fine Bosnian people. His best-known work is *Jazavac pred sudom* [The badger on trial] (1904), a satire. It is the history of an inconspicuous, rather stupid-looking Bosnian peasant who sues a badger for damages. Through this trial of the badger, Kočić ridicules the legal formalism which Austria-Hungary introduced in Bosnia, and places in high relief the common sense of the stupid-looking peasant, as well as his poverty. *Sudanija* is also a satire on the legal system in Bosnia.

Kočić brought out masterfully all the poetry in the life of his people. With few media he skillfully wrought characters almost unique in their love and hatred, or forceful in their extraordinary humour. There were few writers to equal him in creating complete figures by means of a few telling words, allusions and brief sketches. His gift of narrative was both a weapon and an art.

Ivo Cippico (1867—1923) was older than the majority of the Serbian writers of his period when he embarked on a literary career in mature manhood. He was a descendant, on his father's side, of an old noble family from Kaštel Novi, Dalmatia. His mother was of peasant origin. Cippico preferred to live a life uninhibited and simple. He served as a forest warden on the Dalmatian islands and in Dalmatian Zagorje, being in constant touch with nature and with the simple people, and avoiding artificiality and town ways. In 1912 he moved to Serbia. He died in his birth-place.

His collections of stories are: *Primorske duše* [The folk of the coast] (1899), *S jadranskih obala* [From the shores of the Adriatic] (1900), *Sa ostrva* [From the islands] (1903), *Kraj mora* [At the seaside] (1912); his novels: *Za kruhom* [After a livelihood] (1904), *Pauci* [Spiders] (1909).

In his stories and novels Cippico described life as he learnt to know it as a forest warden. His works breathe the knowledge that life is immense and beautiful in its naturalness and instinctive purity, and that the cause of all evil lies in law, in the system of society, in class relations. His work thus reduced to two aspects: he extolled what was in harmony with nature, and hated what the strong had created in order to exploit the weak.

Cippico's novels and stories tell of the free unrestrained life of the sea, on the islands, in the Dalmatian villages. He especially loved the Dalmatian landscape: the sea in its innumerable aspects, the wind, ships, fishing. His characters live a free life untrammelled by convention: they commit adultery, abductions, contract trial marriages; and all this is beautiful in his narrative as long as it is the expression of emotion, becoming ugly only when it is turned into an instrument of gain. In his *Antika* [The antique] Cippico created a type of woman who lives by instinct, refuses to marry, and is happy; and she is full of the joy of life even at the age of seventy.

Cippico, however, dealt also with the reverse side of the social system. He described the effect of laws, social conventions and money on the natural life of his people — farmers and fishermen. These observations inspired works which are a distinctive protest against the hardships imposed on the country people by government, merchants, village moneylenders, employers and the clergy. While he exalted life in nature, Cippico warned of the evils brought to the Dalmatian village by the bourgeois system. In his best works, such as his novel *Pauci*, he described the sufferings of the Dalmatian peasant, who is robbed by all and sundry: by merchants, by government officials, and by priests. Whoever comes to the village has but one purpose: to fleece the peasant; the consequence being that people, who might have lived happily in their simple way, perish in misery, or must seek their livelihood abroad, or unwittingly become criminals and thus lawbreakers.

Cippico was a denouncer of the social system as well as a poet. His two novels, and most of his stories, are terrible documentary evidence of the economic and social conditions in Dalmatia during the development of the capitalistic system and the race for gain, usury, and the exploitation of peasant labour.

Cippico wrote by instinct, spontaneously, without affectation, and often probably without plan. Thanks to his capacity to create characters and types new and original in their freshness, he produced some excellent stories. *Pauci* is one of the foremost Serbian novels in truthfulness of narration, in the psychology of its char acters, in its power of observation and in the iron logic with which its action unfolds. Cippico was a quiet, unobtrusive narrator; but the strength of his narrative lies in its detail. His larger works, such as the novel *Za kruhom*, are disconnected and diffuse, for he was primarily a story-writer. *Pauci* was a success because, like his stories, he wrote it on impulse.

The most outstanding story-writer in early twentieth-century Serbian literature was, however, Borisav Stanković (1876–1927). The contemporary of the younger, western-minded Serbian literary generation, he also went to Western Europe, to Paris, after completing his studies and after a period in government service. Unlike Dučić and Rakić, he was not influenced by Paris; moreover he seems to have even become confirmed in his Balkan, half-Oriental way of thought. On returning to Serbia, he continued his old way of life and his literary work.

Stanković was born in that part of Serbia (Vranje) which, though taken from the Turks in the year of his birth, for long after preserved its old, semi-Turkish customs. He studied law in Belgrade, became a clerk in the Ministry of Finance, and then an inspector in the Ministry of Education, etc. He died in Belgrade.

While still a gymnasium pupil, Stanković wrote some poems, which were published in provincial newspapers. The serious literary magazines rejected his stories. But the publication of his collection of stories *Iz starog Jevandjelja* [From the Old Testament] (1899) brought him sudden success, and he soon became one of the most esteemed Serbian writers. In addition to other works, he published the collections of stories *Stari dani* [Old times] (1902), *Božji ljudi* [God's people] (1902), the play *Koštana* and the novel *Nečista krv* [Tainted blood] (1911), which is still considered to be the best Serbian novel. He published a second play called *Tašana*, and commenced two more novels *(Gazda Mladen, Pevci* – The cocks), but failed to complete them.

On the surface, Stanković continued the traditions of the Serbian realist story-writers who described their own regions. He took the material for almost all his novels and stories from his native town and its surroundings. His works are clearly in the nature of autobiographies or biographies: he described either his own life or the life of his relatives and acquaintances. But in emotion and elaborate treatment of motif they excel over average regional literature.

In his works Stanković depicted a region in which Oriental ideas collided sharply with those of Western Europe. He dealt with that period in which the old economic and social system founded on feudal views and on the inviolable authority of the elders was retreating before the new economic forces and the new ideas of equality and freedom of the person; with the new period of conflicts between the social classes, between individuals, and within individuals themselves.

Stanković describes the old wealthy commercial or feudal families, the way of life and customs of the conservative artisans, the penetration of the peasantry into the towns. The conflicts between his characters are the result of the endeavour of individuals to do away with the old ideas of morality, though society compels them to surrender to it.

While portraying the elder, patriarchal folk, Stanković pictured the struggle of the person against the fetters of the old moral concepts. Most of his colourful and original characters (Koštana, Tašana, Sofka in the novel *Nečista krv)* in that struggle are champions of the right of the individual over social convention and also the victims of the latter.

As a depicter and poet of his region, Stanković described the conflicts between eastern and western elements with especial passion. He described gypsy women, dancers, drinking bouts, hot blood, dissipation; and few other writers have felt the poetry of love, passion, moonlight, youth as he did.

Being a poet of his times and surroundings, deeply torn by conflicting factions, Stanković himself seemed to be affected by the turbulence of the period. At the bottom of his heart he loved the old, patriarchal way of life, which was inevitably being destroyed by the new, although he realized the necessity and inevitability of these changes. Moreover he even openly supported the new forces in their clashes with the old. But he was also aware of the deep tragedy accompanying these developments. His entire work, truthful and profound at the core, is imbued with endless grief, almost hopelessness. It is an expression of longing for beauty, for the past, for dreams which will never be fulfilled.

Although Stanković was occasionally an inferior composer in his principal works, he was nonetheless an extraordinary painter of detail. He described vividly onrushes of passion and despair at the passing of youth. He wrought with particular attention such characters produced by society as beggars, madmen, outcasts and profligates. It was with rare perception that he observed manifestations of degeneration in families once highly esteemed. Endowed with a gift for detail, he revealed that barely conscious state of the soul which individuals do not dare admit. Modelling his characters with diligence and thoroughness, they became in his hands not only the representatives of a passing age, but also types embodying all the passions and pains of his *Vranjanci*. His works are less an illustration of Vranje than an expression of perpetual human striving: from them rises a demand for happiness, for justice and for freedom.

Stanković's style is appropriate to the milieu which he described. Having no similarity to West-European styles, his manner of writing is often involved and almost incoherent, and heavy; but these elements seem to render it all the more expressive of the depth of unconsumed passion, of turbulent blood; it conjures up the vision intimated by his incompletely worded thought, the unuttered, stifled longings, the burden of all that he denied himself.

Stanković's talent and achievements place him among the greatest of Serbian writers: he is unaffected, deeply national, profoundly devoted to his region and period, and a deeply human, genuine and great poet.

The most productive writer of latter-day Serbian literature was *Branislav Nušić* (1864—1938). He was born in Belgrade. He was almost a contemporary of the Serbian realists. He entered public life in 1885. His main literary work comes within the twentieth century.

Nušić graduated in law at Belgrade University, and later held official and literary posts: he was a Serbian diplomat in the regions held by the Turks; he was a theatre director, a district prefect, and a departmental chief in a ministry, etc. For political reasons, he was often arrested, dismissed from service or retired, from all of which he gathered vast experience. Notwithstanding all the hardships that befell him, he was always cheerful and kept his sense of humour.

Literature was not Nušić's means of livelihood; yet he was primarily a writer. His extensive literary work comprises novels, travels, stories, feuilletons, memoirs, tragedies and comedies. His complete works number twenty-five extensive volumes. Furthermore, many of his manuscripts were lost during the wars. What appealed to him most in his public work was drama: in temperament he was primarily a man of the theatre.

His literary and theatre work is of varied purpose and value. As a patriot, Nušić wrote plays on the eve of the war of 1912, the object of which was to raise Serbian national consciousness *(Knez od Semberije* — The Knez of Semberija; *Danak u krvi* — Blood tribute; *Hadži Loja)*.

Nušić continued the traditions of Serbian romantic drama with tragedies on the Serbian Middle Ages and folk poems *(Nahod* — The foundling; *Kneginja od Tribala* — The Tribali princess; *Tomaida)*.

In his unending concern for a repertoire, he wrote plays dealing with problems of blame and retribution, love and hate *(Tako je moralo biti* — It had to be so; *Greh za greh* — Sin for sin; *Pučina* — The sea), and the fantastic plays: *Žena bez srca* [The heartless woman], *Večnost* [Eternity], *Knjiga druga* [Book two].

His travels *(Po Albaniji* — In Albania; *Devetstopetnaesta* — Nineteen-fifteen) have a nationalistic tendency. *Devestopetnaesta* describes the collapse of Serbia in 1915 and the withdrawal of the Serbian Army through Albania.

Nušić's entire work, except for a few of his most important works, is documentary rather than artistic. The real Nušić is the writer of humorous pieces, feuilletons, the novel *Opštinsko dete* [The municipal child] (1902) and a number of comedies on life, the most important of which are: *Narodni poslanik* [The member of parliament] (1883), *Sumnjivo lice* [The suspicious character] (1887), *Protekcija* [Favouritism] (1889), *Običan čovek* [An ordinary man] (1900), *Svet* [The world] (1906), *Put oko sveta* [Round the world] (1910). Between the two wars he wrote the comedies *Ujež* [Short for Udruženje jugoslovenskih emancipovanih žena — The association of Yugoslav emancipated women], *Pokojnik* [The late lamented], *Dr., Ožalošćena porodica* [The bereaved family], *Mister dolar*, and *Gospodja ministarka* [Madame minister].

Nušić's comedies made him the most popular dramatist in Yugoslavia. His plays were performed on every Yugoslav stage, even before the Austro-Hungarian Empire dissolved; and especially so after the founding of Yugoslavia. Both in print and on the stage Nušić provoked the laughter of tens of thousands of readers and theatre-goers in a way never accomplished by any Yugoslav or foreign writer.

His comedies were a picture of the Serbian petty bourgeoisie — the people who neither rise above nor sink below their surroundings. Unlike his predecessors, he showed the other side of public and private life in Serbia: the political intrigues, the ambitions and the methods to which the average Serbian politicians had recourse, petty bourgeois gossiping, the cares attendant upon contracting profitable marriages, the scrimmage for offices and brilliant careers, the feverish race for wealth, corruption in the government, fashion-crazy women. He portrayed with especial gusto the political organs in Serbia, in which primitive characters became statesmen, and their wives exercised influence on government. He censured the oppression and stupidity of the bureaucracy and the immorality of the provincial politicians. During pre-war Yugoslavia, he exposed the struggles for political offices, the utilization of such offices for personal gain, cheating, the race for wealth, the passion for titles, the careerists who strove to win esteem and power at the expense of other people. He remarked the transformation of the one-time petty bourgeois into a business man who swindled and robbed on a large scale. He revealed the comical side of all these manifestations with the object of drawing down upon them as much ridicule as possible.

At first glance, it seemed as though Nušić wanted to entertain the bourgeois and petty bourgeois public by introducing such characters as moved in their surroundings; and his comedies aroused peals of laughter even from the humourless. But actually, behind the mask of the comedian there stood a sorrowful man with a keen sense of observation. His works are a true picture of Serbia during the eighties of the past century, and of Yugoslavia up to his death. He observed the transformation of a small agricultural country into a state of the West-European type, with its banks, its business men, its wealthy class and its careerists. In this break-neck process, conscience was pushed aside, lives were destroyed, resisting upright individuals ruined, and unscrupulous upstarts dominated the scene. His brow clouded and his laughter accumulated growing quantities of gall as this process continued. Once regarded almost as a farceur, historically considered, Nušić now appears as a realist of a higher order, as a typical observer, a daring depicter of reality, and an incorruptible critic. His works are the most complete moral picture of Serbian and Yugoslav society. They are the key which unlocks the door to the things that happened before the defeat of Yugoslavia in 1941.

A picture of Serbian bourgeois society, especially the position of the intellectuals, was given systematically by *Milutin Uskoković* (1884—1915) in novels *(Došljaci* — The newcomers; *Čedomir Ilić)* and in stories *(Kad ruže cvetaju* — When roses bloom).

2. THE CROATIAN *MODERNA* AND ITS REPRESENTATIVES

The literary movement at the crossroads of the nineteenth and twentieth centuries in Croatia was known as *Moderna* (after the German *Die Moderne).* This name did not stop at literature: it embraced the entire national life, and ended a struggle between generations, between the Old and the Young.

A semblance of bourgeoisie of the western type had taken shape in Croatia towards the end of the nineteenth century. With its financial centres outside the country, it adapted itself to the government conducted by Khuen Hederváry. But the gap both in the way of life and in the interests between it and the majority of the people grew wider.

The Hungarians succeeded in impoverishing Croatia with their system of taxation, direct political pressure, and commercial and industrial policy. The number of emigrants multiplied rapidly and dangerously during the early years of the twentieth century, the proletariat grew more numerous, the petty bourgeoisie and intelligentsia became fewer. Croatia became a country of malcontents, particularly as the oppression of the authorities and the deliberate affronts of its representatives grew more frequent.

The resistance of the Croatian political parties against these political conditions was of no avail. The oppressors, with adroit tactics, secured a majority in the National Sabor of Croatia, while the parties of the opposition, blind to the real state of affairs, flew at each other in their hopeless ideological disagreements and quarrels.

Almost the same state of affairs prevailed in literature. The leaders of the cultural institutions and magazines were mostly idealists, who sang vague songs about country and freedom as abstract ideas, but were unable to face facts.

Towards the end of the nineteenth century, the youngest generation began to voice its opposition, demanding more realism in politics and literature. The voices of rebellion became louder as a considerable part of the Croatian university youth, having been ousted from Zagreb for political demonstrations against the Hungarians in 1895, began to attend the universities of Vienna and Prague. Becoming familiar with life in the advanced and free countries, and with progressive views in the world, the members of the younger generation began to publish political and literary papers, which, however, were all of short duration. The Croatian students in Prague who were influenced by Thomas G. Masaryk's realistic philosophy, especially were active. They gradually formed a movement whose echoes reached their very homeland. Its aim was to revise the idealistic principles and to bind the intellectuals more closely with the masses.

The representatives of the Croatian political parties, especially of the Party of Rights, based their entire work on the past, on the state rights of Croatia, irrespective of the present. The younger generation, on the other hand, held that facts should be taken for what they are before they can be altered. Similarly, in literature they demanded that idealistic traditions should be abandoned, and the West-European literature of their period emulated.

The political movement founded in this manner also embraced the progressive elders. The long-standing controversy between the Croats and the Croatian Serbs was forgotten, and a policy was conducted in Croatia based on Serbo-Croatian unity. Contact was also established with the Hungarian opposition, for both the Croatian and the Hungarian malcontents were aware that only Vienna benefited from strife between the Hungarians and Croats. New parties, with an identical negative platform in relation to the government, were founded in Croatia (Agrarian, Progressive, Socialist), based on new philosophical and social conceptions. In 1903 a rebellion consequently broke out in Croatia, during which Khuen Hederváry left the country. In the new conditions the opposition parties gained votes, till, in the end, in 1906, they won the elections. As the opposition assumed power in Hungary, the Croatian and Serbian coalition parties took over government in Croatia, and a brief period of peace ensued.

The agreement between the Croatian and Hungarian parties did not suit the purpose of the authorities in Vienna. Their intrigues again forced the Croats and Croatian Serbs into opposition. Then followed years of serious strife, in which the Hungarian authorities resorted to every possible means to gain their ends, as they had during the whole of the nineteenth century. But the resistance in Croatia could not be broken. The revolutionary state of affairs in the country was clear, and it especially intensified in 1912, when, during the Balkan wars, little Serbia demonstrated what could be accomplished by valour.

The revolutionary spirit in politics had its effect on social ideas. The bulk of Croatian youth were aware that the political support of the broad peasant and working masses should be requited by raising them to a higher social level. A socialist trend was also evident in the progressive bourgeois parties.

The younger Croatian intellectuals first found expression for their dissatisfaction in literature, and towards the end of the nineteenth century literary and semi-literary papers with a common feature began to appear: they criticized earlier Croatian literature and demanded something new. Their criticism was twofold: on the one hand, they demanded that Croatian literature should abandon its framework and approach modern European artistic trends; on the other hand, they demanded an art which would give a realistic picture of life and would be a weapon in the struggle against prevailing conditions. The champions of the former view, mostly the children of the bourgeoisie and State officials, opposed realism and favoured new and different trends: neoromanticism, the Secession, symbolism, decadence, freedom of creation without any bounds. The others, however, the children of the peasants, tradesmen and workers, expected more truth from literature, more contact with reality, more daring. Only the former considered themselves modernists in the full sense of the word; but both divisions were equally opposed to the representatives of the Croatian literature of that time; both demanded more freedom in literature, closer contact with Europe and with art, and more individuality from the artist; both regarded the European literature of the day — notably French, German, Italian, Czech and Polish literature — as the models to be followed. The movement also spread to the plastic and graphic arts.

The appearance of new literary trends perturbed the protagonists of Croatian literature of that period. The leading older writers — Djalski, Kranjčević, Leskovar, Kozarac, Vojnović — were on the side of the younger generation. Djalski, moreover, defended their principles with his theories. But the chief positions in literature were held by men who were supposed to be continuing the best Croatian literary traditions from the times of August Šenoa and the Illyrian movement. In the name of patriotism, morality and idealism they assailed the very idea of freedom of creation and literature as an expression of its period, protesting that the work of the younger generation bordered on pornography, and that it violated ethics and Croatian national interests. The younger generation, on the other hand, struck back at the paper idealism of their elders, their lack of aesthetic standards, the provincial character of their writing. Two bitter and stubborn controversies ensued, which intensified as the younger generation were attacked by the men of the Church and by the conservative politicians. It was during these controversies, in 1903, that the oldest Croatian magazine, *Vijenac* [The Wreath], expired. The younger writers started various new magazines *(Život* — Life — in Zagreb; *Lovor* — The laurel — at Zadar), and eventually, in 1906, they founded *Savremenik* [The contemporary], which survived to become the central Croatian literary magazine.

The picture of Croatian literature had altered considerably in the course of the fifteen-odd years which followed the period of realism. Whereas realism had produced the novel, *Moderna* gave lyrics as its chief category, though it included the lyrical sketch, the short story and criticism. All these categories brought improvements in the mode of expression, views broadened, the area of artistic curiosity expanded. As never before, Croatian literature was susceptible to every outside influence. In one ten-year period Sainte-Beuve, Taine, Croce, Verlaine, Maeterlinck, Dehmel, Hauptmann, D'Annunzio, Gorki, Nietzsche, Pascoli, gained popularity in Croatia.

The wealth of ideas and number of experiments in Croatian literature had never before reached such a level. Side by side with the serious artists stood a multitude of followers of the passing fashion; but in spite of many undesirable manifestations, Croatian literature, in contact with Europe, was richer at that time both in content and in form. As it struck boldly out, it also ventured into fields which till then it had never dared to touch. As it ripened, it gradually discarded everything that was artificial, ephemeral; and supported only those writers who cultivated contact with their country. Having adopted to some extent the subject-matter and mode of expression of Western Europe, they perfected Croatian literary expression, and carried out their duty to their people.

The most outstanding ideologists and organizers of the Croatian modernist movement were Milivoj Dežman Ivanov, Branimir Livadić, Milan Marjanović and Milutin Cihlar Nehajev.

Milivoj Dežman Ivanov (1873—1940) was a most energetic initiator, organizer and founder of newspapers. His chief tenets were that no schools of literature are necessary; every writer must develop his individuality to the utmost; literature must be up-to-date; it must reveal the soul of modern man. He laid particular emphasis in his criticisms on the connexion between his generation and various recognized writers (Djalski, Leskovar). He also wrote stories *(Protiv struje* — Against the current) and plays *(Kneginja Jelena* — Princess Jelena).

Branimir Livadić (1871—1949) most persistently defended the principles of full freedom of creation. Art, in his opinion, must concern itself with every manifestation in life, including sex; but the artistic aspect of a work should prevail over every other. Livadić defended freedom of creation whenever it could be used as a weapon of political struggle against the regime. He also defended it when, on the eve of the first world war, more distinctive national traits were demanded of literature. For many years Livadić edited Croatian literary magazines *(Savremenik)* in accordance with the views he expounded. He also wrote stories *(Novele; Legenda o Amisu i Amilu* — The legend of Amis and Amil) and theatre criticisms.

Milan Marjanović (1879) was the most fruitful critic of his generation. He was prominent as a journalist and public figure, and was among the first critics in Croatia to popularize foreign critics (Taine, Sainte-Beuve, Brandes). At the beginning of his literary career he gave precedence to aesthetic elements over all others; but later he realized that literature could also be a weapon in the struggle for a better life. He demanded that Croatian literature should be the coryphaeus of the political and social struggle. In this spirit he wrote a number of studies on earlier and contemporary Croatian writers, especially on those who shared his views (Kranjčević, Kovačić, Nazor).

Milutin Cihlar Nehajev (Senj, 1880 — Zagreb, 1931) was the foremost connoisseur of the European literature of his generation. He wrote essays and studies about European writers (Zola, Flaubert, Tolstoi, Shakespeare). In his criticisms he demanded that Croatian literature should resemble that of Europe as closely as possible, and that it should be the expression of its period. He considered that the fundamental characteristics of the European of the late nineteenth and early twentieth century were weariness, weakness and general lack of faith. Hating the very name of realism, he extolled romanticism, symbolism and decadence, favouring especially the earlier Croatian writers who possessed characteristics similar to these (Leskovar, Djalski, Kranjčević). He also wrote stories imbued with this zest for life *(Veliki grad* — The big city) His *Bijeg* [Flight] (1909) is the most characteristic novel of the Croatian *Moderna*, a portrayal of the Croatian decadent intellectual. As he continued to develop, he gradually foresook his decadent views, and affirmed the duties of the writer towards his country. His essays on eminent nineteenth-century personages of Croatia (Starčević, Mažuranić) are noteworthy.

The first Croatian lyrist to inspire the modernists and to provoke the attacks of the older generation was *Milan Begović* (1876—1948). Born in the small Dalmatian town of Vrlika, he began to write verse at a youthful age, after the model of the earlier Croatian and Serbian poets. He was especially aware of the importance of Vojislav Ilić, about whom he published an inspired essay, pronouncing him a lyrist of world significance. His studies of Romance philology in Vienna and his command of Italian literature broadened his horizon. His collection of poems *Knjiga boccadoro* [The book of the golden word] (1900), under the pseudonym of *Xeres de la Maraja*, comprised love poetry. He openly descanted on erotism, the beauty of nature, the power of emotion; and rebelled against all convention. The collection is not novel merely in content, but also in mode of expression: in its defiance, cheerfulness and gaiety. This collection brought Begović into the very heart of Croatian literary controversy.

During his later development Begović took up drama. He had written a number of plays by the outbreak of the first world war *(Stana, Gospodja Walewska* — Madame Walewska). Between the two wars he was the most prolific Croatian playwright *(Svadbeni let* — Marriage flight; *Božji čovek* — God's man; *Bez trećega* — Without the third one, etc.). His plays are varied in material, and with their technical ingenuity and the liveliness of their dialogue, they offer excellent opportunities for good staging. Begović learnt to write plays from studying the European dramatists, particularly D'Annunzio, Ibsen and Pirandello; and he raised the drama to a high level. Regardless of whether he dealt with themes from his native region or with characters with no definite nationality or social background, his works are always concerned with affairs of love, especially with love and marriage triangles. His work is sometimes even extremely suggestive. But he wrote everything with such skill and his subject-matter was so fresh that his plays won a place on many European and American stages.

Begović also wrote essays, stories and novels *(Dunja u kovčegu* — The quince in the trunk; *Kvartet; Puste želje* — Vain wishes), which have both the merits and the shortcomings of his plays. He was a writer typical of the Croatian bourgeois public, and his works frequently supplanted their foreign reading matter. His novel *Brak Gige Barićeve* [The marriage of Giga Barić] (1940), whose action takes place during the first world war, contains many accurate observations and details about people and the period. His novel on the ruin of a Croatian aristocratic family

213

(Sablasti u dvorcu — Ghosts in the castle) was published after his death (in 1952). It is also erotic in subject-matter.

Dragutin Domjanić (1875—1933) played a more important part than Begović in the subsequent development of Croatian lyrics. He was educated in Zagreb, where he lived most of his life as a judge. He engaged in all the battles between the young generation and the old, but never in the front ranks. He was retiring, sensitive, ailing, and condemned to the life of a poorly paid Croatian government employee who was repressed by both the social surroundings and the political position of his country. But, lacking the strength to fight, he endured and gave vent to his grief in literature.

Domjanić demonstrated his individuality in his earliest published verses; and he had reached the peak of his development as a writer by the time his collection *Pjesme* [Poems] (1907) was published. Almost everything he wrote later was merely a repetition of old motifs and forms of expression.

Domjanić was the descendant of a noble family which had lost all its property. He was born at Sveti Ivan Zelina. His poems evinced the pessimism of a man of good breeding who could not resign himself to the times of scheming and money. He grieved for the bygone days of gentleness and good breeding, and protested against the system in which gain was the driving force. He described old palaces and parks, and the dying countryside. He wrote of his loves, over-refined and therefore unattainable. He was a poet of self-abnegation, longing, nostalgia, but not a poet of effort and struggle. Following in the footsteps of Verlaine and Pushkin, he created melodious verse, in the rhythm of the most popular dance of that period, the Viennese waltz.

During the first world war, Domjanić began to write poems in the dialect of his region, in which he demonstrated a keener sense of reality, and a sympathy for the Croatian peasants who were sacrificing their lives for their enemy, Austria-Hungary. With a collection of poems of this type called *Kipci i popevke* [Pictures and poems] (1917) he roused the local patriotism of Zagreb and its surroundings. It earned him nationwide popularity among the Croatian bourgeois public, and he became their poet. It is, therefore, easy to understand why his poetry, sentimental and conservative as it was, did not escape sharp criticism in the new conditions.

Domjanić's closest fellow poet was *Vladimir Vidrić* (1875--1909), a man utterly different both in temperament and in the characteristics of his literary work. Strong in mind and body, he was the son of a wealthy lawyer from Zagreb. He received the best education possible at that time in Croatia. While a student, he was one of those who opposed Khuen Hederváry's government, as a result of which he was arrested and expelled from the University of Zagreb. On completing his law studies, he became a clerk in a law office. He died insane at Stenjevac near Zagreb.

A man with a classical education, who was incapable of fighting for career and money, Vidrić became a poet, not because of any literary ambition, but in order to find self-expression. He composed thirty-odd poems in all, which he often recited to his friends instead of writing them down. His only collection, *Pjesme* (1907), contains but twenty-six poems.

In his poems Vidrić never spoke of himself, but he described visions. In his poetry, scenes from life in Rome alternate with scenes from the past of Spain, the Middle Ages, from Slavic mythology, from the surroundings of Zagreb. He described events, not emotions: his poems are poems of wine and caresses; in them satyrs frolic, and the gaze is directed to the beauty and magnificence of the countryside.

Vidrić's poetry is in fact deeply personal, linked with the weighty problems of social and political life in Croatia. Modest and sensitive, Vidrić never spoke in the first person, but expressed himself through the inference of his subject-matter. In his poems he bitterly ridiculed his self-delusion in affairs of the heart; in various romances he enlarged on the wretched picture of the Croatia of the time: on the pressure of the authorities, the psychology of the oppressed, the vast distance separating masters and servants, the horrors of emigration. He presented his sentiments — his anguish, his presentiment of insanity and death — under the most varied guises.

Vidrić's poetic expression is distinguished by simplicity, picturesqueness, artistry, and by an avoidance of literary media, though its form introduced a fresh note into Croatian lyrical poetry.

Ante Tresić Pavičić (Starigrad, Hvar, 1867 — Split, 1949) occupied a special place in *Moderna* on account of his fruitfulness and unequivocal conceptions. Older in age than most of the Croatian modernists, he was their predecessor in literature, his creativeness, the extent of his literary plans and ambitions and his self-confidence drawing the attention of literary circles. Having graduated from the Faculty of Philosophy in Vienna, he lived as a writer and politician, instead of seeking a government post. He wound up his public career as the diplomatic representative of former Yugoslavia in Madrid and Washington.

Tresić wrote poems, plays, stories and novels, and edited various literary papers. He was known for his wide literary erudition; but he combatted the Croatian modernists, endeavouring to introduce principles of neoidealism into Croatian literature. He wrote politically tendentious plays on Croatian past. He put his

215

greatest efforts into the tetralogy *Finis rei publicae*, which describes the downfall of the Roman Republic. In his verse he sought among other things to revive in Croatian literature the old classical metre, adapted to the Croatian tongue *(Valovi misli i čuvstava* — Waves of thought and emotion — 1903). All his works were keyed to a high pitch and full of feeling. For a time he exercised a strong influence on the younger generation.

Ivo Vojnović (1857–1929) was in a way a forerunner of the Croatian modernists. He was a contemporary of the Croatian realists, and began to write at the same time as they did. The general characteristics of his works, however, show him to be closer to the writers of *Moderna;* it was during their period that he reached the height of his creativeness and fame.

Vojnović came of a family of counts from Dubrovnik. His father was a professor at the University of Zagreb, and at home he was brought up on Romance culture. Having graduated in law, he became a government employee. For a short time he was also dramaturgist in the Zagreb theatre. During the period of political unrest in Croatia, when the youth began to yearn for secession from Austria-Hungary, he embraced the cause and joined the most radical faction. He was arrested at the outbreak of the war, but escaped execution thanks to a disease of the eye. Zagreb observed his sixtieth birthday (in 1917) in protest against Austria. After the war he lived in retirement. He died in Belgrade.

Vojnović published his first story, *Geranium*, in 1880; his first collection of stories *(Perom i olovkom* — With pen and pencil) in 1885; the beginning of his first novel *(Ksanta* — Xanthe) in 1887, and his first drama *(Psyche)* in 1889. In their time these were considered to be works of extraordinary merit. Whereas the other Croatian story-writers were enthralled by the Russians or by Zola, Vojnović followed Flaubert. He advanced neither thesis nor tendency, but psychology, his main goal being to work as an artist, to give attention to style, landscape, to the emotions of his characters. He painted, not petty local conditions, but the whole wide world, portraying aristocrats, artists, refined spirits. And when he described Dubrovnik, his native town, it was not in the manner customary among the Croatian realists, in combination with the political and economic conditions of that time, but in connexion with the psyche of its people, with general human problems, unrelated to his own period. Consequently his whole work seemed foreign at the time, and it was only with his drama *Ekvinocij* [The equinox] (1895) that Vojnović succeeded in winning the Croatian literary and theatre public. He employed expressive media in his play similar to those in his previous works; but he took his material from the life of ordinary people from the surroundings of Dubrovnik, and in an impressive manner recounted the conflict

216

between the old local morality of honesty, and the cynical, rapacious representatives of wealth.

Vojnović's most important work is *Dubrovačka trilogija* [The Dubrovnik trilogy] (1900), consisting of three one-act plays on the decline of noble old Dubrovnik, starting with its surrender to Napoleon, and ending with the close of the nineteenth century. During the subsequent twenty years, Vojnović was the foremost Croatian and Yugoslav playwright. His other plays are: *Smrt majke Jugovića* [The death of the mother of the Jugovićs] (1907), *Gospodja sa suncokretom* [The lady with the sunflower] (1912), *Lazarevo vaskrsenje* [The resurrection of Lazarus] (1913), *Imperatrix* (1918), *Maškerata ispod kuplja* [The masquerade beneath the roof] (1922). His short writings — essays, verses, criticisms — are collected in *Akordi* [Chords] (1918).

Vojnović's works are extremely varied in material and technique. He wrote dramas on themes from folk poetry *(Smrt majke Jugovića)*, from the Dubrovnik of the nobility and commonalty *(Dubrovačka trilogija, Maškerate ispod kuplja)*, from the cosmopolitan world of artists and murderers *(Psyche, Gospodja sa suncokretom)*, from the national struggles of the Serbs of his period *(Lazarevo vaskrsenje)*, as well as Utopian works *(Imperatrix)*. Some of his plays are lyrical, others are packed with drama. He was more a symbolist than a realist, animating inanimate things, endeavouring to make the most of what a word conveys. He built up his plays upon the achievements of nearly fifty years of European literary development, starting with naturalism and ending with expressionism. He found something to serve his purpose in Vuk Karadžić and Šenoa, in Ibsen and Pirandello. In the Croatian literature of his period he was the greatest master of word employment.

Vojnović wrote his works primarily as an artist endeavouring to bring out the innermost life of people through their outward expression and in harmony with their surroundings, through the compatibility between man and nature. He is distinguished by aristocratic feeling and individualism; he strove for a nobility of spirit, longing for the unattainable, and detesting vulgarity. In *Dubrovačka trilogija* he glorifies the patricians of Dubrovnik: even in their economic decline they tower above the common people. The features common to all of Vojnović's works are lyricism, exuberance, variety of expression, radiance and gaiety. These were all elements which provoked enthusiasm during *Moderna;* but the next generation was skeptical towards him, for it was able to differentiate between pathos and genuine artistic magnificence.

While Vojnović was the dominating figure in Croatian drama, two other playwrights also gained distinction. They were *Milan*

217

Ogrizović (1877–1923) and *Josip Kosor* (1879). Ogrizović wrote plays based on folk poetry, history and life *(Prokletstvo* — Damnation — 1906; *Hasanaginica* — 1909; *Vučina* — The wolf — 1921). In these plays he demonstrated a faculty for scenic effect. Kosor, who was self-taught, embarked on literature with stories from the world of the oppressed and ostracized *(Crni glasovi* — Ominous voices; *Optužba* — The accusation). During his later development, having now studied European art at its source, he began to write plays which treated chiefly of the primitive human passions stirred up by struggles over land, women, power *(Požar strasti* — The fire of passion — 1912; *Žena* — Woman — 1920).

Of all the Croatian writers of this period, *Antun Gustav Matoš* (1873–1914) was the most familiar with the literature of Europe. He took little part in the literary controversies of his time; but he exercised the strongest influence upon his contemporaries and upon the younger generation. The son of a country schoolmaster (at Tovarnik, Srem), he went to Zagreb as a child, where he attended secondary school. But before finishing his schooling, he was drafted into the army, from which he deserted. As a deserter he passed many years in Belgrade, Geneva and Paris, and he did not dare return to Zagreb till 1908. He spent his years of exile as a journalist, musician, writer, bohemian, without any secure means of subsistence, often enduring hunger and want.

Matoš became known as a writer towards the end of the nineteenth century, when he began to publish stories, essays, criticisms in newspapers in Zagreb and Belgrade. During his lifetime he published several collections of stories *(Iverje* — Chippings — 1899; *Novo iverje* — Further chippings — 1900; *Umorne priče* — Weary stories — 1909), essays and feuilletons *(Ogledi* — Essays — 1905; *Vidici i putovi* — Vistas and roads — 1907; *Naši ljudi i krajevi* — Our folk and our regions — 1910; *Pečalba* — Emigrant's toil — 1913). During his lifetime his works could be found scattered chiefly in magazines and newspapers.

In conception Matoš was an artist. He declared that the only decisive criterion in a work of art should be the aesthetic principle. He regarded art nothing short of a religion, alleging that in the paltriness of other values only art can give meaning to life. The writers who appealed to him most were the decadents and the symbolists (Baudelaire, Verlaine). Later he demanded vigorous modes of expression, similar to those of Stendhal and Barrès. The fundamental characteristic in art, according to him, was style. Consequently he demanded the most rigorous discipline from the artist. While Matoš drew attention to European literary achievements and derided local dilettantism, he nevertheless looked to support on Croatian territory, in Croatian history for his cultural and nationalistic work. He believed that only a combination of elements from the past and the vigour of the present could produce the strength required for national survival. Accordingly, his literary work transcended the bounds of literature, for which reason many regarded him both as a literary and as a national teacher. During the years immediately preceding his death, he was one of the most influential of Croatian writers, the preacher of a rejuvenated Croatism which was to distinguish itself by its high culture and devotion to the country and its past.

Essays, criticisms, feuilletons and travel pieces all had an outstanding place in Matoš's very prolific literary work.

Matoš wrote numerous essays on great foreign writers (Byron, Baudelaire, Stendhal, Verlaine, Rimbaud) and acquainted the Croats with the greatest Serbian writers (Lazarević, Sremac, Veselinović). He also wrote about the most significant Croatian men of letters of his period (Kranjčević, Harambašić).

Matoš published numerous criticisms and accounts of various manifestations in literature and on the stage in the newspapers and magazines of Zagreb and Belgrade; and during a period of many years he was the most productive Croatian critic, showing himself in this role to be an impressionist, regarding criticism as an art. He brought out the aesthetic elements in works of art, protesting against utilitarianism, dilettantism and pedagogical rules in criticism. He especially carried on controversies with the Croatian writer Milan Marjanović, and with the Serbian Jovan Skerlić because of what he called their inartistic approach to literature. In his severity he tore down many a literary authority, chiefly by analyzing the writer's style.

In his feuilletons Matoš for a number of years ingeniously depicted the social and cultural life of Zagreb and Belgrade. He was the first to make conscious use of landscape in describing Croatian and Serbian regions, and described Zagreb, parts of Croatia and parts of Serbia with special devotion. He also wrote a number of travel pieces, which are distinguished by their freshness of observation and by their colour.

Matoš's style particularly appealed to the reading public. His idiom is distinguished by numerous similes, by short sentences, wit, and a search for paradox.

Compared with his essays and criticism, Matoš's stories are only secondary in importance. Interesting as long as they are autobiographical, his stories, which obviously owe something to Poe, must be classified as feuilletonistic narration rather than as works of art brought to perfection.

Matoš's last phase was lyrical: he wrote verse when he was no longer able to play the violoncello, for his hand had grown stiff. As a lyrist he primarily strove for certain formal effects: he preferred sharply defined poetic forms (the sonnet); he sought to compose new rhymes, to create vivid similes. Notwithstanding frequent reverses, being a lyrical nature, he was most at home with lyrics. Through verse he expressed his trials, disappointments, and sufferings, as well as his patriotism, his rebellious nature, and his craving for beauty. By his concise mode of expression, elaborate form, and by the well-balanced order of his poems, he released Croatian poetry from verbalism and pathos, and his work marks the beginning of its further phase of development.

Irrespective of the intrinsic value of some of Matoš's compositions, as a writer he always stood at a high literary level. He clarified literary ideas in Croatia, sifting out the remnants of dilet‧tantism, journalism, well-meaning patriotic poetizing from true literature. A considerable number of his poems, essays, descriptive pieces and criticisms rank among the lasting achievements of Croatian literature.

Vladimir Nazor (1876—1949) was the most fruitful, versatile and influential Croatian writer of his generation. Living to a relatively advanced age, and writing for over half a century, he survived various trends and literary generations. To each he gave something, from each he took something; but through all the tides of taste and trend he managed to preserve his own creative individuality.

He was born at Postire, on the island of Brač in Dalmatia. Having graduated in natural sciences at the Faculty of Graz, he became first a secondary-school teacher, then the director of a gymnasium, and finally a superintendent of orphanages in turn at Zadar, Pazin, Kastav, Zagreb and Crikvenica. During the second world war, in 1942, he joined the National Liberation Army of Yugoslavia in its struggle against the invader. After the liberation of Yugoslavia he was elected President of the National Sabor of Croatia, and then President of the Presidium of the People's Republic of Croatia, the highest public office in his country.

Nazor was the contemporary, personal friend and ally of most of the Croatian modernists. Of the demands which they made on the Croatian writers, he could fulfil one: he was a connoisseur of a West-European literature — the Italian. Besides this, he was versed in Homer's works in Italian translation. Having lived his boyhood in a lonely cove on his native island, without companions, he developed into a retiring individualist. However, he had absolutely no leanings towards modernistic weaknesses, for decadence, pessimism, cosmopolitism. Contact with the countryside, on the contrary, imbued him with joy and with a feeling of strength and faith.

220

Nazor began to publish verse as a pupil in the secondary school, at a time when Croatian literature was succumbing to despondency and disorientation (Leskovar, Kranjčević, Djalski). He established himself as a creative writer with his first book of epic poems, *Slavenske legende* [Slavic legends] (1900). Like all the modernistic works, it was a departure from realism as a trend. Unlike the works of the realists, it lacked details of life: it was a world of myth and fancy, presenting figures from Slavic mythology, from folk poetry and from history, but in such a way that the poet expressed his own emotions through these figures. As distinct from the sentimental and pessimistic note of the majority of Croatian poets of that time, including even the younger ones (Domjanić), Nazor gave utterance to the joy of living, to love for the countryside, to the beauty and gaiety of youth, to faith in the strength of his country and people. At the same time he broke away from the Croatian poetic mode of expression which was based mostly on rigid metrical text-book rules. On the contrary, his rhythms are the reflection of the sentiment which inspired him to create. Consequently his verses flow, long and apparently irregular, like an endless swollen river.

Thence up to his death, Nazor continued active in literature. He distinguished himself in all fields of creation: in lyrics, in epic poetry, story-writing; as a novelist, essayist, critic, polemicist. He also translated Dante, Goethe, Hugo, Heine, Leopardi, Pascoli; he was a writer of travels, an editor, etc.

His principal collections of lyrics are *Lirika* [Lyrics] (1910), *Nove pjesme* [New poems] (1913), *Intima* (1915), *Pjesni ljuvene* [Poems of love] (1915), *Knjiga pjesama* [A book of poems] (1942). His epic poems are collected in: *Živana* (1902), *Hrvatski kraljevi* [Croatian kings] (1912), *Medvjed Brundo* [Brundo the bear] (1915), *Utva zlatokrila* [The duck of the golden wings] (1916), *Ahasver* [Ahasuerus] (1946). His most important volumes of stories and his novels are: *Veli Joža* [The giant Joža] (1908), *Istarske priče* [Istrian tales] (1913), *Stoimena* (1916), *Arkun* (1920), *Priče iz djetinjstva* [Tales from childhood] (1924), *Priče s ostrva, iz grada i sa planine* [Tales from the island, from the town and from the mountains] (1927), *Šarko* (1930), *Zagrebačke novele* [Stories from Zagreb] (1942). His criticisms and polemical articles are collected in *Članci i kritike* [Articles and criticisms] (1942), *Na vrhu jezika i pera* [At the tip of the tongue and pen] (1942). His lengthiest work is his novel *Pastir Loda* [The shepherd Loda] (1946), in which, alluding to the immortal Greek satyr, he tells in allegory the history of the island of his birth up to the second world war.

Nazor's works are varied in expression and subject-matter. At certain periods he would concentrate upon the antique pagan world, to step forth directly afterwards as a true Christian. He would often live in the world of his dreams, and then immediately after write pages of completely realistic prose. He occasionally wrote poems which violated every rule of Croatian metrics, and then in his subsequent book he would present perfectly regular verse. The characteristic of his work is constant mobility. Whenever he seemed to have exhausted one field or trend, he would cease writing for a time; then, upon emerging again, he would have something new to say. Ostensibly a subjectivist and social writer, a mystic and a materialist, Nazor was actually always simply a lyrist with a rich inner life. The most fundamental trait in his work is his strong imagination, which helped him to build new worlds out of negligible creative impulses, expanding the dimensions of his observations to immensity. As he always lived with the images of his dreams, his works were equally suggestive of a striving for freedom and a search for better forms of life, confident that the world of dreams can and must materialize. Because of these traits his poetry was revolutionary both politically and socially. Accordingly the literary categories most congenial to him were the tale, the myth and the legend, for in these his imagination reached the acme of its powers (*Utva zlatokrila, Medvjed Brundo*, etc.).

Nazor exercised a strong effect on several Croatian generations. With his works on Istria (*Veli Joža, Istarske priče*) he aided the cultural and national development of the Istrian Croat during both the rule of Austria-Hungary and that of the Italy of the fascist era. During the years preceding the first world war, and during the war itself, he influenced the younger generations which strove for the liberation of their nation from alien rule by his lyric and epic poetry (*Lirika, Nove pjesme, Utva zlatokrila, Medvjed Brundo*). With his poems, both lyric and epic, which were full of the joy of living and pervaded by an attachment to nature, he wrought a beneficial influence on a number of younger people who were inclined to pessimism. But the climax of his work came with his participation in the struggle against the invader, during the second world war. Although advanced in years, and of a reserved nature, he demonstrated by so doing, that poetry was life for him. During the war years and later, he published additional books (*Pjesme partizanke* — Partisan poems: the diary *S partizanima* — With the partisans; *Legende o drugu Titu* — Legends about Comrade Tito).

Nazor's work stamped a seal upon Croatian literature in the course of nearly fifty years of its restless, difficult existence. Much as his mode of expression and his subject-matter bespeak West-European traces, especially the influence of Hugo, D'Annunzio, Pascoli and Heine, he is both national and personal as an artist.

222

Everything he adopted from them he assimilated, and expressed individually and nationally.

In the story and novel the realistic trends were continued only by *Viktor Car Emin* (1870) in regard to subject-matter and technique. Born in the region of Istria, he was one of the most distinguished cultural and national workers in his region, enduring every change that befell Istria both under Austria and under Italy. In a number of novels and stories *(Pusto ognjište* — The deserted hearth; *Usahlo vrelo* — The dry spring; *Iza plime* — After the flood tide) he discussed the economic problems of his region in connexion with the disappearance of the sailing vessel and the transformation of Opatija into a fashionable seaside resort. He depicted seamen *(Vitez mora* — The knight of the sea) and described events from the past of Istria *(Pod sumnjom* — Under suspicion; *Presječeni puti* — Blocked roads; *Suor Aurora Veronika)*. He also wrote about his political experiences during the occupation *(Danuncijada; Udesni dani* — Fateful days). His works are distinguished by sincere narrative and profound patriotism.

The most distinctive narrator of *Moderna* was *Dinko Šimunović* (1873—1933). But he had no connexion with the modernist movement; rather, he developed of his own accord in contact with Croatian literature, the folk poem, and generally in contact with the people among whom he lived.

Šimunović was the son of a schoolmaster, born at Knin. He too became a schoolmaster, and in his advanced years a teacher at the handicraft school at Split. He died in Zagreb. All his life he felt like a vagrant, ostracized and alone. With the feeling as though something had broken in him, and burdened by the sense of being a foreigner, he kept his eyes wide open for the manifestations about him, and his senses extraordinarily sharp to appreciate the beauty of the countryside and man. He became a writer during his thirties; and by the time he had completed his first book, *Mrkodol* (1909), he was a mature artist, with his own way of observation and with a completely individual style. In his subsequent books of stories *(Djerdan* — The necklace — 1914; *Sa Krke i Cetine* — From the Krka and Cetina — 1930), in his novels *(Tudjinac* — The alien — 1911; *Porodica Vinčić* — The Vinčić family — 1911) and in his autobiographical pieces *(Mladost* — Youth — 1920; *Mladi dani* — Youthful days — 1912) he would give forth an occasional new note; but in essence, the literary features shown in his early work remained unchanged.

In his novels and stories Šimunović described Dalmatia as he had learnt to know it while a scholmaster. He had taught in regions of extreme poverty and backwardness, and in regions in which beauty and strength were still the supreme principles of life. He had seen in all its hideousness the backwardness into which the impoverished peasants were hurled by bankers, by the authorities, and by the Church. On the other hand, he was elated to see people who still lived a patriarchal life, according to tradition and the folk poem — proud, bold and healthy, remote from the degeneration of the average bourgeois.

Šimunović portrayed the Dalmatia of capitalistic penetration, with its manufactures, banking and new customs, all of which were ruthlessly doing away with the old order. In a series of stories, and in the novel *Porodica Vinčić*, he dealt directly with the effect of these things on the Dalmatian countryside. Some of his tales are a picture of the resistance put up by the patriarchal village; some show the ruin brought by the new order. Šimunović was not content with merely looking on at this process: he deliberately rose in the defence of the old system, against the bankers, the usurers, the cultural retrogrades — against the fatal influence of the town on the village folk. With all his being he fought against the domination of money over heart and beauty.

But Šimunović was no economist: he was a poet who sang about people and not about economic development. With the sensitivity of a rare artist he depicted the characters of gentle and refined village girls. With enthusiasm he portrayed men whose attraction lay in their vigour, strength and handsome figure. He depicted the beauties of Dalmatia with the skill of a painter: the ancient towers, woods, brooks and poplars. He portrayed with unconcealed admiration the patriarchal peasants, who were mostly illiterate, but noble in their bearing and feeling of complete independence, and in their firm attachment to their land. He described almost with hatred the mean, calculating petty shopkeepers, the bureaucrats, the degenerate townsfolk. And he entered with rare lyricism into the psyche of the lonely, over-sensitive intellectual such as he was himself.

During his time Šimunović was the most distinctive Croatian story-writer, the deeply national voice of his country. His works contain some slight doctrinal sign of modernism. But he was above all an artist, he was himself; and he composed his stories with a masterly hand, using an unusually pure popular tongue, sensitive to all its nuances.

Like Šimunović, *Franjo Horvat Kiš* (1876—1924) and *Ivan Kozarac* (1885—1910) described motifs from their regions — which the realists had already been doing — in an artistic fashion, and more lyrically. In his stories (the books *Ženici* — The bridegrooms; *Zašto* — Why; *Nasmijani udesi* — Smiling fates) Kiš suggestively and sadly recounted the life-roads of the intellectual and village proletariat. Kozarac in his tales *(Slavonska krv* — Slavonian blood; *Djuka Begović)* and in his verses revealed the poetry of Slavonia, delved into the psychology of pleasure and dissipation, severely criticizing manifestations in society.

A great similarity with Šimunović is shown by *Ivana Brlić Mažuranić* (Ogulin, 1874 — Zagreb, 1938), the grand-daughter of the poet Ivan Mažuranić. Her two books *(Čudnovate zgode šegrta Hlapića* — The strange adventures of the apprentice Hlapić — 1913; *Priče iz davnine* — Tales of yore — 1916) revive the world of tales, with their fairies, elves and Slavic gods, packed with strange and uncommon adventures, with a variety of events, her heroes and victors being the small, weak and unprotected, in their struggle for justice. Similar in purpose is her novel *Jaša Dalmatin* (1937).

3. THE SLOVENE MODERNISTIC MOVEMENT

Like the identical movements in the countries of Europe towards the end of the nineteenth and at the beginning of the twentieth century, the literary struggle among the Slovenes had the original objective of departing from realism and adopting what were then modern European trends. The literary movement also among the Slovenes was connected with similar endeavours in the plastic and graphic arts. But a specific mark was impressed on Slovene literature by the national and social conditions in Slovenia.

Towards the end of the nineteenth century, Slovene national life was still in the throes of a struggle between the Young Slovenes and the Old Slovenes, between the zealous Catholics and the liberals. The representatives of the Young Slovenes, however, were no longer poor writers, such as Levstik had been, but members of the Slovene bourgeoisie. They were already powerful, both in the economic and in the political life of the Slovene regions. They owned the most important literary papers *(Ljubljanski zvon, Slovan* — The Slav), and literary institutions *(Matica slovenska).* Theirs was a struggle, not only for principle, but also for position. The liberal Slovenes found justification for their struggle in the fact that the reactionaries in the ranks of their opponents were becoming stronger. The militant clericalists, in the name of ecclesiastic principles, condemned all the more progressive and superior Slovene literature, from Prešern to Tavčar. The relationship between the two groups, however, was not so simple as during the time of Levstik and Stritar.

Capitalism had penetrated into all aspects of Slovene national life by the end of the nineteenth century. The Slovene peasants were leaving their homes in growing numbers; emigration was mounting, and the small Slovene nation was dispersing all over the world. The proletarian section of the population was becoming more numerous, while the political representatives of the Slovene liberal bourgeoisie, fighting for liberalism, were simultaneously the representatives of their class. The patriotic and Slovene slogans were empty phrases. They screened the interests of groups and individuals. The bankers, the village shopkeepers and the lawyers pretended they were liberal and God-fearing in order to receive the protection of the political parties. It was precisely among the Slovene clergy, who were closer to the village, that there grew up a conviction that the peasantry should be given economic assistance. Peasant cooperatives were founded, peasant economic life was organized and credits were granted to the farmers, the result being that the church organizations again intensified their influence upon the broad masses. And all the while a Slovene socialist movement, headed by progressive, intelligent leaders, was becoming stronger.

The young Slovene writers who appeared towards the end of the nineteenth century were nurtured chiefly on the works of the Young Slovenes. They published their more valuable works in *Ljubljanski zvon*. Anton Aškerc, in a fashion their patron and teacher, also attracted the young men with his broad-minded views on literature, with his struggle against superstition, intolerance, social inequality, and with his sonorous verses. The political representative of the Young Slovenes was the writer Ivan Tavčar. But the young and old writers and public figures were soon torn by strife, and the younger ones went their own way.

The members of the young Slovene literary generation differed from the old in that they were concerned, not so much with the struggle between liberalism and clericalism, as they were with the problem of delving into the core of the Slovene national issues. In so doing, they were critical also of the Young Slovenes. As they acquainted themselves with the works of European writers in the original, they sought models beyond the domestic poets. They were especially attracted by the French and German literature of their period. Their own literary activity began during their school years. The best-known representatives of the younger generation, Ivan Cankar, Oton Župančič, Josip Murn Aleksandrov, Dragotin Kette, Ivan Prijatelj, while gymnasium pupils, constituted a group which endeavoured to reach the highest attainments of the European literature of their day. They broadened their outlook during their university studies, chiefly in Vienna. Through Cankar, Župančič, Prijatelj and others Vienna, in a fashion, became a Slovene cultural centre again, particularly so as several talented painters were also there during this period.

A characteristic common to the whole Slovene modernistic group was the striving of the Slovene writers to assimilate the features of form and subject-matter prevalent in European literature, with its decadence, individualism, impressionism, symbolism; and with its considerable tendencies towards despondency, pessimism and over-emphasized erotism.

The appearance of the Slovene modernists provoked the reaction of the conservative elements. Bishop Jeglič of Ljubljana had the entire edition of Ivan Cankar's lyric poetry, *Erotika* (1899), bought up and burnt, for he regarded it as a threat to morality. During the first ten years of the twentieth century the conservatives affected indifference to the writings of the Slovene modernists, assailed them, and distorted their purport. Their controversies were bitter and ruthless, and occasionally ended in the ruin of reputations.

There were times when even the foremost Slovene modernists were not certain as to their objective. They faltered between decadence, symbolism and naturalism; between blindly imitating European literary trends and the requirements of the Slovene people. Art for art's sake, which they expounded, provoked resistance among the people, who held that the Slovenes require books from which they can benefit in their national and economic struggle.

The position of the younger writers was difficult, for they had provoked both the conservatives and the successors of the Young Slovene movement, such as Aškerc, whose later works were criticized by the younger writers for being the product more of a craftsman than of an artist, for their rhetoric and vacuity, notwithstanding his significance as a public figure.

Hesitation and internal weakness also provoked strife in the ranks of the Slovene modernistic movement. But as individual writers came into closer contact with Slovene reality, peace soon reigned.

During the first ten years of the twentieth century, the Slovene bourgeois elements, notwithstanding their dissatisfaction with political conditions among the Slovenes, gave official support to the government, which was in the hands of the Germans in Austria; and, having secured a firmer social position, the Slovene conservative and the Slovene liberal bourgeois elements began to follow in the footsteps of the German bourgeoisie in economic affairs: like the bourgeoisie of every nation, they sought to accumulate wealth. Although Slovene cultural life had reached a relatively high level, secondary education in the Slovene regions was still given in German. Nor was there any prospect whatever of founding a Slovene university. The repeated demands for greater political independence were answered by the authorities with greater pressure. As a result of this, the majority of the youth turned revolutionary, the old slogans lost their meaning.

A similar process was evident in literature. The modernistic principles regarding individualism, freedom of creation and other

227

principles had helped the younger Slovene writers to improve their mode of expression. But as they became inspired by European literature, they adopted some of its turns of expression in order to advance Slovene literature, and not simply for the sake of emulation. As they gained experience, they abandoned decadent and cosmopolitan principles, and turned back to their own country and the best traditions of Slovene literature: to Prešern, Levstik, and to the folk poem. They raised Slovene literature to a height it had never attained before: it became profoundly artistic and deeply Slovene. In the Slovene tongue they found unexpectedly rich sources of expression. Finally the achievements of the Slovene modernistic movement were accepted by some of the more conservative writers who still rallied round the magazine *Dom in svet*, and their works became more readable, broader in subject-matter and richer in expression.

Slovene literature at the beginning of the twentieth century produced no ideologue or critic of major importance. The principal controversies over trends and literary values were carried on by their originators, chiefly by Cankar. Nevertheless, Slovene science and literature benefited by the movement, for it produced the two most significant Slovene literary historians and theorists: Ivan Prijatelj and France Kidrič.

Ivan Prijatelj (1875—1937), the son of a peasant from Sodražica, near Ribnica, studied Slavic philology in Vienna. After his studies he stayed in Russia for a time, and travelled in western and northern Europe. He worked in the Court Library in Vienna up to Austria's defeat. From 1919 he was a professor of Slovene literature at the newly founded University of Ljubljana. His scientific work consisted of a study of the aesthetic elements in the works of the major Slovene writers and the effect of social conditions on their work. He concentrated particularly on those periods of Slovene literature in which the Slovenes built up and consolidated their national sovereignty. His main works are *Janko Kersnik* (1910—1914), *Duševni profili slovenskih preporoditeljev* [The spiritual aspect of the Slovene renaissance writers] (1921).

The life and career of *France Kidrič* (1880—1950) resembled Prijatelj's; only, Kidrič occupied himself scientifically with the earlier periods of Slovene literature. The result of his work is the extensive *Zgodovina slovenskega slovstva* [The history of Slovene literature] (1929). He also began an exhaustive monograph on Prešern, but failed to complete it. Kidrič's scientific work sprang from the same source as that of Prijatelj: from the desire to comprehend the evolution of the Slovene nation.

Ivan Cankar (1876—1918) was the most important figure in the Slovene modernistic movement and, with the exception of Prešern, the greatest Slovene writer.

Cankar was one of a large family of children of a poor craftsman. He was born at Vrhnika, near Ljubljana. His upbringing
and education were chiefly due to his mother. Although living
under conditions of want and humiliation, he graduated from
gymnasium and proceeded to study engineering in Vienna. Poverty
and love of literature, however, prevented him from finishing his
studies, and he began to support himself by writing. He lived mostly
in Vienna until 1907, when he returned to his own country. He
first settled down at Rožnik, near Ljubljana, and then in 1917 he
moved to Ljubljana, where he died.

Like all the outstanding members of his generation, Cankar,
influenced by Aškerc's strong personality, began to write while
still a gymnasium pupil in Ljubljana. But on becoming acquainted
with the West-European literature of his time, he freed himself
from Aškerc's spell. Profoundly read, sensitive, he was first carried
away by the artistic trends of the period — decadence and symbolism; but he soon discovered his own bent, which was completely
personal — Cankarian.

Cankar's first better lyrical pieces were his sketches and lyric
poems. His first volume of poems, *Erotika*, provoked unexpected
attacks from the conservative writers. Later he abandoned verse
and devoted himself to prose. In just over twenty years he published
numerous works, the principal among them being his volumes of
sketches and stories: *Vinjete* [Vignettes] (1899), *Knjiga za lahko-
miselne ljudi* [A book for the lightheaded] (1901), *Ob zori* [At
dawn] (1903), *Hiša Marije pomočnice* [The house of Mary the
comforter] (1904), *Gospa Judit* [Madame Judith] (1904), *Hlapec
Jernej in njegova pravica* [The servant Jernej and his rights] (1907),
Zgodbe iz doline Šentflorijanske [Tales from Saint Florijan's Val-
ley] (1908), *Milan in Milena* [Milan and Milena] (1913), *Moje
življenje* [My life] (1914), *Podobe iz sanj* [Dream visions] (1917).
His novels are *Tujci* [Foreigners] (1901), *Na klancu* [On the cliff]
(1902), *Martin Kačur* (1906). His plays are: *Jakob Ruda* (1900),
Za narodov blagor [For the welfare of the nation] (1901), *Kralj
na Betajnovi* [The king of Betajnova] (1902), *Pohujšanje v dolini
Šentflorijanski* [Sacrilege in Saint Florijan's Valley] (1908, etc. He
also wrote a considerable number of criticisms and polemics.

Cankar found the material for his works among the Slovene
petty bourgeois and rural folk, and in the life of the proletariat
and Slovene intelligentsia. He dealt with the process which, having
commenced among the Slovenes about the middle of the nineteenth century, especially intensified during his childhood and
youth: with the pressure of capitalism in the Slovene regions, the
pauperization of the Slovene peasantry, the formation of the proletariat and *Lumpenproletariat*, the education of young Slovenes
from the country, and their employment in government posts. In

229

a way typically his own, Cankar described the controversies between the Slovene liberals and conservatives, socialism among the Slovenes, the attempts of cultural organizations and groups to influence the Slovene countryside.

In ideology, Cankar became an opponent of the clericalists and liberals during his later development. Having lived in the workers' quarter of Vienna, he familiarized himself with the labour section and became a socialist, and once he also stood for election as a socialist candidate. Originally akin to the Slovene liberals in cultural matters, he soon realized that, as the representatives of the bourgeoisie, they too supported the views of their social class in relation to the peasantry and workers. During the years preceding his death, of all the Slovene politicians, Janez Krek appealed to him most, for he was just as concerned over the prosperity of the Slovene peasant as he was over the political freedom of the Slovene people.

In the course of his literary career, Cankar passed through several phases: he was in turn a decadent, a symbolist, a champion of art for art's sake, and an advocate of tendentious literature. At different periods he stated his views on political and social problems in different ways. Yet through all these phases there remained a constant note: he strove to make Slovene literature the full and free expression of the individual and nation; he sought to render it distinctively Slovene, and an instrument with which to develop a new and happier social order. Cankar's strength, however, does not consist in the theoretical principles of his art, but in the manner in which he expressed his world.

Cankar is primarily a poet of longing, a poet of the heart. His best-defined characters in his different works appear again and again under different names. They are all people who yearn for something finer, for something almost unrealisable; yet they are incapable of adapting themselves to everyday life. Owing to this, they suffer when they come into conflict with the harshness of life and the ruthlessness of those who are better fitted to cope with reality. His most frequent characters are "eternal" students, aged and poor workers, maidservants and manservants, unsuccessful artists. The philistines regard them as failures; but in fact they are all full of anticipation and hope for a better life. On the other hand, Cankar portrayed the typical petty bourgeois, with his plans, rapacity, and his cruelty towards the weak.

Cankar's analysis of the psychology of ordinary people in their endless sufferings, helplessness and inability to resist violence is remarkable. He possessed a special gift for fathoming the psychology of children, for that horrible anguish endured in silence which, though invisible, leaves ineffaceable traces on the character and future of the adult. With almost autobiographical fidelity he described the blows endured by the soul as the child suffers injustice, or is branded and punished for offences which it has not committed. He was a master in exposing the pain which eats into the human soul, like an incurable sore which has been opened by humiliation suffered in childhood.

Cankar's characters are extremely sensitive and, consequently, unhappy and incapable of self-composure. These characters he forgave; but it was with the scourge of satire that he lashed the philistines and the hypocrites, who exploited the weak and helpless, masking their actions in terms of piousness or patriotism. A number of his plays and stories satirize Slovene cultural and economic conditions. Cankar found pleasure in portraying the average Slovene townsfolk with their God-fearing respectable types, who were at heart voluptuaries, usurers and judicial murderers.

In his plays, long stories and novels Cankar was primarily a lyrist. He was never an objectivist in relation to his subject: he felt for it either sympathy and admiration, or scorn and hatred. The literary category most typical of him is his lyrical sketch, always a piece of perfect artistry, chiefly autobiographical in subject-matter. It is in this form that he described both his childhood and his youth, as well as the last years of his life. From the most commonplace events in life he would produce works of exalted poetry. His mother occupies a special place in his works: a rather plain, but tenacious and selfless woman, whom Cankar regarded as a superior being, with her immeasurable love for her children and with her intense feeling for justice.

At the core all of Cankar's work is a cry for justice and beauty, for forms of life without the oppressed or the oppressor, without the hurt or the wounded.

Cankar is the greatest prose writer in Slovene literature. He was attracted by Levstik and Trdina; but he created his own, distinctively Cankarian idiom, which is immediately recognizable in everything he wrote. His style, simple and precise, yet colourful, contains rare tenderness, penetration, melody, gradation. Cankar arrived at the heart of the matter in a few words, using short sentences, paradoxes, special turns of phrase and significant suggestive breaks in his narrative. In him the Slovene language found an artist who revealed its boundless possibilities of expression, and raised it to heights till then unanticipated.

In his grasp of the entire life of Slovenia, Cankar was not merely a writer. All his work is distinguished by a profoundly realistic tone and topical thoughts; and it is only their expression that is distinctively poetic, often bordering upon symbolism. But Cankar was aware of his goal, and it was no less obvious to others. He was, consequently, attacked by the reactionaries, which is why he applied himself to criticism and polemics, his controversies with his opponents frequently carrying him to extremes. He often had to fight alone, and was wounded, hurt, bruised. At first stigmatized and assailed, in the end his works brought him the fame of a writer over whom the several sections of Slovene society vied.

With distinctive realism, even with naturalism, *Alois Kraigher* (1877), story-writer and playwright, approached Slovene reality. In his novels *(Kontrolor Škrobar* — Inspector Škrobar — 1914; *Mlada ljubezen* — Young love — 1923) he gave a bitter picture of the Slovene petty bourgeoisie, with its readiness to compromise on national matters, with its weakness towards money, its shaky morals.

Slovene lyrics were raised to the highest level by three modernists: Dragotin Kette, Josip Murn Aleksandrov and Oton Župančič. Each in his own way accepted the achievements of the various literatures of Europe, assimilating them and making them Slovene and their own. Dragotin Kette and Josip Murn Aleksandrov were unable to develop to the fullness of their talent, for death cut short their career at an early age.

Dragotin Kette (1876–1899) was the son of a country schoolmaster. Having graduated from gymnasium, he was drafted into the army, in which his health broke down. Shortly afterwards he died in the old Ljubljana sugar mills which had been turned into a poorhouse.

Although he was barely twenty-three years old at the time of his death, Kette was already an independent artistic personality. Though reading the works of many European poets, he fashioned a mode of expression all his own. Profoundly Slovene at heart and attached to the country, he preserved his peasant straightforwardness, his contact with nature, his humour and cheerfulness. In his poems he exhibited all these traits with the directness, naturalness and whole-heartedness of a bird singing on a branch. His poems evince a gay and carefree mood, and only rarely do they become pensive. In the course of his further development he successfully employed the sonnet form, in which he revealed his philosophical views, his attachment to nature, and a kind of pantheism. His collection of poems, *Poezije*, was published after his death (1900).

Josip Murn Aleksandrov (1879–1901) was the illegitimate son of a maidservant. He was brought up in the country as an orphan. Having made his way with difficulty through gymnasium, he went to Vienna, but no study offered sufficient attraction to arouse his interest. He returned to Ljubljana, and there, in the same conditions and in the same room in which Kette had died before him, he also expired.

Like Kette, Murn was a mature poet even during his schooldays. His poetry has something timid, gloomy and vague about it; and longing, despair and discontent issue from his verses, which, though formed without sufficient practice, still have a profound directness. They are deeply impressive in their awareness and presentiment of early death. His poems were collected in a book called *Pesni in romance* [Poems and romances] (1903).

Oton Župančič (1878–1949) was the only prominent Slovene modernist to develop fully, for he lived over seventy years. He experienced the many stirring changes which the Slovene went through in the twentieth century, and lived to see the political liberation of his people. After the second world war, in which he fought actively as a poet on the side of the fighters for freedom, he lived to experience the highest honours the Slovene nation could confer upon him.

Župančič was born at Vinica, a small town on the Slovene-Croatian border. He attended gymnasium in Ljubljana, and studied at the Faculty of Philosophy in Vienna. He spent some time travelling in the countries of Western Europe, where he acquainted himself with West-European literature. He returned to live in Ljubljana, where he was dramaturgist in the theatre, among his other activities.

Župančič embarked on literature during the last ten years of the nineteenth century by writing for children's magazines. He introduced himself with his first volume of poems, *Čaša opojnosti* [A cup of bliss] in 1899. Then followed other collections: *Pisanice* [Easter eggs] (1900), *Čez plan* [Across the plateau] (1904), *Samogovori* [Monologues] (1908). During the first world war he published two books for children: *Ciciban in še kaj* [Ciciban and something else] (1915), and *Sto ugank* [A hundred riddles] (1915). After the first world war he published two volumes of lyric poems *Mlada pota* [New roads] (1920) and *V zarje Vidove* [The dawn of Vid's day] (1920). He wrote no more poems during the following twenty years, but in 1924 he published *Veronika Deseniška*, a play. He was also a prolific translator (Shakespeare, France, Rostand). His last collection, *Zimzelen pod snegom* [Snowbound evergreen], a forceful, topical and artistic collection, was born of the circumstances engendered by the second world war.

His first book of lyrics was in a manner a manifesto of his modernistic views. It contains cosmopolitism, fiery passion, decadence, individualism, as well as a blasé disposition. The personal element in his subject-matter was as yet not strong. Nevertheless Župančič revealed talents during that period which later soared to the supreme degree of development: a gift of employing the Slovene tongue freely, of making the most of the wealth of its material of voice and form. He wrote with directness, almost with a child's guilelessness. While close in form to free verse and the free division of a poem into stanzas, he was perfect in rhythm and fluency of expression.

233

As he continued to develop, Župančič soon abandoned various fashionable modernistic tendencies, and gave prominence to whatever formed a link between him and his country. Although he availed himself liberally of both the achievements of West-European literature and the fruits of Slovene peasant poetry, he was the slave of neither. As a supreme artist he throve upon the spirit of folk poetry, while remaining an independent creator.

Župančič succeeded in expressing his internal world as few lyrists before him have done: the world of the educated bourgeois intellectual of the first half of the twentieth century, which he would connect with the sentiments of a man attached to his village by firm ties. His poetry is the expression of vacillation, suspicion, of the love and longing of the educated European of his period. At the same time, there emanates from his poetry the gaiety and abandon of the young Slovene rustic, the breath of the village idyll, the freshness of the countryside, cheerful and gay.

Župančič was aware both of his own position and of the position of the subjugated Slovene nation in the prevalent political and social circumstances, and he revealed his subjective loves and hatreds, and criticized Slovene conditions. Besides this, he called attention to the poverty surrounding the Slovene, whose life-breath was spent in foreign lands in his struggle for subsistence, while at home the authorities drained the last ounce of strength from his family by means of economic and political pressure. He was an idyllic and merry poet, as well as a fighter for political freedom and social justice. His *Duma* is a touching and sensitive picture of Slovenia on the eve of the first world war, strife-ridden, depopulated, impoverished and helpless.

Before the first world war broke out, Župančič was actively engaged in helping the generation of young Slovene intellectuals who were preparing a revolutionary bid for liberation from Austria, in conjunction with the Croatian and Serbian intellectuals.

He wrote his poems for children during the war. They revealed his amazing understanding of the child soul as it begins to become aware of the outside world. His poems are distinguished by their childlike serenity, their directness, and by the purity of their verse.

Župančič's only play, *Veronika Deseniška*, is a portrayal of the omnipotence and tragedy of pure and innocent love. Both its virtues and its faults lie in its lyricism.

Župančič's significance in Slovene literature is immense. After Prešern's poetry, his poems indicate the further strong rise of Slovene lyrics to towering altitudes, with a wide, unusual range of emotions and a supreme sureness of expression. Although he was an unwavering individualist, Župančič succeeded in depicting the whole life-course of his nation during half a century of his own life, and in becoming a poet who was national and Slovene, in the fullest sense. At the same time he raised the Slovene poetic language to such a pitch of perfection that it has become a marvellous organism, capable of uttering the most delicate shades of emotion and feeling. Taking up the thread of Prešern's work after the intervening lapse of time, Zupančič is witness of the vitality of the small Slovene nation, as demonstrated by its ability to produce such works of art.

The group of writers gathered around *Dom in svet* contained several who were regarded during their period as among the most outstanding in the whole of Slovene literature (Ksaver Meško, Anton Medved, and others). The foremost among them was *Frančišek Sal. Finžgar* (1871). He was born in the country. After taking orders he served in many parts of Slovenia, ultimately settling in Ljubljana. He had, therefore, a profound knowledge of the psychology of the peasants, the workers and the intellectuals. He wrote poems, plays and criticisms; but his favourite vehicle were the story and novel. With a keen gift for observation, and being opposed to compromise, he dealt with the same material as Cankar: with the penetration of foreign capital into the Slovene regions, with the first conscious resistance of the Slovene workers against exploitation, with the cynical behaviour of the servants of capital towards the workers *(Iz modernega sveta* — From the modern world — 1904), with the position of the Slovene intellectuals among the parvenus *(Sama* — *Alone* — 1912), the village rich and poor *(Dekla Ančka* — The maiden Ančka — 1913; *Stara in nova hiša* — The old house and the new — 1900). In his descriptions of human relations Finžgar is on the side of the weak and downtrodden. But being a clergyman, he often dealt with events and persons in a specific manner: he sought solution of conflicts and disputes on religious soil. Consequently the greater part of his stories are in a certain way didactic. The most artistic are his pictures of nature *(Na petelina* — The grouse shoot), and his historical novel, *Pod svobodnim solncem* [Beneath the free sun] (1906—7). Uninhibited by his calling or by political considerations, he wrote of the conflicts between Slavdom and Byzantium in the sixth century. The novel is full of pictures of battle, suffering, defeat, love and intrigue; and winds up with the conclusive victory of the young Slavs. Finžgar's novel, with its pictures of corrupt Byzantium, had a relation to conditions during the Austro-Hungarian period; and, faithful to his views, Finžgar stood by his nation during the first and the second world war.

235

BETWEEN THE TWO WARS

1. THE DEFEAT OF AUSTRIA-HUNGARY; THE CREATION OF YUGOSLAVIA AND CONDITIONS IN IT

The modernistic note in Yugoslav literature had lost its appeal at the beginning of the second decade of the twentieth century. Among the modernists themselves there had developed differences which were immediately obvious, and they became acute before the outbreak of the first world war. The achievements of the modernistic period — a taste for artistic values, delicate shades of expression, contact with Europe — still survived; but in regard to the political and social conditions, literature had already assumed another trend. The writers who continued to advocate unrestricted freedom of creation, artistic individuality and cosmopolitism were strongly opposed by writers who asserted that art should deal with its own nation and period. These tendencies were evident in all the three Yugoslav literatures, but they did not manifest themselves in all three with the same intensity, or at the same time.

Literary life was the most unrestricted in Serbia. The endeavours of Austria-Hungary to prevent Serbia's development and national aspirations provoked the Serbian people to resistance and defiance. This particularly found expression in literature. Even the extreme pessimists gave vent to their feelings with songs of strength. The representative and advocate of the new views was Jovan Skerlić. He launched a fierce attack against modernism, against affected pessimism and pseudo-aristocratism, demanding daring, national literature as the expression of the progressive social forces. His influence spread beyond the boundaries of Serbia, for his *Srpski književni glasnik* published contributions by all the most outstanding Yugoslav writers, and reported every major manifestation which occurred in the three literatures. On the eve of the war he started a movement to eliminate all differences in the literary language and script of the Serbs and Croats, by pursuading the Serbs to accept the Latin script and the Croats to accept the eastern speech development of the *štokavski* dialect.

Owing to the behaviour of the Austrian and Hungarian authorities towards the Slavs, the conviction grew in the Croatian and Slovene regions of the Dual Monarchy that neither the Croats nor the Slovenes, nor finally the Serbs, could expect anything in the Austro-Hungarian empire, and that they must seek liberation and unification outside it. The revolutionary tide first rose among youth, who soon received the support of the foremost older writers (Vojnović, Tresić-Pavičić, Nazor, Marjanović, Župančič and Šantić), and literature soon began to reflect the new state of affairs.

The principle of freedom of creation, resistance to trends, lost meaning in the new conditions. A struggle was launched in the ranks of the one-time modernists for national, realistic and tendentious literature. Even Matoš, the most consistent advocate of art for art's sake in Croatian literature, found a way to connect his aesthetic views with the duties of a writer towards his people. While among the Serbs and Slovenes the new movement was supported by the foremost literary journals such as *Srpski književni glasnik* and *Ljubljanski zvon*, magazines were founded among the Croats, notably *Književne novosti* (1914), to oppose the consistently modernistic *Savremenik*. New periodicals *(Srpsko-hrvatski almanah*, the scientific magazine *Veda)* were started, in which Serbs and Croats, or Slovenes and Croats cooperated. These literary papers endeavoured to attract contributors from among the Serbs and Croats and Slovenes, while literary institutions began to publish the works of Serbs, Croats and Slovenes without discrimination.

The movement spread to the plastic and graphic arts: Ivan Meštrović, a Croatian sculptor, conceived as his first great work of art the *Vidovdanski hram* [The *Vidovdan* temple], with images of characters from folk poetry connected with the Battle of Kosovo (fought on June 28, 1389). During this period folk poetry had gained in eminence as the most direct artistic creation of the broad peasant masses and because of its extremely national subject-matter and mode of expression.

Austria-Hungary endeavoured by force of arms to prevent the Yugoslav peoples from drawing together: it attacked Serbia in 1914, precipitating the first world war. Exhausted by the wars of 1912 and 1913, little Serbia succeeded nevertheless in defeating its superior enemy in a number of battles. But when it was also attacked by Germany and Bulgaria in 1915, the Serbian Army was forced to withdraw from the country. It left unvanquished, however, and crossing the mountains of Albania, it reached the sea. With Allied assistance it was re-equipped for further operations. Meanwhile revolution began to spread in the Yugoslav territories of Austria-Hungary and the State began to break up. In 1918 the Serbian Army returned victorious to its own country; and from the ruins of Austria-Hungary rose the new State of the Serbs, Croats and Slovenes, later renamed Yugoslavia.

During the war the Austrian and Hungarian authorities prohibited the publication of anything that they considered even remotely harmful to their interests. Courts-martial were set up and rigorous military censorship instituted in occupied Serbia, and in Croatia and Slovenia. Nevertheless the Croatian, Slovene and Serbian writers found means to state their views, particularly during the latter half of the war, when there was no longer any doubt as to its outcome. Several important works were written during the war itself, significant for the views of the Yugoslav writers towards it: *Podobe iz Sanj* by Ivan Cankar, *Prorokovana* [Prophesied], a novel of war by Frančišek S. Finžgar, *Sikara* [Brushwood], an allegorical poem by Vladimir Nazor. Their anti-war note and their faith in the final liberation of their nations are obvious.

The Serbian writers who had remained in the country wrote for the Croatian magazines. The writers who were in exile with the Army published books and periodicals in the countries which had given them asylum.

The common State of the Yugoslav peoples was founded during the years of growing class antagonism in the world, the year following the Russian Revolution. During its earliest days, various problems appeared in all their acuteness.

The several national bourgeoisies of Yugoslavia had now attained full power for the first time, but they were incapable of adjusting their interests. A struggle ensued between the idea of eliminating completely the previous boundaries and traditions of the several nations, in favour of total centralistic organization, and among the several Yugoslav nations to preserve their interests and national individualities. The centralistic Constitution, which had been written against the will of the Slovene and Croatian majority, accorded full hegemony to the Serbian bourgeoisie, the result being that the majority of the Croats, Slovenes and Macedonians, and considerable numbers of the Serbs, went into opposition against the central Government. Although the authors of the Constitution declared that it was the result of the desire of the Yugoslav peoples for unification, they forgot that these nations had been kept apart for centuries, and that each nation had traditions distinctively its own.

Adopting the methods of the West-European bourgeoisie, the Yugoslav bourgeoisie, as the ruling class, sought to emulate the West-European capitalistic States in way of life and business affairs. Instead of concentrating upon constructive work in the interest of the broad masses, the members of the bourgeoisie started

239

a get-rich-quick race, with corruption, bribery, blackmail as means to easy profit. Banks and companies were founded, factories sprang up, the forests were ruthlessly cut down, mansions were built; and all the while the masses steadily sank deeper into wretchedness: the peasants were deep in debt, the workers poorly paid, unemployed, persecuted. The resistance of the latter, most of whom were organized in the Communist party, was broken when the party was banned in 1919 and went underground. The resistance of the Croatian peasant masses, organized in the Agrarian party under the leadership of Stjepan Radić, however, lasted almost up to the second world war.

The fascist-like dictatorship set up by King Alexander in 1929 only rendered the situation more acute, the internal antagonisms more intense; and the result was that in 1941 the fascist invaders simply walked over Yugoslavia.

An attempt was made after the unification of the Yugoslavs to break down the barriers separating the several Yugoslav literatures. The slogan of 1850 was again launched in literary life: One nation — one literature. The result were attempts to unify the Yugoslav peoples in script, speech, orthography; to enlist cooperation in literary magazines, to reconcile literary and cultural organizations. Almost all the writers, from the distinctive nationalists to the extreme Marxists, at first agreed to this. Several years later, owing to the political differences and political strife, the idea of literary unification was slowly abandoned: the several literatures drew back into their own confines, their writers gathered around their own magazines, while the cultural organizations throve in the main on their national soil. Notwithstanding this, the most prominent writers endeavoured to preserve a general Yugoslav horizon even during the years of the most acute political strife.

Almost immediately after the war, an attempt at the revaluation of literary merit appeared in the literatures of the Yugoslav peoples. The tempo of life, the connexions between the Yugoslav writers and the writers of Western Europe, which were closer and easier, facilitated the exchange of cultural acquirements. Thus West-European literary trends soon became evident in the literatures of the Yugoslav peoples.

As in Western Europe, the old slogans were forgotten in Yugoslavia, the old literary authorities repudiated, modernistic slogans and new champions taking their place. Thus, expressionism of different shades and names invaded Slovene and Croatian literature, while surrealism with all its consequences for style and idiom was introduced into Serbian literature. Some features of expressionism were also adopted by writers who belonged to the left, and by distinctively Catholic writers (among the Slovenes, for instance).

During this struggle of trends and generations, new magazines were founded, or efforts were made to bolster the old ones. Between the two wars, apart from the revived *Srpski književni glasnik*, a number of new papers were founded in Serbian literature: *Raskrsnica* [The crossroads], *Misao* [Thought], *Svedočanstva* [Testimonies], *Naša stvarnost* [Our reality], *Umetnost i kritika* [Art and criticism], *Život i rad* [Life and work], etc. In addition to *Savremenik*, *Hrvatska revija* [The Croatian magazine] was founded in Croatia as the organ of the more conservative writers, which had been preceded, among others, by *Plamen* [The flame], *Književna republika* [The literary republic], *Književnik* [The writer], *Juriš* [The onslaught], *Literatura*, *Savremena stvarnost* [Contemporary reality], *Kultura*, *Izraz* [Expression]. The Slovene *Ljubljanski zvon* survived up to the beginning of the second world war. Other magazines were *Modra ptica* [The bluebird], *Sodobnost* [Contemporaneity]. Apart from the magazines and newspapers published in the literary centres of Belgrade, Zagreb and Ljubljana, a number of important journals were also published at Sarajevo and Novi Sad. Newspapers of a Marxian shade were the link which held the writers of the three Yugoslav nations together in close cooperation, especially those which were edited and published by Miroslav Krleža *(Danas* — Today; *Pečat* — The seal).

The first writers in the three literatures of Yugoslavia who overcame the troubles of experiment were the writers who championed a definite social ideology, and reverted to some form of realism or other. Some of them, after the model of the French surrealists, in theory justified the logic of development from surrealism to Marxism.

The political and social fermentation in Yugoslavia also affected literature. As never before, the life of the worker, of the peasant, the wretchedness of the proletariat, the narrow-mindedness of the bourgeoisie and petty bourgeoisie, the severity of the clashes between the classes, etc. found expression in literary works. The Yugoslav authorities, especially during the dictatorship, persecuted literature for fear that it might encroach upon their interests. Most magazines with a Marxian ideology were banned.

2. THE MOST IMPORTANT REPRESENTATIVES OF YUGOSLAV LITERATURE BETWEEN THE TWO WARS

During the years which preceded the last war, there were many writers in Yugoslav literature who championed new literary trends. Most of them, however, soon withdrew; but there still remained a considerable number who contributed greatly to the development of the new literature.

In Serbian literature the chief names are Ivo Andrić, Miloš Crnjanski, Branimir Ćosić, Isak Samokovlija (story writers); Desanka Maksimović, Dušan Vasiljev, Milan Dedinac, Božidar Kovačević (lyrists); Marko Ristić, Milan Bogdanović, Miloš Savković Velibor Gligorić, Velimir Živojinović-Massuka (critics and essayists). Side by side with them stand the prolific members of the older and the middle generation: Bogdan Popović, Jovan Dučić, Veljko Petrović, Isidora Sekulić, and the youngest, Branko Ćopić, and others.

The leading writers in present-day Croatian literature are Miroslav Krleža (lyrist, story-writer, playwright, essayist), August Cesarec (story-writer, polemicist), Julije Benešić (dramaturgist and translator), Slavko Batušić (poet and travel writer), Ljubo Wiesner (lyrist), A. B. Šimić (lyrist, critic), Ljubomir Maraković (a representative of Catholic criticism), Tin Ujević (lyrist and essayist), Gustav Krklec, Dobriša Cesarić, Dragutin Tadijanović, Vlado Vlaisavljević, Vladimir Kovačić, Frano Alfirević (lyrists); Vjekoslav Kaleb, Slavko Kolar, Novak Simić, Ivan Dončević (story-writers); Stanislav Šimić (poet and critic), Mihovil Pavlek Miškina (story-writer, a self-taught peasant).

The more important names in Slovene literature are Alojz Gradnik, Srečko Kosovel, Tone Seliškar, Igo Gruden, Pavel Golia, Mile Klopčič, Anton Vodnik (lyrists); Prežihov Voranc, Vladimir Levstik, Ivan Pregelj, France Bevk, Anton Ingolič, Miško Kranjec Boris Pahor (story-writers); Bratko Kreft (a playwright), Josip Vidmar, Vladimir Bartol, Božidar Borko (essayists), and Juš Kozak essayist and story-writer.

Of significance in Croatian literature is the appearance between the two wars of regional writers, who wrote in their native dialects, continuing to some extent the traditions of Frano Galović and Dragutin Domjanić. They are, among others, Mate Balota (the nom de plum of Mijo Marković), Dragutin Gervais, Pere Ljubić, Marin Franičević (in the *čakavski* dialect), Nikola Pavić, Ivan Goran Kovačić (in the *kajkavski* dialect).

Members of the older generations (Milan Begović, Dinko Šimunović, Vladimir Nazor, Viktor Car Emin, Frančišek S. Finžgar, Oton Župančič) were also active in Croatian and Slovene literature.

All the writers mentioned, and many others besides, developed their talent between the two wars, most of whom are still active. The foremost among them are Miroslav Krleža, Ivo Andrić and the late Prežihov Voranc.

Miroslav Krleža (1893) was the most prolific, forceful and influential writer in Croatian and in Yugoslav literature between the two wars. Born in Zagreb, he was first an officer, but after graduating at the military academy in Budapest, his national enthusiasm took him to Serbia in 1912 to serve in the Serbian Army. His offer was rejected. He wanted to take part in the war of 1913 against the Turks, but the Serbian authorities arrested him as a suspect and sent him back to Austria. During the first world war he was a private in the army of Austria-Hungary. After the war he became a writer with independent means. He also distinguished himself by his ideological work in the workers' movement. During the occupation in the second world war (1941—1945) he was persecuted and repeatedly imprisoned by the Ustashi. In present Yugoslavia he is Vice-President of the Yugoslav Academy of Science and Arts, and Director of the Lexicographic Institute, to mention but two of the offices he holds.

Krleža entered literature on the eve of the first world war with *Legenda*, a symbolical sketch of Christ. His first volumes of poetry were published during the war *(Pan, 1917; Tri simfonije — Three symphonies — 1917)*. From 1918 onwards, he displayed immense literary activity, publishing stories, novels, essays, plays, and carrying on polemics. He contributed to all the major Yugoslav magazines, and initiated new literary papers *(Plamen, Književna republika, Danas, Pečat)* either alone or with other progressive writers. Most of them were short-lived, for they were quickly banned.

His principal books of lyrics are: *Lirika* (1919), *Knjiga pjesama* [A book of poems] (1931), *Knjiga lirike* [A book of lyrics] (1932), *Pjesme u tmini* [Poems in the darkness] (1937). His plays are: *Golgota* (1932), *Vučjak* [The wolf-hound] (1923), *U agoniji* [In agony] (1928), *Gospoda Glembayevi* [The Glembays] (1929), *Leda* (1930). His stories and novels are: *Tri kavalira gospodjice Melanije* [Miss Melanija's three gallants] (1920), *Hrvatska rapsodija* [The Croatian rhapsody] (1921), *Hrvatski bog Mars* [The Croatian god Mars] (1922), *Novele* [Stories] (1924), *Povratak Filipa Latinovicza* [The return of Filip Latinovicz] (1932), *Hiljadu i jedna smrt* [A thousand and one deaths] (1933), *Na rubu pameti* [On the brink of reason] (1938), *Banket u Blitvi* [The banquet at Blitva] (1939). His essays and polemics are *Moj obračun s njima* [My settlement with them] (1932), *Eseji* (1933), *Evropa danas* [Europe today] (1935), *Knjiga studija* [A book of studies] (1936), *Eppur si muove* (1938). His journey to the Soviet Union is described in *Izlet u Rusiju* [A trip to Russia] (1926). Since the second world war Krleža has written numerous ideological articles, impressions, reflections on matters of principle in art, and on the position of the peoples of Yugoslavia in the culture of Europe.

Krleža demonstrated his strong individuality in his earliest work. To literature which, on the model of the modernistic traditions, was spending itself in helpless formalism and literary motifs, Krleža contributed new ideas expressed generously, freshly

243

and forcefully. In his early books of poems *(Pan, Tri simfonije)* he made a striking effect with his unusual lyricism, which was a repudiation of every verse pattern, letting the Croatian tongue speak in its natural rhythm and with the fullness of its voice. His plays, stories, novels, essays and polemics are especially conspicuous in Croatian literature. In these he has had the courage to broach new material, to give it expression in his own way, and to approach it from his personal standpoint, which almost always differed from the standpoint of the average Croatian intellectual.

What decided Krleža's position in the cultural life of Croatia after the Russian Revolution, was his definite position on the social left, his adamant opposition to the bourgeois order and his championing of the workers' movement. This was especially pronounced in the subject-matter of his works, in his position towards various cultural, political and social problems as they appeared in Croatia, and in Yugoslavia in general for that matter.

Krleža's works picture ordinary people in Croatia, the peasants principally, in the vortex of the first world war, when they suffered and perished for foreign causes. He treats of the psychology of the Croatian petty bourgeois intellectual in his inability to adapt himself to the wretched Croatian petty bourgeois conditions, and to reach broader horizons. He exposes the Austrian military, which did its duty with calm, impassivity and narrow-mindedness, killing souls and bodies as a natural every-day chore, invoking social standing and officer's honour the while. He especially depicts the feudalists and the higher bourgeois class who, associated with the high oficialdom in Austria, had for centuries exploited Croatia in their own behalf and in that of the foreigners. On the other hand, he vividly portrays Croatian and other personages who distinguished themselves either by their progressive views or by the strength of their individuality. Widely-versed in both literature and science, Krleža deals in his articles with every problem of cultural, social and political life, handling skillfully vast expanses of time and space with remarkable literary power. He once again proved that any event, be it even the most commonplace, can be turned by the poet's fancy into a work of art.

Krleža's analyses of Croatian conditions are completely objective. Being a keen observer, the miserable, reactionary, hideous Croatian petty bourgeois conditions, the backwardness, suffering and agony of ordinary people in Croatia in the past and in his time did not escape his notice. He ruthlessly laid bare romantic falsehoods couched in pious terms, which the Croatian petty bourgeois political and cultural figures had used to stupefy the Croatian people in the course of twenty years. With equal ardour he sang the praises of great Croatian figures (Kranjčević for example).

As a portraitist and critic Krleža is never dull, and never presents himself as a man who sees clearly and always perceives the truth: expressions of doubt, hesitation, helplessness, and wandering are interwoven in his works, and imprecation and grief often alternate. But all his works carry such individuality, such strength and temperament, that they always make a lasting impression. A special place in his work is occupied by *Balade Petrice Kerempuha* [The songs of Petrica Kerempuh] (1936). In a series of poems written in the *kajkavski* dialect, Krleža produced a synthetic picture of the whole tragic and bloody past of the Croat, whom the feudalists, the Church and the bourgeoisie had tormented for centuries, and who was even deceived by his cultural leaders.

Krleža cultivated his own mode of expression. Continuing the work of Matoš and learning to some degree from Zola, he smashed the moulds of the modernistic style. He wrote lucidly, with many similes, many antitheses. He employed expressions from everyday speech, with naturalness, freshness and novelty. He distinguished himself by succinctness, a wealth of association, and by an ability to regard things from an original point of view. His rhythm is exuberant, strong, irresistible. He combines keenness of observation with strong lyricism, which permeates all his work.

Krleža soon won the admiration of the progressive literary public of Croatia. He won popularity, and his renown spread all over Yugoslavia, especially among the progressive writers. In his criticism he exposed the backwardness, mediocrity, bourgeois paltriness that impeded the normal development of Croatian cultural and social life. Because of this he was often persecuted by the authorities and attacked by the backward critics, which called forth his numerous polemics. But for this very reason he was often the idol and teacher of the younger generation, both in literature and in life.

Ivo Andrić (1892) was born at Dolac, near Travnik, Bosnia. He attended gymnasium in Sarajevo, and studied Slavic philology at the Faculties of Philosophy in Zagreb, Cracow and Vienna. As a member of the revolutionary Yugoslav youth he was imprisoned at the beginning of the first world war. Completing his studies at Graz after the war, he was accepted in the Yugoslav diplomatic service. He reached the peak of his diplomatic career as Yugoslav Minister in Berlin. Since the second world war he has occupied himself exclusively with writing. He has been the President of the Federation of Writers of Yugoslavia for a number of years.

Andrić began his literary career by writing poems during his gymnasium days in Sarajevo. In 1914 he contributed to *Mlada hrvatska lirika* [Lirics of young Croatia]. His book of lyrical pieces *Ex ponto* (1919), which are distinguished by delicate shades of expression and a feeling of humanity and forgiveness, is the fruit of his years in prison. Immediately after the war Andrić wrote a number of lyrical prose pieces under the title *Nemiri* [Restlessness] (1919), and then devoted himself entirely to story-writing. His first outstanding story was *Put Alije Djerzeleza* [The journey of Alija Djerzelez]. Between the two wars he wrote three books of stories (Belgrade, 1924, 1931, 1936), which were originally published in magazines. Directly after the second world war he published three full novels *(Na Drini ćuprija* — The bridge on the Drina; *Travnička kronika* — The chronicles of Travnik; *Gospodjica* — The lady) and a number of stories in magazines, some of which have been collected in the book *Nove pripovetke* [New tales] (Belgrade, 1950). In addition to these, between the two wars and since 1945, he has written a number of essays, literary studies and reviews.

Andrić is a rarely tender, lyrical, retiring nature. His earliest verses were distinguished by a reticence of expression, devoid of glitter, fashionable tricks and affectation; they were reduced to bare essentials. *Ex Ponto* contains not a single nationalistic utterance, not even an exclamation of hatred for the enemy whose prisoner he was. It is a picture of profound human suffering, but devoid of powerful protest. His first story, *Put Alije Djerzeleza,* marks the completion of his profile as a story-writer. His hero is a figure from the Bosnian Moslem epics. He is a braggart and the terror of everyone; but he cuts a ridiculous figure in his venture to conquer a member of the opposite sex. The central question for him, a hero without equal, as he sees himself, is how is it possible that he cannot accomplish what the meanest wretch can. In this story Andrić clearly defined his artistic process: the source of his subject-matter lay in Bosnia; but in it he sought the common human element. His *Alija* is not merely a Bosnian braggart, but man in general confronted by the eternal problem presented by woman.

In his further narrative work Andrić drew mostly on the Bosnian scene, on its past, on old records and legends for his subjects. Bosnia, a country which was oppressed by different invaders, with a population divided by three religions and by national, economic and social inconsistencies, had for centuries been the arena of differences, conflicts, wars, murders, blood and suffering. Andrić wrote about Catholic friars, Hajduks, Turkish beys, Moslem theologists, Austrian officers, porters, merchants, Turkish pashas and their Christian mistresses, the rich, the poor, with their passions, sorrows, intellectual horizons, customs, speech, conduct, enthusiasms, despairs. He always preserved the characteristics of the place and time of his narrative; yet he elaborated every motif to a general human significance. In writing of Bosnia, he writes of man on this earth, and his stumblings and staggerings caused by love, hate, delusion and the passions of civilization and culture

Andrić composed his works in measured language, apparently without emotion, careful of every word as though he were carving stone to last into the distant future. He weighed each sentence, endeavouring to avoid any unnecessary or false note, discarding everything that might obtrude with a note too vociferous or personal. But for this very reason his stories teem with subject-matter, especially his short ones. Each of them seems to contain one of the problems concerning man's relation to eternity. Written in perfect popular speech, without affectation, they are all as impressive as masterpieces, and each is worthy of a place in anthologies.

Andrić did not produce at his full capacity between the two wars. But since the last war he has eclipsed every other Yugoslav writer in the volume of his work and its comprehensiveness. *Na Drini ćuprija* and *Travnička kronika* are novels from the history of Bosnia. *Na Drini ćuprija* describes the erection of a bridge across the river Drina on the boundary between Bosnia and Serbia, the events which it witnessed through the centuries, and the course of human destinies in connexion with it and in its vicinity. *Travnička kronika* tells of the period when a French consul came to Travnik during the time of Napoleon. His arrival, as well as the arrival of similar officers representing other States, in the small Oriental town, touched off a number of shocks, conflicts, tragedies. The fundamental characteristic in these two novels is identical, as it is in his stories: he portrays individuals with their hopes, weaknesses, afflictions and passions in connexion with time, which waits for no one, and with the indifference of nature.

Gospodjica and *Nove pripovetke* deal with people and problems closer to Andrić's own period. Here he treats of the psychology of the rich, the time of war and the post-war period, the formation of a new society. But his artistic process continues the same: absolute artistic conscientiousness, dispassionate creativeness, the motifs being elaborated to the extreme.

There is a sadness in Andrić's art even while he seeks to sound an optimistic note. It gives the impression that everything is futile in view of the ubiquitous presence of death and general nothingness, in view of eternal change along with the indifference of nature and things. Like Njegoš's art, however, it is profoundly national, firm and invincible as the past of Andrić's Bosnia and the past of the Yugoslavs in general. Awareness of the passing of things and of misery are present in it, but so are strong feelings of courage, faith in man's struggle, sympathy for his sufferings and afflictions. For this reason it is no wonder that Andrić observed so closely and revealed so clearly many of the traits which distinguished the personages who best expressed and represented his people (Njegoš,

Vuk Karadžić). Andrić's works may be said to be among the highest attainments in Yugoslav literature.

Prežihov Voranc is the nom de plume of *Lovro Kuhar* (1893–1950). He was the son of a poor peasant from that part of the Slovene region of Carinthia which was artificially divided by the peace treaty between Yugoslavia and Austria after the first world war. Kuhar was completely self-taught. He attended elementary school only, and then worked on the family farm. Later he attended a higher cooperative school in Vienna for a time, and there he heard about socialism. He was in the front lines from the outbreak of the first world war. Regarding Austria as the enemy of his people, he deserted to the Italians, for he had faith in the liberation slogans of the Allies. The Italians imprisoned him and released him several months after the war. In Yugoslavia Kuhar carried on ideological and propaganda work among the workers, and became a member of the Communist party in 1920. He fled to Austria with the establishment of the dictatorship in Yugoslavia, from where he proceeded to other countries. He spent most of his life abroad — in Vienna, Paris, Prague, Bucharest, etc., always the victim of persecution or arrest. He returned home only seldom, and then secretly. He spent the second world war in Nazi concentration camps, returning to Yugoslavia after the liberation.

Kuhar began to write while still a young man in the village. In 1925 he published a book of stories entitled *Povesti* [Stories]. It was brought out during the period of expressionism in Slovene literature. Being distinctively realistic, his book passed unnoticed. But Kuhar continued to work and write, especially in prison, for he had now become familiar with life from very many angles and with European literature. He emerged again in Slovene literature in 1935 with the story *Boj na Poživravniku* [The Battle of Poživravnik], which was published in *Sodobnost*. He signed it with the name *Prežihov Voranc*, which came to be a new name in literature. This story, apparently by a beginner with its perfect realism and perfect idiom, was a revelation, and heralded the appearance of a new and strong talent, similar to Cankar's.

Thenceforward Prežihov Voranc wrote much and energetically. He published a book of stories entitled *Samorastniki* [Self-made] (1939), the novels *Požganica* (1939), *Doberdob* (1940), *Jamnica* (1945), two books of travels *Od Kotelj do Belih Vod* [From Kotelj to Bele Vode] (1945) and *Borba na tujih tleh* [The struggle in foreign lands] (1946), notes from the national-liberation struggle *Naši mejniki* [Our boundary stones] (1946) and a book for young people *Solzice* [Tears] (1949).

Prežihov Voranc's novels, stories and notes in the main describe his homeland proper and his life at home and abroad. Most of his books are documentary, being in a manner material for his biography. His artistic work gravitated towards the novel and story.

Although Prežihov Voranc was a worker by profession and one of the foremost leaders of the Slovene workers' movement, he wrote of the Slovene village and its immediate neighbourhood. His characters are villagers, men and women, from Carinthia, the northernmost part of Yugoslavia, and from that part of the province which belongs to Austria. In his novels he confined himself to a short period of time: to the last years of Austria-Hungary, the events connected with the Paris peace conference, and the early years of pre-war Yugoslavia down to the dictatorship. His novel *Doberdob* — named after a Slovene town for which Austria and Italy fought bitterly during the first world war — is a description of events between 1914 and 1918. He depicted the psychological development of the Slovene soldier, from his first suspicion that he was the victim of injustice, up to the moment when his being rebelled and he displayed conscious revolutionary strivings. The novel is not actuated by nationalism: it is a portrayal of the representatives of the different nations in the Austro-Hungarian Army during the war. *Požganica* describes the last years of Austria, the anticipation of its disintegration, and the struggle for that part of Carinthia which subsequently went to Austria after a plebiscite. The novel *Jamnica* is a picture of peasant life in the Slovene countryside during the first ten years of the existence of Yugoslavia.

As an artist Prežihov Voranc is completely objective towards his subject: he is above ordinary political and cultural catchwords, and brings out the salient traits of his characters.

Prežihov Voranc's ideology is quite clear. He succeeded in showing that the interests of classes and associations are couched in different slogans. *Požganica* bears out the supremacy of capitalist interests over national feelings and over the interests of the Slovenes. *Jamnica* is intended to be a text-book example of how social and economic conditions — the strength and rapacity of capitalism — gradually impoverish and pauperize the peasantry: of necessity, a once wealthy nationalist draws near the workers' movement.

The artistic merit of Prežihov Voranc's work lies, not only in his presentation of his characters as abstract figures in order to explain the economic laws of society, but in his exposure of their innermost qualities. He was such a keen observer that under the apparently unvarying physiognomy of his peasants, who are nothing out of the ordinary at first glance, he was able to point to countless distinctions. In his small and confined countryside he thus found a multitude of types, and described them at their everyday work: diggers, wood-cutters, ploughmen, timbermen, their wives, their children, village priests, merchants, officials, with all their idiosyncrasies, limitations, common sense, stupidities, selfishness, spitefulness and nobility, speech, curses, movements; and with an unexpected medley of human virtues. His intractable blasphemer turns out to have the goodness and innocence of a child. The woman who is regarded by the villagers as licentious demonstrates an exceptional capacity for sacrifice and creativeness. Prežihov Voranc understood deeply the psychology of the people who were attached to their niggardly, lean land, and grappled with it till their last breath. His novels contain scenes deeply human and touching in their display of man's misery, weakness and helplessness on one side, and man's magnificence on the other. Prežihov Voranc was a master in presenting his profound knowledge of man and of his innermost workings with precision of expression, conciseness of narrative, directness of touch and mellowness of speech. His characters, peasants and workers, who come from a limited area, remain in the memory of the reader as mighty, stalwart representatives of mankind along the difficult and thorny road to happiness.

Kosta Racin is the only writer who dared to write in Macedonian between the two wars. He was born at Veles in 1909. He finished two grades of gymnasium, and then had to give up school in order to work as a labourer. Like his father, he also worked at the potter's trade. But he continued to give his spare time to his cultural advancement. Since his earliest youth he was a member of the workers' movement, and persecuted and imprisoned for his views. He was killed in battle in 1943. He published the collection *Beli mugri* [White daybreak] in Zagreb in 1939. It contains poems on the hard fate of the worker and peasant, on toil for the benefit of others, on poverty and self-abnegation. Finding inspiration in the style of Macedonian folk lyrics, Racin found a simple, direct, penetrating and touching mode of expression. His extensive literary plans were cut short by death.

PRESENT LITERARY TRENDS

The fascist armies coming from Germany, Italy, Hungary and Bulgaria overran Yugoslavia in April 1941. Upon the ruins the invaders set up a number of so-called independent states and at their head they placed the obedient executors of their orders. They also annexed considerable parts of Yugoslav territory (Dalmatia, Macedonia, parts of Slovenia, Croatia). In the quartered and mutilated country they instituted a regime of concentration camps, gallows, massacre and deportation. Whole villages were burnt down, whole classrooms of pupils were shot, thousands of people pushed over the edge of abysses. In order to facilitate the extermination of the Yugoslav peoples, they sought to engender hatred among them by

250

stirring up old political differences. The fratricidal war which ensued presented some of the ghastliest scenes in occupied Yugoslavia. But the effect was contrary to what was expected: the Yugoslav peoples realized that the same danger threatened them all, irrespective of nationality; and forgetting their old differences, they sought to save themselves as a nation. Although there had been signs of resistance at the very beginning of the occupation, in July 1941, at the call of the Communist party, an uprising burst forth, developing as time passed from isolated guerrilla attacks into organized military resistance. Seven offensives were directed against the National Liberation Army under Marshal Tito's command, but they all failed. The heavier the enemy pressure became and the greater the number of villages burnt and innocent people killed, the greater became the number of new fighters who came from the occupied territory to the liberated areas. Parts of Yugoslavia — Macedonia and Serbia — completely recovered their freedom towards the end of 1944, the remainder of the country being cleared of the enemy by May 1945.

The new Yugoslavia was organized as a federal people's republic, with six republics (Serbia, Croatia, Slovenia, Montenegro, Bosnia and Herzegovina, and Macedonia) and with a Federal Government in Belgrade to administer their common affairs, each Yugoslav people enjoying national and cultural autonomy. A social revolution has taken place, with socialism as its goal: Yugoslavia is to transform rapidly from a backward agricultural country into a country with an advanced industry, free of the economic dependence in which the several peoples had been living for centuries.

The literature of the Yugoslav peoples never faltered either during the occupation or during the most trying years of fascist terror and the struggle against it. Books and brochures, mostly with militant trends, circulated in the areas which were even temporarily liberated by the National Liberation Army. Many of the Yugoslav cultural workers were in prison and concentration camps, but an even greater number, especially young men, had fled to the liberated territory, where they carried on their cultural mission. One of the older writers who joined the National Liberation Army was Vladimir Nazor, whose literary work continued even under the most difficult conditions. Oton Župančič also inspired the struggle with his verses. A number of works brought out during the war are valuable, not merely as documents, but also for their artistic merits *(Jama* — The pit — by Ivan Goran Kovačić; the poems and plays of *Matej Bor*, the nom de plume of Vladimir Pavšič; *Pjesme partizanke* — Partisan poems — by Vladimir Nazor; the poems and stories of Branko Ćopić, and others). In *Jama* the poet, who was murdered by the Chetniks, describes a ghastly massacre of innocent Serbs, committed in Croatia by hirelings of the

251

enemy. During the war poetic distinction was gained also by Jovan Popović, Skender Kulenović (with the poem *Stojanka majka kne-žopoljka* — Stojanka the Knezpolje mother), Vlado Popović (with the poem *Oči* — Eyes), Karel Destovnik Kajuh (with poems in Slovene).

In the new Yugoslavia, literature is evolving in step with life generally. Each Yugoslav people now enjoys the opportunity of literary development. Even the Macedonian people has for the first time in its history been given the opportunity of creating in its own language. New literary papers have been founded in each of the republics: *Književnost* [Literature] (Belgrade), *Republika* (Zagreb), *Novi svet* [The new world] (Ljubljana), *Nov den* [The new day] (Skoplje), *Stvaranje* [Creativity] (Cetinje), *Brazda* [The furrow] (Sarajevo), etc. Of the older magazines only *Letopis ma-tice srpske* in Novi Sad, and *Hrvatsko kolo*, among miscellanies, have been revived. The older literary institutions *(Matica srpska, Matica hrvatska, Matica slovenska)* have been set up on new foundations. The writers, organized in Republican associations, are united in the Federation of Writers of Yugoslavia.

Literary life in Yugoslavia was especially lively during the early post-war years. Many new talents joined the mature writers of the older and the middle generations, and publishing has greatly increased. The translation of foreign works, particularly the classics of world literature, is also very intensive.

The main objective of the writers during the war was to help the struggle for freedom from the fascist invaders and their domestic hirelings. Immediately after the war and during the subsequent years, the main subjects were scenes and personages from the war, as well as pictures of construction in new Yugoslavia. Thus several diaries were written during the war *(S partizanima* — With the partisans — by Vladimir Nazor; *Zapisi iz Oslobodilačkog rata* — Notes from the liberation war — by Rodoljub Čolaković; *Dnevnik* — A diary — by Vladimir Dedijer; *S Titom* — With Tito — by Čedomir Minderović), as well as a number of collections of lyric poems, of stories, and several novels.

The greatest success with the critics and with the reading public has been won by the Slovenes Ciril Kosmač (the stories *Sreča in kruh* — Happiness and bread) and Matej Bor (verse); by the Serbs Oskar Davičo (the novel *Pesma* — The poem) and Dobrica Ćosić (the novel *Daleko je sunce* — Distant is the sun), Mihailo Lalić (stories); by the Croats Ranko Marinković *(Proze; Ruke* — The hands), Petar Šegedin (novels and travel pieces) and Mirko Božić (the novel *Kurlani).*

New names have also appeared in rejuvenated Macedonian literature. The national minorities (Hungarians, Italians) have also produced writers of their own.

Instead of exclusively following foreign models, the Serbian, Croatian, Slovene and Macedonian writers laid heavier emphasis on the need to add to the achievements of their own past. The observation of the anniversaries of past writers, and the celebration of the jubilees of some outstanding living writers were not merely a view in retrospect, but also an occasion to ask what of this cultural treasure could be adopted by the new generations. Thus the Slovenes observed the anniversaries of Prešern, Trubar and Cankar; the Serbs observed the anniversaries of Njegoš, Vuk Karadžić, Jakšić, Svetozar Marković, Radičević; the Croats celebrated the anniversaries of Mažuranić, Marulić, Kovačić, Kranjčević. These are the writers who, having found a literary expression of their own, which was, at the same time, national, most successfully resisted foreign influences. Most of these jubilees were observed by all the Yugoslav peoples.

They also reflected the fundamental trend in the literature of the Yugoslav peoples: that they must evolve to the greatest possible degree; that they should also recognize the achievements of other nations, but only in the spirit of the best traditions; that they must accept from others what they require for their own cultural advancement while being true to themselves both in subject-matter and in mode of expression.

Dr. ANTUN I. BARAC

Academician and University Professor

Anton I. Barac, a historian of literature, was born at Kamenjak near Grižani, Hrvatsko Primorje (the Littoral), on August 20, 1894. He died in Zagreb on the 2nd November 1955. He attended gymnasium at Sušak, studied Slavic philology at the Faculty of Philosophy in Zagreb, at which he also gained his doctorate. He was a secondary school master at Sušak and in Zagreb. In 1930 he began to lecture on later Yugoslav literature as docent at the Faculty of Philosophy in Zagreb, and later as full professor. He engaged himself wholeheartedly in the organization of the Slavic Institute. He has been in France, Germany, Italy and Czechoslovakia for purposes of scientific research. He tyrned to writing just before the beginning of the first world war, and has written numerous articles, dissertations and criticisms for the foremost Yugoslav magazines. His studies of Nazor, Matoš, Šimunović, Vojnović, Gundulić, Šantić, and to some extent of Šenoa, Djalski and Novak, are in the nature of essays. In his most important works (Mirko Bogović, "Hrvatska književna kritika" — Croatian literary criticism — Vidrić, Mažuranić) he produced psychological portraits of the writers, in which he emphasized their subjective traits in the prevailing political, social, and economic conditions, analyzing their world of ideas and their attitude towards reality, and examining the artistic elements in their works and their influence on their literary and social environments; he does not attach special significance to the influences that may have played a part in the making of his subjects. He advanced principled views on problems of verse and the folk poem as a poetic source in his studies of Vidrić and Mažuranić, in which he gave exhaustive analyses of poetic expression and metrics in composition. One of his most important works is "Hrvatska književna kritika", an informative dissertation with many judgments on critics, starting with Vraz and ending with Matoš, and on their methods. Among his most interesting later compositions are his articles on Vraz (1951), Preradović (1952), and Nazor (1953). His mode of expression is nearest to realism with a slight leaning towards subjectivism; but he has also shown a keen liking for every literary trend except for the most extreme trends. In his study of Croatian literature he has given special treatment to the period between Illyrism and 1918, often reverted to earlier literature and kept in pace with contemporary literature with brief critical dissertations. He has devoted much attention to Mažuranić, Šenoa and Vidrić; but there is almost no minor writer about whom he has not written. He exerted every effort to be constructive during the period of destructive and biased criticism between the two world wars, primarily seeking the positive traits in his subject. He has also given living portraits of Šenoa, Vidrić, Kranjčević, Matoš, Šimunović, and rescued minor writers, such as Botić, Veber and Horvat-Kiš, from oblivion. As editor of »Mladost« he has exercised a beneficial influence on a number of Yugoslav writers. His works, which are rounded compositions, constituted the foundations of a history of Croatian literature.

(Enciklopedija Jugoslavije, Zagreb 1954, Vol. I)

NOTE

This survey comes on the initiative of the Committee for Foreign Cultural Relations as a source of information. Hence, it contains a limited number of names and events, and in many cases fails to deal with matters the reader might expect to find in a book of this type.

The literature from 1918 down to the present has been given brief treatment, only mentioning trends, and introducing one representative writer of each of the several nations whose literature is dealt with. As a part of contemporary literary creativity, this period of literature cannot be presented according to the methods of literary history employed throughout this survey. Many events hardly noted by later generations are often important to the literature of the day, just as the opposite may also frequently be the case. The fact, therefore, that the names of only a few writers have been recorded, whereas the great majority have not, must not be taken to mean that judgment has been pronounced on them one way or another.

INDEX OF NAMES

This Index contains only the names of writers and those historic figures directly connected with the development of literature. It does not contain the names of other figures and rulers who are mentioned in the text.

CONTENTS

VII. THE NINETEENTH CENTURY

The Foundations of Modern Yugoslav Literature

FROM ROMANTICISM TO REALISM

REALISM

VIII. THE TWENTIETH CENTURY

Facing Europe

Between the Two Wars